Tory Dent

Collected Poems

TORY DENT

COLLECTED POEMS

THE SHEEP MEADOW PRESS

Designed and typeset by The Sheep Meadow Press
Distributed by The University Press of New England

Library of Congress Cataloging-in-Publication Data

Dent, Tory, 1958-2005.
[Poems]
Collected Poems / Tory Dent.
pages cm
ISBN 978-1-937679-50-7
I. Title.
PS3554.E586A6 2015
811'.54--dc23

All inquiries and permission requests should be addressed to the publisher:

The Sheep Meadow Press
PO Box 84
Rhinebeck, NY 12572

CONTENTS

BLACK MILK

EARLY POEMS

Preface

by Sean Harvey*

Tory once told me in jest she imagined that, if she were to be remembered at all, it would be as "some crazy character who churned out wild poems in an attic somewhere as a matter of survival". As I revisit these poems in collected form many years after her death, I'm afraid that this tongue-in-cheek bit of self-parody is the only reflection of hers about how she wanted or expected her poems to be received posthumously that I can recall. Tory Dent was a lot of things, most of them quite lovely and mundane. She was certainly no madwoman in an attic. But knowing her as well as I do, even this comment evokes a couple of truths about her and her attitude toward her work that are worth remembering.

First, she did indeed write poetry not as a profession or in expectation of accolades or even external appreciation, but because the joy of creating and expressing, of using her gifts as a writer and pushing them to extremes, was for her absolutely a matter of survival, a declaration that she was still vividly alive as she struggled pretty heroically with HIV over the last seventeen years of her life.

Second, despite the seriousness of her subject matter and the unsettling nature of some of her poems, when she stepped away from the writing table she never took herself as seriously as one might imagine. Tory had a rare ability to laugh at herself, and a general sense of fun that was never compromised even in her last days, despite the unfair portion of human suffering that she experienced. She would never have devoted so much of herself to poetry if she hadn't enjoyed creating it so much, if it didn't thrill her or send a chill up her spine. If it wasn't fun.

As I look at these poems again after so many years, all brought together in a single volume for the first time, I'm surprised to find that her sense of play shines through and pervades the work every bit as much as the seriousness of her subject matter. I can sense the joy of creation traveling along as equal partner with the black-bottomed well of personal and collective pain that she was brave enough to delve into again and again. Both are essential components in understanding and appreciating her accomplishments as a poet. The vivid imagery, metaphor piled upon metaphor, long unruly lines of rhythm bursting the seams of their form and even the page itself, a disorienting chain of high and low cultural references stitched together like a line of breadcrumbs left along an alleyway at night, a call and response with the work of other poets and popular songs, exquisite and personal pearls of truth pieced together with bits of a magnetic poetry kit sold as a novelty impulse buy at the checkout line for Barnes & Noble. Taken collectively it reminds me of nothing so much as getting lost in one of those magnificent, surreal, disorienting de Chirico landscapes that she loved so much.

Whether or not Tory Dent's work still matters is for other people to decide. It sure mattered back when she was alive. She was one of many amazing and vibrant voices that arose in the first years of the AIDS epidemic here in the US. She spoke to a lot of people and was important to a lot of people, and for that reason she will always have a measure of historical importance.

But there is a lot more than nostalgia waiting for you in this book. I hope you can find some of that same thrill of creation that Tory felt when building this strange city, the same chill that ran up her spine.

There are so many writers and artists who were essential to Tory's craft and community that it would be impractical to list them here, but I would like to thank all of them, both the living and the dead, and devote this collection to them with gratitude and love. I'd also like to express my tremendous gratitude to Stanley Moss for his publication and total support of Tory's work during her life and even after her life, as well as Michael and Karen Braziller who gave Tory her first shot by publishing her first book. You brought a great deal of happiness into Tory's life, and everyone who loves Tory and her work will always be grateful.

* Sean Harvey was Tory Dent's husband from 1999 until her death in 2006.

Introduction

by Greg Miller

This edition includes the three books Tory Dent published in her lifetime, along with early unpublished poems that, astonishing in themselves, throw new light on the poems so many already know, now in one unique volume. In assembling Dent's *Collected Poems*, Sheep Meadow Press, publisher of *HIV, Mon Amour* and *Black Milk*, came upon a folder of Tory Dent's early poems, a few dated 1981. Publisher Stanley Moss remembers Dent felt these poems unworthy of publication; however, given the passage of time, Moss, her husband Sean Harvey, and other poets close to her have concluded it would be wrong not to make them available to readers. Her reasons for hiding them were often not literary.

Tory Dent's chief subject is survival: her fight against AIDS. Her fugal counterpoint is creation's power: taken again out of herself, she finds her way home: "Welts rise up on the youth of paper / Where lead drags a tiny trail across its torso / As if threshing a path home / Trenchant and narrow" ("Blue Ruin"). Dent's poems confront the void of nonbeing, testing the construction and limits of consciousness, scaling the night, skeptical of "transcendence," registering a longing for transcendence.

If "Silence Equals Death," to use the slogan of ACT UP and AIDS activists of the 1980s, then Dent's poetry, her speaking, is a force for life.

> Being sick is terribly redundant, and I think my writing seems to cheer me up, that it always surprises me in terms of what I'm feeling, what I'm thinking, how I'm able to express the emotions and the physical discomfort I'm going through, and that makes life still within the elements of surprise that normal, healthy people seem to experience all the time.[1]

These "elements of surprise" are not only the poet's; because of Dent's gifts, the reader experiences with her: bracing, startling mixtures of diction, imagery, and narrative. Take, for example, one of Dent's meditations on language, its potential to engulf us, to cut us off, to isolate us. The imagery of "Death as a Language" takes us to Paul Celan territory:

---

[1] Interview with Michele Norris. "Tory Dent's Poetry on Life with AIDS," January 3, 2006, 12:00 p.m. EST. National Public Radio.

Because we know, an extraordinarily complex but organized web
wraps with cognition its soft shearing between us like a pact.
It drapes and folds, togalike, yet immaterial as the weather;
erotically charged as a black lace nightgown
is the feral, black lace evening that branches out around us.
The cloudy room ferrets with speech we love to hear for its own sake,
a metalanguage made up of actions, accordances, predilections,
mutual destinations, and private thoughts
which, when etymologized,
break down to the white noise of our anticipations.
Like white noise the white water flows evenly at night,
lace rafting along the river.
The lofty branch, lost but present, sleeps . . .

Adrienne Rich describes Dent's distinctive linguistic alchemy and human directness, the way it can "veer from great elegance to brutal realism, the revelations of the sense of betrayals of her body, disfigurements, infections, and yet the language transcends morbidity, as great poetic language can."[2] If Death here is a language, Dent's "lost" "lofty branch" offers a *glimpse* of transcendence.

If Dent's language is not morbid, neither is it merely elegiac, a genre that activists at the beginning of the AIDS pandemic saw as complicit, part and parcel of the machinery of death put into action by the silence and inaction of the Reagan administration, and the culture at large. Many early death notices used euphemisms to deny AIDS and all the unacceptable deviancies it implied: being gay or bisexual, an I.V. drug user, Black, foreign, "other." I personally remember friends who died in the 80s and 90s suddenly, miserably, and sometimes alone, isolated from their partners or friends by their families or the state, or the two in collusion. Erasure, literal and metaphoric, governed reality. Dent writes moving elegies; they are one part of a poetry that fights for more life.

Part of the wonder of Dent's poetry comes from her transgressive, radical joy of speaking truth heedless of consequence, the sheer pleasure of invention, the poet doing what cannot be done. Great poetry often rises through the pressure of what's left unsaid, the implied, the implicit: Emily Dickinson's gnomic implosions, Seamus Heaney's distilled lyricism. Dent's language continues when you think it can only stop. Her spring replenishes itself. The singular voice does not cease to amaze: the play of language, the delight in consciousness itself.

---

2   Ibid.

> I touch the keyboard. The cold plastic alphabet
>
> singes, strangely forbidden, therefore erotic. I realize slowly, as if in orgasmic
> stages of cunnilingus, that the most elementary effort of extending toward the
> familiar, of taking control of my body, of pushing out articulations, has become
> transgressive . . . .
>
> ("Fourteen Days in Quarantine, 7")

Exuberance *in extremis.* The joy of making, or discovering what one thinks, in the
act of writing, of being alive in body and spirit.

In other poems, Dent is more clearly distrustful of the visionary impulse,
her ability to shine forth her inner light in the experiencing of it, in part because she
is simply unable to "take control" of her body.

> I reach inside for the wild goose, a spot somatically deficient as scar tissue;
> A soreness deep inside the solar plexus where the meat hook disengaged itself
> Just before death a lot time ago. Like a Wordsworthian spot of time
> It occludes my vision, the dark end of the spectrum equivalent to blindness.
>
> ("Cinéma Vérité")

As the fairy tale teaches, you can't kill the goose to find the golden egg. Literally,
scar tissue has weakened Dent's eyesight. As a result, Dent is losing the ability to
see, to dream. This unrelenting poem nevertheless has much in common with W.
B. Yeats' "The Circus Animals' Desertion" or George Herbert's "The Forerunners":
great poems written about the inability to write, though it is not growing older
that dampens the fire of Dent's creativity, but AIDS and a shortened life. "So sema-
phoric signal flail in the twilight, ecstatic as if winged" ("Accidental Poetry"). It is
important to understand that if the plague of AIDS had not occurred, Dent was a
great poet who would have fought for life, beauty, love, and language itself.

Dent rages against her illness, the dying of the light. In an important ear-
ly poem, Dent explores one deep source of her anger in her relationship with her
mother:

> Thank you for the hell-hole of that social smile, mother,
> the cavernous imagining of your throat that leads to your stomach
> your intestines, your asshole—
> my hate turned you inside out, attempted to dissect you
> like the generic frog in ninth-grade biology, I pinned back your legs and arms
> to render you as helpless and as victimized as I felt,
> to demystify, de-sublimate your enormous power,
> which had always eluded me in terms of its source, dog-eat-dog

in its ability to excuse itself—the self-justifying mentality
of those devoid of a consciousness convinced of the morality of their motives
like Klansmen, like McCarthyism.
("Peter the Great")

Dent rages to become herself, to break free of an omnipresent, belittling, engulfing maternal gaze, voice, and body—a mother complicit with larger cultural forms of oppression. "Mother" embodies fate, the voice sentencing her to permanent unhappiness. Such intimate violence in mother/daughter or father/son relationships is not all that unusual: projection and displacement (a hall of mirrors and hammers, meanness and mercilessness). I know of no other poem that gets to the heart of that primal dynamic with such compelling force. The poem, when I first read it, did to me what Dickinson said poems should do. I walked around missing the top of my head.

What can one do with such rage? At times, Dent would like to believe in the divine, to be able to construct a deity to whom she might pray:

But I thought of the concept of forgiveness and mustered up my ambition.
I thought of pretending it was a noble and organic site for God.
("Many Rivers to Cross")

In a poem about sitting in a hospital chapel with a woman in devout prayer, Dent in the end is not comforted, only "empty." She feels no release from "the grief-work that is living" ("The Interfaith Chapel at New York Hospital"). Finally, in "Black Milk," Dent imagines what she calls "closeness" as an alternative to faith traditionally conceived:

XXXI
What then after faith for the lost? Just flesh,
Unreliable in its warmth, fickle in its tendernesses,
As fragile and sickly as you? Yet closeness
Is what makes anything matter, ineffable or otherwise.
It's why we try.

*

Hissing against loss, the "void," Emily Dickinson often saw language as inadequate: "You cannot solder an abyss / With air." Tory Dent's blow-torch blasts a road of molten metal mid-air into the void. You watch it cool and harden: "Cindered, I test the overwrought sky for reality, / pink-gray like the grieving mind . . ." ("Ash"). Dent's poems demand that we travel with her, listen to the unthinkable, see what no human should ever have to see. Everything around looks different than it looked before.

What Silence Equals

Words Aren't Cheep

in memory of Richard Horn

Into an aptless metaphor for this,
into its conceivable, metastasized equivalent:
iconically blue, ephemeral of course, void of stars
or the washed pink center of that
which we've felt only a fraction of—
we guess but we don't know.
You're dead and you died at thirty-four.
So left without recourse, stupefied, we stare
at the sidewalk where the timbered body fell,
the chalked silhouette veined into the pavement,
unstable as a fresco as it is.
We don't know what it's like
for the world to underworld into your enemy overnight,
troops that enumerate like ants in a hill,
for just in the complex and necessary gesture
of getting on with our lives,
we leave you, out of reflex, behind,
leaving you amazed that it is you who is left
to witness Darwinistically the train diminish into tracks,
your future planed down, freakishly retarded,
shriveling up with the accelerated growth
of a child who turns sixty-five before he's twelve—
like the site of a ghost accident where cars slow
to glance at a stretch of grass
when the smashed car was towed weeks ago,
so we stare at the grass, at the pavement,
at each other, into our lupine pupils for some clue
that transcends the deterioration of flesh like teeth,
a trace of the pool your body has evaporated into—
we breathe for a while, then circle back
to a crowd of likeness, hair and skin,
wondering what it's like for the furniture to shrink,
for the carpet to spread, looming larger than its floor,
wolf-gray as the train platform we project,
the pavement that separates you from the abyss
you ultimately stumble into

and sink into the pile, the viscous cement,
like a tourist into quicksand.
The chalked outline of your body fades like a film.
Although it should, it doesn't matter what you died of,
your sickness made sublime (much too) by our contracting lives,
by our ornery fear,
by our love suddenly experienced
with ludicrous unconditionality now that you're gone,
so that we love instead as representative of you
the entire loaf of sky,
all specious things as if they were trees,
even the incredibly ugly skyscraper
because we regard it, however conciliatorily,
in the way and not in in the way
you did.

Spared

My hair, quotidian, my hair ululates like a cut peony
that only dogs can hear. The ebony handle of my brush,
black as Snow White's hair, draws, strand by strand,
my hair into its guts to tumble in penurious mass on the floor.
Profligate, it falls almost willingly from my scalp,
while the cruel and exemplary barber appears
mountainous against the cacti of my form,
his shadow made up of my missing hair
expands to signify my futurelessness.
I watch vigilantly as its circumference floods forward,
the setting sun poured like hourglass sand.
We stare each other down in the beauty parlor mirror.
He snips with satisfaction close to the pellucid cap of my head.
My hair, my hair, as much me as my legs or breasts,
affectionate, recalcitrant, straw doll at my chest,
removed with anesthesia merely for experiment,
enough to stuff a mattress, spin shirts, or weave five wigs.
Perhaps this is my necessary penitence.
When will I know if I've been spared?
When will I know that I won't lie
with a tube in my throat, the weight I was at fourteen years old
the K.S. lesions, leeches fulminating my body,
while I can only listen to the receiver placed by my head
to the voice of the benevolent caller
at the hand of my benevolent bedside friend.
When will I know that my immune system won't crumble
precipitantly and conclusively as the city can say it once predicted,
the condemned building that collapses onto its healthy vermin.
I can feel the people waiting for me to make statistical sense.
Let my hair grow then, furiously, seditiously, in protest.
I'll make it really hard to stick
the straw doll that resembles me malevolently with pins;
hard for the insipid sky with its impotent vastness
a matte baby-blue and seemingly so innocent
when I ask it why it guides the barber and his well-intentioned friends
to force the door upon me as I'm pressed against the dirt,
stone by stone piled upon my bones that begin to crack

while they shove doses of the wonder drug down my throat.
Let my body subvert itself then, rise irrepressible,
mysterious as waves in the ocean or homemade bread.
Let my strength rejuvenate with indemnifying reserve
against the door, the sky, the barber, even the benevolent bedside friend;
keep fighting, keep fighting, like the weathered admiral
who's become so accustomed to the surrounding slaughter,
unconsciously he's learned to thrive upon it
and wills to repair the body within the body,
always kept occluded from him as a ship within a bottle.
And when they've lined us up, those people,
prisoners they're determined to punish for something petty,
counting every third person to be dragged out and shot,
let my hair grow livid and flamboyant, grow even longer up to the minute,
if I end up where the finger is pointed
among those not counted as number two or one.

Apology to the Doctor

The consultation room blurs around us as for a noyade does the ocean.
The plate glass window convexes beyond its means
in a last ditch attempt to reach the world,
and the world, empathetically, concaves as a sail pivoted leeward
by our conversation, our ballooned cheeks puffing madly to save us.
Lifted like a ghost ship, a slaughtered rabbit, a tray of personal effects,
in suspended animation afore such inexplicable refusal the sky-cult shows us,
aft the earth which has become a roof, ubiquitous and shoddy,
sheltering a tenement of graves, slaves in a galley.
We navigate by default, for there is no right decision.
Spotlit by our situation we extemporize some outdated existential play,
divulge the way strangers passing en route might,
when sharing the same compartment or guilty Catholic albeit at heart
atheistic who seeks confession as the most efficient method of unburdening.
The souls lean closer, avert their heads to the better ear;
we sense the pressure as if their breathing could be heard.
"I've lost so many patients over the past eleven years." I imagine
their bodies felled with expedience into a pit just beneath us.
When I mention my dead friends I envision a bed of red tulips,
then the nothingness of pavement, then nothing at all.
We stare into our separate abysses for a moment almost like prayer,
but I wonder if either of us really prays anymore.
Your office posits itself like a Buddhist shrine,
haunted, thus protected, and stripped of religious innuendo.
The single desk survives on its own, statuary and symbolic:
the desire to heal—a sheet of water eternally poured on the octagonal rock.
The two leather chairs of community and isolation:
the desire to heal—a drilling for water; a searching for the doctor.
The body a given, a gift, a limitation, also a mystery
of which there be no end to the cruel suspensions of its mystery.
Over my interiority as if, paradoxically, outside myself
how powerful am I, Doctor? You who know and do not know the body,
how powerful are we? Our differences as doctor and patient
fall away like personas instantly absorbed by the industrial carpet.
The mass grave gives a rumble, a volcano threatening activity.
Our ineptitudes, perceived through a stauroscope, form in a myriad that crowds us;
The deaths so recent, their faces still excruciatingly fresh in the morning,

the throng of their voices pitched at an acoustical intensity
we can no longer hear ourselves think in the locked auditoriums of our minds.
We stare instead, thirsty and bewildered, at our stupidity
as if it were a talisman, mesmerized by its depth and black comedy
of its proportion, gargantuan in authority over our plebeian knowledge.
We stare as if our ignorance, like knowledge, were something to be applied,
that taken far enough might turn, inadvertently, on a dime into luck.

What Silence Equals

for André François Villon

Where the homogeneous wind beats the wild grass closer to the quiet ground,
Homogeneous, wild, quiet
Homogeny in a pretense of superiority
Beats wildness to wither into nothingness,
The quiet ground enveloping all that is askew, unorthodox,
The chaff of the world.
If we keep our heads bent in equal direction
Like plow horses pulling against the elements,
The plow will conform into manageability the unharrowed.

The plow will conform into manageability unharrowed.
Plow, conform, unharrowed
Like strong men at the circus with handlebar mustaches.
We hold up this principle while the applause meter goes berserk.
We watch mute and emotionless as you pace in your cage,
Your frenzied wildness eating you up alive,
Giving back to the god-given earth what you took.
If we're not better than you, what are we better than?
Let the saber-toothed plow of silence reign.

Let the saber-toothed plow of silence reign.
Saber-toothed, silence, reign
We watch you rise fitfully with fever in your apartment,
Your eyelids bruised from crying.
Mute and emotionless we watch you make phone calls
And talk a steady stream of what you need and believe.
Your so-called friends sit paralyzed on the other end;
They've said they love you,
But what good can be done really for a drowning man?
In time your talk will collapse onto itself like a Chinese box.
They'll admire the inlay of pain on your face.
They just want to commute conscience-free to their jobs.
Like a Chinese box you'll be buried with all your secret drawers locked.

Like a Chinese box you'll be buried with all your secret drawers locked.
Box, buried, secret

Ugly angels like buzzards circle overhead.
Your prayers, their prey, they carry clenched between their teeth.
On the horizon we stand, appointed klansmen waiting,
Impatient for the riffraff around us to cancel itself out.
Our tuft heads in the distance project a cryptic kind of village—
We're just a discriminating denomination, folks.
You sink, rightly so, in the swamp of your made bed,
Far enough away so you can't infect the kids in our schools.
The sky cuts you off like a sun roof as it should.

The sky cuts you off as a sunroof as it should.
Cuts, off, should
Your screams billow up, clouding the glass.
We watch your face, contorted, shrink and whirl away
With a high-pitched cry like a helium balloon losing its air.
We watch several faces follow yours
As if severed from some grasp,
Each with that high-pitched ringing noise.
They shrink and whirl away behind the cloudy glass of the sky.
We watch until that irritating ring stops in our ears,
Comforted by the solid surface of the god-given earth
Where the homogenous wind beats the wild grass closer to the quiet ground.

The Mind vs. the Brain

The sky sequences itself like a digital alarm.
The telephone has become, always becoming, Heideggerian.
In your aptitude for highlighting you show a flair for color.
Yellow always emphasizes, no matter the market value.

Like being in the pink, we're in the black again.
How luxuriant the matching plastic upholster of the taxi
and the street, absolutely filthy, where chart the pedestrians,
self-centered, ambitious, but for the most part, kind-hearted.

Eschewed by me, as if of their own accord, my goals ricochet
like tennis balls. What deranged epiphany
sirens centrifugally from their fluorescence stuck in the fence;
cycloptic gods, idiotic as we've evolved in our late century.

Sadistic underpinnings must have been at play all along.
Astonishing the courage a blind man administers at the crosswalk.
And sometimes I admire paper, predictably, just for its ancestry.
If I had one year to live, this is how I'd live it.

At the Dark End of the Street

written to the song by Percy Sledge

At the dark end of the street, I can see only your jacket
and the shadow of your head emblazoned on its leather.
At the dark end of the street, that's where we'd always meet up
talking on the phone late at night. Our love kept coming on strong,
the cradle on my desk burnished by my desk lamp, but the cigarette,
a python hypnotized by our ever more quieted voices,
remained in complete possession of the field of my hand.
We confessed, eventually, somewhere around the second hour into it
the way the gross anatomy of lovemaking gives way to its interiority,
bends supple as if broken already beneath the weighty implosion,
the photographic recall of its fantasy, the vivid details hidden always
in that netherworld of what we'd all be pushed to do if given
the tools and context. Through the perforated plastic
like a confessional screen come the dirty secrets cornered in our brains,
I offer each to you, a lump of sugar on my flattened palm,
what in our work and our daily public gestures we lie blind to get past
hold hostage in the attic what actually makes us the happiest.
Now you lick up, desperate tongue, along my lifeline every crystal.
At the dark end of the street, we follow where it narrows into need.
Led by the stench of the cobblestones underneath
until with amphibian dexterity underwater we breathe and exist off
the ocean replete, a perfect replicate of our labyrinthine revisionism
that reduces and expands like a pupil under flashlight examination
fear and desire coupled as if narrative, adulterous, connubial.
We knew time would take its toll: we'd have to pay for the love we stole,
looting each other when we felt most vulnerable until raped
by the metaphysical force of our love foreseen only in glimpses
through the oblique passageways of our mouths when we talked.
Our teeth lit up like skeletons in the night, our hands gloved by darkness
would take on another persona the way leaves replace stars and stars leaves.
We would loiter with half-empty glasses of champagne on New Year's Eve
and study the second hand for the actual end of the century,
so that sleepy-eyed but not drunk enough at least we'd have done our bit
and could return to the cold but familiar singularity of our beds.
And assuming the fetal position, the way the elderly become more childlike,
we'd be comforted enough by the fact we'd gotten through it

by the last-minute realization before falling asleep that the older we get
the less we seem to need, that rations can satisfy the stomach like a meal.
O they're going to find us! O they're going to find us!
Together reading the same sentence in silence, an epitaph or litany
of the dead carved on black marble that curves helically downward,
the tunnel to our souls we so dread to explore
we must be forced to the brink to our own deaths to start,
for surely hell will be the endpoint, the many evil thoughts added up by now.
At the edge of Antarctic territory I stood erect as an icicle,
and stared incredulously at the uncanny precision of the cut
where suddenly my future, an iceberg, simply broke off as if a punishment.
My life, totaled in an indifferent instant to a disappointing sum,
now rushed along the rapids, a houseboat out of whack, valleyed then peaked
before eclipsed finally by the sun's hissing that must have hated me all along.
Where had that hatred gestated, ready to watch when, sufficiently weakened,
undoubtedly I would keel? How long (and with such longing) had it festered?
What brilliant tactic to camouflage itself in the heart of the man I loved.
At the dark end of the street I'd just finished you with typical greed
when you kicked me so hard straight over I fell,
a statuette kilned in the position of genuflection.
I cracked predictably at the neck and knee. I broke, as you had hoped,
irreparably. Out spewed my teeth like lumps of sugar. Out spurted
your semen that evaporated immediately, drops of water on a warmed skillet.
Out burst my heart from my jaws pried apart like the wagging tongue
of a mad dog or the still pulsating meat of a clitoris.
There you left me as if after autopsy at the dark end of the street.
I melted the way a mantra does into the thoughts until there are none.
The agony condensed into a kind of ascent, a repetition of sound
that obscures over time into the absolute of nothing.
I listened until the silence filled up my ears with the water
where the iceberg of my future has ultimately gone.
Now like a Swedish summer my city is doused in daylight, twenty-four hours.
Now like my shadow my fears and desires to see you mimetically follow.
Perhaps one day you'll surface amidst the silence I'm used to,
appear internally lit, the shrine of my future,
patronizing me by positing a monument to its nonexistence,
that valleys then peaks like its would-be predecessor for a titillating moment
before eclipsed finally by the sun's hissing that must have hated me all along.

Accidental Poetry

Countless pinpricks mar the body, a hundred years ahead of their time.

Parables break like wet sticks, torn ligaments.
Sentences, once only verbal, now granted, Romanize into wings.

In a snap they've alighted from an archaic branch,
frenzied but arranged.

I talk on the phone, jot a memo, communicate to you what I mean;
what I mean, the blameless arena where as spectator
I participate in the Christians thrown.

Circumspect, this pernicious vernacular
articulates itself both in the lion's tooth and in the Christian soul.

Perhaps if I stood in front of a funhouse mirror
the text, like the prophecy of a talisman would make itself shown,
rise like a Todtenbaum on the stagnant river,
a letter bled to death on the surface of a swimming pool.

It would materialize again like any text or Christian soul
into the many versions of interpretation, already known
only to dematerialize back into its mold.

My sense of ongoing assemblage, as if pared through a sieve,
sets itself up to be pulled out from underneath,
left to drown in turn to be saved.

A noyade, it pools outward in proportion to tragedy proper,
bruises into the pavonine of absolute ocean or sky.

Like the practice of taxidermy, it looks and feels lifelike,
albeit basted and thatched and contrived
the way grass huts mimic their prototype, the tree:
the bricolage of what I've been told and hence believed to mean.

So semaphoric signals flail in the twilight, ecstatic as if winged.

Barely decipherable from their pavonine context
each sign subsumes its absolute, prototypical of ocean, sky, or parable.

While I, a seraph, fated to fly backwards in order to move forward
like Hebrew or the helical structure of DNA,
concede to the holy, to the literate, to the blank;
to the dead animal who, in my flying, I'm fated to imitate.

Only Human

When the violins and cellos mount, legatissimo, their notes,
and the soft hills burnish with an afterglow,
and the houses plump up and light like jack o' lanterns in the distance,
I imagine you at your piano listening to the same concerto,
your body encasing my view like a sheath carried in the field.
Your hands play softly like hills these notes, my poems you compose
in your humanness, that which I cannot stop thinking about.
You said many times, "We're only human," "I'm only human,"
the rhetorical phrase fishhooked my throat, cryptic in its riddle,
so here I am still flapping on the pier months after,
wondering about what humanness is, your humanness in particular.

Used for generalizing it's an apt expression,
human contrasted as a species to, say, Vulcans,
with the kind of disgusted acceptance of the former's incorrigibility
pontificated by Mr. Spock when witnessing Captain Kirk's actions.
Or when analyzed in comparison to mammals and reptiles
that we love to humanize in illustrated storybooks for our young,
bunnies by Beatrix Potter or some crusty alligator
propped up in an easy chair with book and pipe like a professor,
narcissism reveals itself
as one of those incorrigible human qualities.
Or the kind of humanness brought to light in an epic novel,
preferably by Dickens or Dostoyevsky, where large scale paradoxically
miniaturizes into something like the underworld of the Borrowers,
and human society viciously undermines itself with its humanness.

The older I get the weirder I think people are, frankly,
the more like animals who herd suddenly away
at the slightest stir from the bush.
But when you love someone, their little humannesses turn into rarities
so precious you're happy to stare at them all day long
with the sense of false epiphany that belongs to a dope addict.
And the qualities that are actually inconsequential,
like hair color or preferences in literature,
provide the metaphorical and metonymical devices
with which you interpret the textual soul of the person you love,

writing them opulently and expediently out of the reality of who they are.
You love more and more the tenebrism of faults and attributes,
that tenebrism abstracting into what you love more than them.
It's the complexity of shading, the variations of gray
that lend depth and mystery and fascination
to the freshwater pond of their character.

Later alone at the kitchen table, looking out the window at nothing
in particular—a solitary lawn or tree
that appears so vividly analogous to your state of things—
you recall with a numbing mixture of forgiveness and betrayal
those uncompromising and inexplicable ways of their being human,
as if they were obeying some invisible, omnipotent master,
the modification of "human" allowing for a margin of fallibility
gray and wide and completely opaque
as the fog that closes in and strands an island.
In that way you sat at the island of your piano
you played "nothing," as you put it,
concentrating intently on the nothing that you played.
That's what I thought of as your humanness then,
but of course, in the long run, not what you meant.

The fog that emanated from the walls
and kept my face stranded from your hands is what you meant.
The humanness of the legs upon which you left.
The humanness that demonstrated itself as if a supernatural force,
tearing limb by limb our intertwined bodies apart.
The part of your brain, or was it your heart, that caved in;
the termites of fear that burrowed in and burrowed in and stayed there
drilling at the same time with the same pressure
until exhausted and half-insane you inserted your hand,
ripped each one out, and fled like a nomad into the horizon.

It was the way I changed hallucinogenically before you,
my wood-colored hair matted and graying,
my blue eyes circling like crazy dice in my head.
All that materialized before you was somebody HIV positive,

another one of those silhouetted figures interviewed on David Susskind,
my true self, ghostlike, condemned to the back of your mind.
Your humanness sealed me in, shut the door airtight,
hoping that my spirit would run out of oxygen—
a mercy killing of a kind.
That my body still pumps away like an old Navy engine,
stands full-bellied and armed, a Red Army barrack,
serves only to remind you of the pink attic room
you both spitefully miss and abhor for its preservation.
If only its walls would cave in like that part of your brain or heart,
emanate enough fog to obscure me forever,
show that humanness, while cheered on, you gambled against.

The post-mortem poems you carefully compose now
supply tragic event for rich content.
My wood-colored hair, my drivenness,
subordinate into adjunct souvenirs that merely embellish.
But it'll be your humanness that will bring an eerie tone to this music,
and that ironic sense, almost olfactory, palpable but impossible to pinpoint,
will leave your audience sufficiently bewildered
with an odious sense of déjà vu they don't often experience.
For my poems and your music more human than us
fulfill the wish of the wishbone of us pried apart,
the sound of the tuning fork that reverberates as a sign
calling up our humanness from the ocean inside;
though in keeping with our humanness, only belatedly do we understand
like a bottled note ejected onto the deserted shoreline.

The Murder of Beauty / The Beauty of Murder

"If you cut off my hands, I'll offer you my stumps."
If you knock out my teeth, I'll still go down on you, conscientiously,
vine along a trellis, and suck you with my gums.
If you smash my toes, employing an ice crusher, one by one,
I'll heal myself with such truancy that someday I'll run on my knees.

"If you cut off my hands, I'll offer you my stumps,"
and orchestrate a standing ovation with the memory of my hands
representing each that are dying, each that are dead,
each forgotten that we refuse to remember like the lost hands of stumps.
So much misery in plain sight like tears streaming down a face;
so much misery hidden like the eventuality of the anti-Christ;
and so much incognito like the accompanying instruments of a torch song:
like the fire in the torch itself, like the torched interior of the song.

If you cut off my ears, I will listen with my eyes
to the spitting death of cavalrymen as they're roasted over an open fire;
to the smallest bones snap, dry as sun-seasoned kindling
of the young and truant witch when she's pressed by a thousand stones;
to the brave convulsions of the communist
strapped in the electric chair, dying by degree . . . not unlike the commonfolk
plucked from the village, arbitrarily, one last December night,
stripped to the flesh and heaved high into the freezing air
upon a whittled stave, tall and sharp, thrust deep into the asshole
they die by degree, ever so slowly and often only
(if not by freezing first, which, if merciful, God deems)
when the wooden point finally pierces the brain, brain-dead already
from the mauve anticipation and ear-splitting prerequisite of pain.

If you cut out my tongue, I will write you a letter,
a love letter lovelorn for that taste of your tongue.
If you fuck me hard I can never make love again,
I'll plant hyacinth bulbs in an effort to replace my abolished fecundity.
I will turn eternally on my side and pull down my pants
and listen to you masturbate while fantasizing about my ass.
I'll admire the willow out the window when I hear you come
and allow as if in tribute to the times I used to participate,
a vague expression of pleasure, albeit contrived to wash across my face
the way my desire for you, real as a willow, once had done.

Poems in American Sign Language

for Daniel Meltz

try becoming brilliant like the spring
hard as change
hard as death

try becoming like 20 chickens
or 5 beautiful women
hard as life
and forgotten as a family

try becoming an expert at forgiving
other people for living
differently from you

yes, I love 45 things about you
all mostly nice and good

people always assume they have a future
but only the sick know
how life is very, very short

please rest next to me
so we can grow like good conversation
or a happy home

my dreams and my life are very different
I wish they were the same
each day they grow further apart
I'm helpless to change my dreams
but I'm not helpless to change my life

you know it's hard
and you know it hurts
and you feel so alone
if I ask the earth, it says
"Too fucking bad!"
am I right?

all I want is to live with my friends
on earth as wonderful as heaven
and not far from here

I'm sorry
I wish I could help you
but all I can say is
that I love you
very, very much

Let

If it can be done then I do let, I'll let it be done
and done again, from my hands that close in
on themselves like a bedroom
my coat I hold wrapped loose around me like a bathrobe
my body the church I admire for its beauty
but cannot bring myself to wholly believe in,
I will begin to loosen the grip, to let, to let flee or emit
not wrench, not dig with steel teeth in my chest, my abdomen, my uterus
screwed tightly to my head and yanking my hair
like an electric chair cap or my mother's cervix.
I will let instead, watch with care, slowly
my fingers as if another's open like a bulb, an arthritic hand
freed of pain that stiffens and limits my movements just the same
underpinning like clothesline pins,
a clothesline of life's events, each known intimately and worn again
the synchrony of them played out against the schizophrenic day.
Like a family picnic table of tasteless but edible food,
I will let the red-and-white checkered cloth blow innocuously in the wind
the way it is, the way it was, the way it will always be and was meant to,
let the beetle's blood be in its miniature veins
and watch silently the wallflower watch the waltz
smelling the gardenia, extinguishing, in her bosom.
I watch her objectively from a distance, she being myself
with equal examination as she does the waltz.
The personified curtain or full-length window I reflect
perfectly, a full-length mirror, letting her loose from the mirror's image,
letting her loose from my wish that she were different,
letting the suffix *let* act with diminutive force my discontent
as she evaporates like fluid spilled onto the kitchen floor.
The milky substance of semen, her buttery dress
lost as a wallet, a wallet of hopes between the linoleum cracks
made up of her baleful desires, deserted by both her body and the gardenia.
I watch myself from a distance, the personified cabinet or broomstick
kneeling on the floor and peering into the cracks
looking intently for something for hours, a wallet perhaps (?).
I permit, I permit with monolithic tolerance my own frustration,
understand my own misunderstanding, if it's possible.

If it can be done then I do let,
the handmarks that once made wildly red my face
the door that locked definitively to my room,
the pants that were pulled down, then pulled up, then down again
out of my control, the carte blanche world where anything goes,
and projects itself onto the blank face of my isolated doll.
Her tiny pink sweater flew of its own accord above me at night.
The solid black ceiling that served as my version of the sky
served me well as it came to symbolize what I missed,
what I waited for and waited for and waited for
what I wished upon so greedily that there weren't enough stars.
Poor helpless and powerless stars I stubbornly let to my need, to my lacks
and concentrated on and concentrated on
until as if by the increasing intensity of my glare
they would finally submit and burst into a million pieces
like the creation of the earth,
proceed, an infinitive following like the verb itself *let*
fall with discretion as light rain on this devilish child
and alter down to the most unruly specifics her commonplace situation.
I watch her, the invisible persona of the pink sweater.
From this view it's so much easier to take, you know?
To let the belt undulating without remorse in the air, a serpent
whose poisonous tongue stung the small spine not out of spite
but some off-the-wall righteousness ingenuously followed like lineage.
So the ignorant stumbled out of bliss as stockbrokers did in '29
their limbs wriggling the way a spider descends
into a void of volition where their dreams clearly seen
from the window's ledge, spiraled in helical descent forever
and because they never really hit bottom
paradoxically they were caught and suspended indefinitely
within their own ignorance that grew wider and wider
like several so-called second chances
or a spider sleeping within its sprawling web.
Let us walk, permit us to suffer to walk, to watch
the child grow up, a thought distorted by its own insights and perceptions,
the baleful desire, a spider's den of glistening black eyes that burrow in
and watch her, scrutinize her, as she runs with trepidation,

with agility throughout the museum,
carrying to capacity her thoughts and insights and perceptions
while bombs crack the ceiling and blow out into the newly emancipated air
its wings and walls and limbs of the statues
wriggling in midair like spiders or stockbrokers.
I let, I let, if it can be done, her hideout in the desert, in a hutch
self-constructed of expensive oils, typed poems, and decaying toys
a hybrid of fag hag, nouveau-riche industrialist, and mental patient
mixing her own cures, ad-lib, within the wacky universe of her belief system.
I'll let the novice campfire recede into the distance
watch the blurred embers eventually dispel like trash
or all the helpless, powerless stars with total recall I remember.
I'll rub between my index and thumb the woven wool of the tiny pink sweater
wondering how it was done as I survey its weathered unraveling.
No urge to repair, no wish it were new again;
What other held object I wonder
has been observed with similar curiosity and befuddlement?
The love poem, the other's keys, their alien clothing, the spontaneous present
the tarnished silver ball that rolls, rickety-rock, along my desk.
Now, for the life of me, I have no feeling for it whatsoever.
How it played itself more than once, insidiously and schematically
like the tender chimes themselves trapped inside the silver ball
deep inside the bricks and mortar of the solitary cell
where a single shaft of light casts illumination on a single bowl
where uncountable particles of dust whirl nefariously within the fallow ray
mullocky in its color as counterfeit money or the mass production of anything.
Let, let my desires spring off in a finale, a chorus line,
a flock of birds taking off together.
Leave me to my gravity shoes irreversible as a photograph
laminated to preserve it, resentful
of the lightweight living things as they choose to leave
effortlessly as a striptease these shoes, my gravity.
I can only let, allow, accept, forgive the birds their ease
as they soar even higher, leave the terrain to its churlish disposition
left like a treasury note to me.
Let eternity be interpreted as it pleases
out of my control as these superior birds
that whip through sheets of NutraSweet clouds
severed and dismissed by their iron beaks, their emotionless eyes

while puffs of air continue to replenish their commitment
as if steam jets from a coal-engine train.
Buying up eternally their bony wings, they ride like a ride,
or a cantering horse, their sultry, indiscerptible wave.
I'll, I'll let, I'll let most painfully
what you've come to mean to me mean less
which no one can understand the depth, including you, despite your depth,
if that's what's convenient, if that's what you need.
Like the silver ball that rolls uselessly on my desk
though not entirely so if it can be used as an example:
feelings will be diffused, even eliminated
if impoverished long enough, if absence be accepted completely
and let as blood is let to bleed its longing by silver leeches
in small silver dishes tarnished as silver balls.
Let my hours be let loose from the lease of sixty minutes,
hour by hour, not wrenched from my arms
as a bundle might be when it consists of one's livelihood,
a locket from the loof of one's fisted hand,
but let to mean less, to wane, a corsage or sad Irish song.
Diminished by the diminutive force of *let*, let my hours become just *hourlets*.
Let, in turn, the presumption of a future putter on
in the minds of others with their inflatable clocks
like the invention of the wheel they assume it's as large, as noble
until witnessed in the tricycle, the limousine, or the golf cart.
I watch experiencing a kind of permanent jet lag
these good citizens follow in homage giant wagons on the road to Rome.
I let without any equity of spiritual recompense
no comfort in fate's novelistic intent,
no loyalty to God and his right-hand man,
nor in the judicious recycling of reincarnation;
nor even in its opposite, the hardened conviction, albeit political
when I lift my eyes all too knowingly to the bluestocking sky.
I'll settle for the implacable and prudish irreversibility
that composes, laboriously, my tomorrow and my today,
trailing a certain aftertaste, a numbing sheen to my perception
like lacquered wood or Windexed vinyl.
I'll let, I'll let, for all this brutality
the infinite dimensions within my last hourlets
penetrate and soothe, tiger's balm the gaping schism

that splits as the earth in an earthquake, or chicken breast, bleeding
to my very core where fear fills me up like guts.
Let, tactfully, the ravine between us and our love
the false reality of our ever growing closer
waver above me balloonlike with all my other dreams,
crowded as an airport by now.
Let them entertain me well so they will
in my last will and testament in which I leave you
such well-written fiction it exists as the essential and palpable gift of oxygen by air.
I watch her from the distance of my emotionless eyes.
My bony wings swoop down, zeroing in on my girl in the chapel
trying to believe in her body if only for its beauty like a church
or this more humble chapel, asking for more time,
fixated on the crucifix as she did those helpless stars.
Let as snow is let from a swollen cloud,
duck feathers busting out from their pillow,
let disperse throughout the earth the way her ashes would
that have yet to be made,
yet to descend even further underground to where a furnace burns
eternally in a cellar, cold and damp with no doors or windows
where the disparaging souls look on as my soul is let to take place among them.
Escorted by guards with webbed wings and toes, emotionless eyes
and the faces of those I've ever felt betrayed by,
my enemies surround me and let me watch the fire that never dies.
Let to be strapped to a chair, forced to stare, unblinkingly, as the embers
blur, the lonely campfire I never wanted to remember
into the splitting wood where each handmark on my face slaps back,
each undulation of the belt snapping on my spine.
The tiny pink sweater, a squeaking bat, makes its nest in my hair.
The waning hours, pared down to minutes, then minutes into seconds,
brings back the panic in complete rendition, the sad Irish song.
No corners cut, no pennies pinched, in the chorus assembled
the high soprano voices, narrow and perfect, pierce my skull
like acupuncture needles with the refrain I could sing note by note,
that underscored my nights and a good many days
one song, one scene encompassing everything, its theme
all pervasive, fully fleshed out, never lets up, never lets up,
no recitatives at all
from being left, of being alone, of being lost in a city that looms taller

while you shrink in proportion, smaller and smaller, floating away,
an astronaut with his hose cut, floating on and on in space
shriveling up, instantly, from the sight of the crew,
their faces pressed against the modular window a minute longer
as if in memoriam after you've disappeared from their view.
No one can hear you or see you and eventually it's only a matter of time
before they can't remember you exactly, what you actually looked like
the sound of your voice or your laugh in particular . . . .
just that they liked it when you come and go in their minds one day
like a cloud that trespasses momentarily before their eyes.
Let the cloud pass then, pass like a cloud
dainty and pretty and pasted in childlike fashion to the sky.
Let the cloud pass, billow up and be absorbed
into an atmosphere, empathetic and intelligent.
Like the chalky white dust of disinfectant
freshly shoveled on a mass grave where your corpse has been dropped
wrapped in burlap secured by two safety pins,
let the trespassing cloud, the chalky white dust,
rise, a phoenix that does not fail transformation.
Let glide into the aimless, amiable sky,
beyond where my dreams still huddle, a beloved but defeated team,
onto and into some vague sensorial fling
undergone only olfactorily, or sexually, or the way a certain weather condition
a certain temperature can make happiness burst suddenly
in surprising places in your body like sunlight
through stained glass in a church.
O let, o let, let, let, o let, please, let that happen
let me rise up into that pleasure with all its gradations
so blue and green and white and pink and brilliantly textured
as water, medicinal and base,
let love be an element and let me amongst it,
let me be in it, a pine tree in a pine forest.
Let me, let me, let me, let me, let me, please, at least be its metaphor
and fulfill no less soberingly the destiny of a spore.
Let my silly life break swiftly, fail-safe as a Timex
scatter its parts, hither and thither, on the egalitarian landscape
leveled at last (as if in an afterlife) with the pinecone and its mulch
no less graceful than the pinecone, no less purposeful than its mulch.

Walking Away I

Persimmons spurned underfoot the churlish path where no path exists.
Already the famous shimmering from the unguarded pond up ahead,
the lavender love letter that revises itself by resurfacing again and again.
Your face, smoothed like a stone overturned by the sea in my brain,
the incorrigible memory contrived to its seafaring metonymical place.
Beloved, the stone weighs me down necessarily, analogous to the weights
used by astronauts and sea divers to achieve equilibrium in their voyages;
the stone, the love letter overturned in the poem I rewrite like a love letter.

Certainly there's promised a clearing beyond the forest all of us believe in
if only subliminally when we glance at the fuschsia horizon and wish
if only subliminally, as we always do, that things were different.
Toward the clearing, toward the horizon, upon the sea, within the street,
persimmons, movie stubs, exquisite odds from the ocean's bottom
spurn underfoot while we caress their natural likenesses in our pockets.

Walking Away II

Into the underbrush of black and charcoal smudged landscape, the houses
and cars in their driveways serene with dark blessing, unexpectantly.
Into the cold and vinyl waves that swell and heave with a hissing
as if a great respiratory system attempting to sigh, to shed its darkening
like the star that winces you identify with in its need for so much attention
so much affection from us in its need for our wishes to keep it alive.
It's hard to refuse a star, the symbol of wishes granted never granted until
indifferent we become, grateful only for the light, the tiny, tiny light

satisfied by the darkening that obliterates methodically all within sight.
Satisfied we become by bleakness, by erasure, by starkness fulfilled
paradoxically by its nothingness, by pebbles deleting themselves, magically
by the empty house, the light switch, the needy star that ultimately needs
nothing, not even us to wish upon it, finally, for nothing, to want nothing,
to be happy with nothing but the black underbrush, but its tiny, tiny light.

Walking Away III

Walking away from the ravenlike night that slips easily from your hands
from your insides as if you were made up of string or filigree
dismembering pleasantly in the wind like breeze sifting through your hair,
walking away in some strange metaphysical yet bodily climb, bead by pearl
unfurling, the altitude shifts inside where all comes apart, poetically
like straw held up to the wind held together so fragilely from the start
the loss, liberating, your flesh assimilating into the cool blue air
light blue and airborne as air, air above underbrush or persimmons spurned

the way the blade inside shreds you apart delightfully, propels you forward
your evolutionary heart, evolving backwards like the clock of negation
your limbs unfolding automatically in fetal position, your dying words,
a cry for milk before all words muffle into the rosy egg where you sit
like a chick then a yolk that bursts into a rosy cloud, vast and plentiful
in the cool air that bursts, bead by pearl, into cool blue air.

from A Two-Way Mirror

II

The omniscient threshold, threadbare and glistening from your lack of pity
looms with iron proficiency like the ocean in winter, cruel waves
that counter each other like Christian souls in a competition of suffering.
When life has become so precious you're afraid to touch it, the child saint
who miraculously never deteriorated but to kiss her would be her desecration.
It's this constant miracle that throws cold water on every conscious moment
like a slow but exculpated loss of sight as it ekes out a path of exile:
one puff of wind and tiny leaves alight all at once, future days and past,
confusing the air like snow flurries, the ground with a glinting mosaic
of immediacy, panic, peace, for which no amount of exposure acquires the taste.
The large shadows shift as if earth plates beneath me, recall my flirtation
snagged once again back into the undertow, the Gregorian beating of my heart.
When I say that I'm jealous of the dead, you turn away, partly in disgust
and partly in agony, for you can't provide for me what the dead know already.
My brain splits apart, hemispheres of apology and longing to be understood.

XIII

Will there ever be a point like a riptide that divides me from this fight
and delivers me as if in the wake of Mercury unto my dignity, contrived as courage,
the Captain who remains erect, though trembling, when he salutes the abyss,
the heather-hued ocean that devours him and his ship and a hundred dependents.
Perhaps such saving-face gestures of protocol, once fail-safe, snapped and broke
in the course of trying, the last resort like retirement savings piled up,
gambling chips, on a long shot, a leap of faith where realization came in midair,
you'd never make it; the upshot of the great hand you sank your teeth into
and held on to, scrapping, ready to take it to the bitter end, even if bitterness
be the outcome, your skin gone gray with sweat, your hair, lanky and tremendous
in the past, cropped angrily almost to balding, your eyes ringed with exhaustion
exempt themselves from compassion, from cultural interests, from the peripheral
vision of human potential: family, community, enrichment, your stare set solely
on survival for so long, digesting metal, drinking urine, it's become albino.
You spit into the heartbreakingly beautiful faces of the dead, enemy children.

XVIII

When you go you go alone, giving good head to a loaded gun. That's what we're afraid
of. From the git it's an ongoing love/hate rapport with that iron barrel, whether fed
from breast or bottle, operative always an ulterior agenda played like a music box
in the milky sky. Whether a spoon of nickel or silver, the moon shattered on the Aegean
a bed of needles, a nude of marble, unstable and cryptic and of a rape mentality.
Whether the sex of the beloved, bending its back almost to agony over a kitchen table.
Its bound arms blur to plastic, its pawky ass rubberized within the myopia of
eroticism, fragmented like a page torn out of a porno magazine. The potentiality to
dismember your life, utterly, remains set to spring just an earshot away. You picture
the omnipotence amidst the black grasses of your unconscious ready to be revealed
like a lightshow. That desire will become confused with fear is what we're afraid of.
In dread of being terrorized one more time our desire will mount like a stallion.
At the point of climax we look up at the milky sky and pray for intervention. We open
our mouths, O-shaped like an angel's, lick our lips thoroughly as lubricant. Our eyes
roll back into their sorrel interior. Out of our exploding heads spurt feathers.

XXVI

Sometimes I step out of my suffering and stare at it, self-contained as a miscarriage.
I move toward myself as if aimlessly, a bottle tossed on the waves, in contrast
to the static figure finally put out of pain like a chloroformed body on the table.
I touch her glass-cold face with a glass-cold hand extended, a conduit for three
generations, the matrilineage of myself. I turn my aging grimace away from the sun
to regard, existentially displaced as a blurb, myself kneeling inside the pink sphere
of my recollection, both belittled and exploited on the dirt stage of its amphitheater.
No one was there as the beholder but us, when you lifted your face to mine with what
Diderot would call a "naïve" expression of terror. The broken elevator slid another
twelve floors. The counter-day of fluorescence twitched on and off, mutating
all color unto the quality of black-and-white film the way ashes deliver themselves
to the wind. The forest shifts simply to darkness, barely gradational against
the sheen of an overcast sky. I acknowledge the white sheet that eventually covers
my head: black iris of a dark forest against the skull-and-crossbones white
of an overcast, marbled sky; my silhouette erased in the process of acknowledgment.

XXIX

If you know that you will die alone, like a coyote, like a Yugoslavian, then you
can do anything in life. The innocence of abyss arches its trajectory of deletion
across the image repertoire of your failures, mitigating the conjecture of tragedy
in the process, a processlessness that reads like a palindrome: matte white on glossy
white, white rose on sepia rose, the smoothed cascade of muscular infrastructure in
the marbled back of Rodin's mistress, the myopic teardrop to which we supply
the hermeneutic signified of "miserable." Your death floats always beside you, a kayak
stranded on the parched surface of the desert. Swaddled inside the Todtenbaum of your
negative future you break down like a particle, only the idea of which is fearful.
You guard your carcass, O papoose, that lies beneath the liturgical purple, blue tarp
of a lean-to flapping in a nebulous definition of fresh air, while underneath awaits
either a bed of nails or a bed of sweet william, the marriage bed you never consummated
but kept the repetition compulsion of excess and supposition going like some quartz
mechanism, hand between legs, nose pressed against the conundrum of your perception.
You wonder if it's worth the risk of slitting your wrists to shatter the glass. It is.

Listen

In your prison, your ochre cell, big as a couch, you toss on the cot and read the same poem on the ceiling, on the walls of your brain and heart and watch drop by drop the mist bead up cold and damp on the porcelain toilet next to your head, where you're forced to sleep with the symbol that epitomizes your prison life and therefore your life in toto it seems, the conclusion the all-encompassing pain that spreads throughout your body like a genetic formation, down to your toes, which if pointed and bare would graze the bars when the guards pass, their heels on the cement execute a torture all their own, the brass rings of their keys, that bob against their waists like an Indonesian earring, tease with a kind of hideous and addictive music, as if listening to the keys, to the chime of them together with such intensity, you can almost hear each one individually and find the one that is yours, as if listening to them could let you out, give you the power to open your cell effortlessly like drawer; listening, listening, you walk through the village of corridors and notice, oddly, how your heels sound different from the guards', notice how odd it is that you have time to notice the change underfoot from institution to courtyard, the sun suddenly thrown on your head like a burning blanket, your shirt catches fire and you listen to the burning; you fall in love with fire, walking from city to forest, listening to the leaves burning, to the trees burning too, to the rain sad and cool and feminine that relieves you in the smallest way at first, pinpricks your face and then, as if letting go at last herself, soaks your shirt, your pants, your hair, your hands—as you approach with no specific direction but with this strong sense of destination into the thick of the forest, the way you would enter a church and heading toward the altar as if pulled by something magnetic and good, toward the sweet gate and iron cross hung at an angle, Christ's body bowed like a sail, you turn to measure how far you've come, when abruptly you behold a couple making love on the velveteen pew and listen surreptitiously to their breathing like keys to the chime of them together with such intensity you can almost hear each one individually, hers short and warbling, his long and raining, and thinking of rain remember that your clothes are dry now inside the soft stones of the church, and comforted, you inspect without method, though meticulously, the architecture, the rafters, the stained glass, the tall brass tubular columns of the organ, the eyelets on the altar cloth, listening to the various creaks and cracks amidst the polished wood so quiet, and then as if increased in volume to only the breathing, hers short and warbling, his long and raining, and yours yours as you hold her writhing in your arms, entering her like a church, her hair falling in your face like fire, her hands sad and cool like rain splayed against your face, like keys loosened from their ring, like an Indonesian earring, listening to the music hideous and addictive and magnetic and good.

Square One

Afore the tombstone "Hotchkiss" and aft the pathway yet to be
a stick is stayed to mark the spot of the hole you insist on digging
yourself on the shadeless hill, on the steep, on the knoll
where no flattering description, for the life of me, can be made.

Under a rock I've lived and waned and waxed and worn
the rock like a hat or a frock or pushed like a wheelbarrow
bending the four corners as if the making of another plot.
I've dug with one hand well into the evening
by the light that's not light but the eye's adjustment to the dark
(the way the eye of a cat can adjust), tiny, miniature graves
like those of a troll or a chipmunk.
Within them I've placed ritualistically the tender thoughts
that contrived my tender hopes, not stillborn but short-lived.

These are infants' graves, stars we know are there on a starless night.
So many of these I've dug, a nursery of hopes has become one grave
like passengers on a boat sailing leeward on the ocean.
So many ghosts, remembrances of these hopes, I can hear them
clearly, the way Joan of Arc claimed the voice of god in midday—
no clambering all at once like a kindergarten but alternately
as if called upon, though I can never really make sense of what they say;
just tropes or clauses, nonsequentially uttered
and audited, wisps of advice or folkloric phrases.
Sometimes I've taped them with minicassettes
or typed them verbatim like a stenographer, my spine erect,
little orange spheres hanging by little chains from my lobes.

Irrevocably, interminably, they love to hear themselves talk
and I am more than happy to listen, to lean my head like a cameo
on the custom-made easel of my arm
and soak up what they say with placid expression
so jaded to their enthusiasm experientially I've become.
Pushed to confess I'll admit I'm grateful
for anything or anyone that alters if only abstractly like bonbons
or bourbon or beeswax candles or carnal sex
wrought askew from interpretation into true lovemaking,
the monotone traversing of my view.

I'm only capable of glancing across that mutant fields that adumbrate
ad nauseam shades of beige.
And despite the flecks of wildflowers, albeit white, albeit yonder,
internally I'll always demand a hell of a lot more,
and stare, not glance, with contempt at the imperial sky
gorgeous and pompous as the imperial palace of Pompeii
happy to listen with placid expression like a cameo
resting on the custom-made easel of the horizon.

I hate the resemblance, its nudging imitation,
the soft blue walls and the soft green hills that coexist
in a false sense of Zen equilibrium, a Zen contrivance.
Sometimes I wish I could throw a monkey wrench into the works,
chuck my naked body wriggling with discontent out into the ocean.
And not just watch but like an atom split, provide
what unearths the earth with volcanic implosion
to resettle with delicacy as the ruins once lay in Dresden
where I with the camaraderie of my hopes hike upon the rubble.

The pleasure I take in the discontinuity almost comforts me in my loss,
for wasn't it always this same landscape I felt carved within me
like metaphysical surgery or inserted barbarically, the handmade altarpiece,
for which my fingers were smashed publicly for its many flaws?
What relief I sought in the chalky rubble, the glad identification
with the ruined city which within me its scenic rendition
like an architectural model had long since bombed.

Appropriately among the ruptured cobblestones propped the remnant of a steeple
sitting askew like a dunce cap or sailboat sailing obliquely.
I placed the heavy structure on my head with inhuman fortitude
and continued on nomadically, as if crossing a desert or ocean
upon which a most unstable ferry tossed, a toy, to and fro
enveloped eventually into the horizon as if swallowed surreptitiously, whole.

So they will gather again and again one foggy morning
on the porch of their home to mourn the toy and its history.
How they loved the toy each they'll voice,

the father of the toy even more poignantly than the wife.
He'll stand up and announce he's the father of the toy
explain briefly the immeasurability of his grief.
Toy! Toy! Toy! For the specificity of the toy we ache.
For the specificity of the toy we long, we long
with a longing disproportionate to fate.

We long so long at last your eyelids pop open
your spirit coiling upwards as if conjured up by flute and turban.
I long until at last my hopes follow your spirit as once did children
the Pied Piper into disappearance, into flecks of wildflowers, yonder.

Jab a sprig here and there in my hair, smudge my face with dirt,
the markings of a tree, a sapling, I tiptoe sideways across the gritty stage,
gnomes having made their homelike hibernating chipmunks in my belly.

Like a gnome someday I will be laid, a toy, into a seemingly miniature grave.
Like the scrawny vegetable garden Candide could not surpass
always within the same square, without demarcation, we begin and end.

Like heather and hay, the beige field varies only by the wind
and sun, a slant on the invariable that's made up of glint.

Beyond Belief

Hateful ferns like harlots
tease the sky where dreams have melded for centuries.

White caps, driven, dive forward, a school of dolphins
obedient to the militant mum-faced blue, tearstreaked
at the most appropriate moments as if sympathetic to us like one of us:
Purposeful yet confused.
Alternately self-flagellating and self-forgiving.

True, in my prayers I'll confess my atheism
and actually believe in an atheistic god whose understanding
would bridge all my conflict.
I'll find the manifest Christ handsome and rationalize my attraction
as an admittance that allows for more of an ingenuous devotion,
bolstering my beliefs with twigs and cotton balls and poems and foam rubber
and most of all desires that expand organically like yeast at my acknowledgement.

Desires like dolphins, driven
obedient, tearstreaked, sexy.

Death as a Material

I lose, I lose beneath black lace clouds, the black lace house
that once bloomed or broke out of black lace itself.

Out of black lace woods I crept at night on all fours, feral,
my hair a cluster of briars,
my eyes of an animated sparkle like zircon diamonds.

Lofty branch, be my loss and lean against my body, barely, like lace.
Lean as loss leans
against my faith, a diary, a sleeping infant,
easily irruptive, combustible, and innocent.

The large starless night swings open with pantheon expansiveness,
onward and outward like intention or space.
Where long ago we capitulated to be born into this world
and exemplify, as if our previous experience, the experience of stars.
As tiny and as burdened with expectation,
we radiate by virtue of our ability to die, extemporaneously
but slowly and so eternally shine, though dimly,
for lit by our unfortunateness we are like any shrine.

We know then, already (and have always), in the back of our minds
what it's like to be dying, to be lost like a lofty branch
in the feral, black lace of night.
We know the way we know that entering a diary entry
our experience will disappear instantly in its exemplifying,
into the same starless evening at the back of our minds.

Because we know, an extraordinarily complex but organized web
wraps with cognition its soft shearing between us like a pact.
It drapes and folds, togalike, yet immaterial as the weather;
erotically charged as a black lace nightgown
is the feral, black lace evening that branches out around us.
The cloudy room ferrets with speech we love to hear for its own sake,
a metalanguage made up of actions, accordances, predilections,
mutual destinations, and private thoughts
which, when etymologized,
break down to the white noise of our anticipations.

Like white noise the white water flows evenly at night,
lace rafting along the river.
The lofty branch, lost but present, sleeps, a panther, among the loss,
feral though safekeeping as a fault plane.

We point to a couple pointing to a rainbow of cups
our branch of lace that glows in negative illumination
like an x-ray or white object under a black light.
The water, black lace or white, flows extemporaneously, forever,
while we, its gesture,
reach like a river across the rioting fog.

Caught in Your Own Reaching

Was there a specific matrix, a decision
formulated as an object of desire is formulated into an object
apart, pristine, veneered, African violet violet-blue
where I drifted, surrendered to drifting as a cloud may seem to?

Whenever I visit (or rather come upon) the pile of tombs,
everything becomes read and painful in that I'm still in my youth;
in that I use the word *still* when I use the word *youth*.
Everything becomes violet-blue in its density, disturbing as a tomb.
I am as close to death as I am far, like a visitor of a tomb,
still an object of desire the way I'm still in my youth.

From that sense of *still* is where I drift, you know?
And so in my stillness am mobile, passionate, and decision-making,
though caught, as *still* implies, still as a bureau.
Woven around me, a mire of my own doing, my own bureaucracy
of longing, translucent and untenable, like Rapunzel's hair,
as crippling as it is phenomenal.

Ash

Cindered, I test the overwrought sky for reality,
pink-gray like the grieving mind, almost garish in its stricken
state, the tearful clouds, the throaty lament of the wind,
a state that should succeed by the marginality of extreme.
The fuchsia highway lone along the anemic hills,
a hemophiliac's vein varicose with what its bleeding means,
and the sheep-sheared valleys, benign to feeling, their emotive curls
shake with refusal above in a kind of suspended hell,
curlicue the screwed-up eye sockets, the distorted face that weeps
afresh as one ratching thought after another plays like atonal music.

Cruelly all around me flaunts the disclaimer that there's no repetition
in nature, but why then does the primal scene, the taste of petites madeleines,
so to speak, belatedly retrieved, present a dead catfish,
snagged instead of caught, reeled in only to be tossed out again?
The paradigm necessitates the production of its own paradigm
as a modus vivendi for its endless dismantling, the way a four-poster bed
which acts as staves when the decapitated heads of traitors
still defend themselves in a whispering, necromantic legatissimo
beseeching from primacy the belatedness of evidential manufacturing
that would be their defense, their blinking eyes let to close at last
the four-poster collapsing like a Murphy bed into a wall lavishly blank.

Therein goes all our vivacious hatred for fare, so life-affirming,
into this invisible figure eight, infinite and hence unhelpful.
Only architecture, personalities and plant life impinge themselves on absence,
providing in the process at last the pretense for some answers
as if all the world were an exposition we as interlopers could experience
in a deferred relationship, our hands on interaction sensed secondarily
though pronto like room service or masturbation.
Otherwise we have the option, always, of elegance, of erasure,
of allowing the truthful unknowingness of space to surround us with vacancy.
Of grace, of efficiency, we have the option of accepting ourselves
as at once amid the absence and also of it; as both impotent and ingenious.

Like the late, lace-blue sky weighed down by the intercourse of its lacking,
by the graceful intentions of noneffort, a sublimity

made by an infrastructure of what's missing,
it sways with expensive sadness, as does a single blue lantern,
or a wind-tortured branch of cherry blossoms, or the sour-dark chartreuse
hallways of an apartment complex, lit in commiserating unison at midnight.
The vast, once spiritual, often offsets the solitary by defamiliarization
unto an astringent loneliness as the basement does a fluorescent tube,
or as the fluorescent tube does your face, a bas relief, in the bathroom mirror.
It never takes long for anything to disappear from your view,
but diminishment from within requires a kind of metacentric conversion.

Like paint thrown against a wall with anger in the arbitrary gesture,
anger at arbitrariness itself for you're jealous of its freedom;
the shocked grace of missing places permits a launching, reallocates
the point of buoyancy self-wrought as the human condition.
Unless mostly of lace, of water, of absences we make ourselves
although with excruciating intentionality like the late, lace-blue sky—
its display of nothing so genuine we wantonly absorb its pain in acquiescence—
then of only anchors, of only amulets outworn of their medicinal properties,
of only anniversaries planted insidiously inside our bodies
where seasonally enslaved to their roots we behave as never anything but dirt;
unless mostly of rice paper we make ourselves, of paper, of rice, of ash.

Many Rivers to Cross

Written to the song by Jimmy Cliff

Many rivers to cross,
                     but I can't seem to find my way over.
Maybe you wonder why I'm not stronger.
Maybe you wonder if I've lost and lost badly.

Yet you tell me it's of no matter
                 (while thinking all the while I'm not stronger).
Maybe you believe me when I say I'm going insane,
                         day by day
and too easily picture me ending up conversing with a tree—
no longer able to distinguish my place setting from my food—
barely audible are my mutterings of water torture in another world.
They strapped me down and just a drop hit my forehead, dead center
every fifteen seconds, for seven years, or ten or was it twelve, I can't remember.
It was the endlessness of it all that killed me, not the water.

Wandering, I am lost
                   as I travel alone, white cliffs of Dover.
How I envy and resent and admire the white cliffs of Dover,
              kneel surreptitiously upon what's left of a rotting belief in them.

I demand from the rock some iron, for I know I'm failing.
I sob and hate the whiteness. It does nothing as it watches me fail.
How I wish I knew what it felt like to feel hope again.
How hopeful the white cliffs are indeed, regardless.
How I hate them all the more for their lack of regard.
I sob, my tears the would-be snow of the white cliffs of Dover.

Many rivers to cross,
                   and it's only my will that keeps me alive,

as if I had crossed many rivers already;
somnabulistically treading the currents, Christ-like, with bare feet,
both vulnerable and omnipotent,
both the protagonist and bird's eye voyeur of the protagonist
deep inside the beautiful, omniscient double vision of my sleep.

I awake, soaked in sweat, panting from the droves of dead bodies
that awaited me on the other side of the riverbank.

I've been licked, washed up for years
              like a slave collared and leashed by my way.

For in my heart of hearts I know that probably I'm dying.
For in my heart of hearts I know that I'm going to survive.

How I know this exactly splits my skull in half with a chisel,
no longer human, the hemispheres of my brain have turned to marble,
a Modernist material born like a runt, a last resort
from the supplemented content of my thoughts, i.e., my "pride."

Before I could hear my molecules eat me alive like locusts,
                         ravage the fiber of my body,
I had a nightgown white as the white cliffs of Dover
and liked walking upon light, though it burned my feet,
                  when crossing the desert.

O the sun throttled me a good shake and I had no choice but to stand it.
And I merely survive because of my pride:
the promise of pride my pride provides for me.
I wear the promise every day wrapped like a sarong around me.

This leaves me topless, so I negate my breasts like a man.
Sheared like the white cliffs of Dover, my chest reaches final closure.
But their tenderness, their weight, their meaning won't go away.
Why are men surprised that breasts could mean as much as a penis?

I thought of turning, once more, to the white cliffs of Dover,
of pleading my case to its classical veneer as if it were an altar,
though God knows they fucked me over
              with the good white stuff they never did deliver.
But I thought of the concept of forgiveness and mustered up my ambition.
I thought of pretending it was a noble and organic site for God.
I thought if I repeated the words in lieu of a god
maybe they would work by the virtuous power of their vernacular,
        and a god would be produced—even a pretend god would be useful:
with the fulfillment of a wish the carte blanche sky clouds over,

hailing in a nimbus, a dark fist which tightens and gathers up
the fragile atmosphere that screams like a woman in its grip;
who puts me on par, at last, with the cliffs and damaged seacraft.

And this loneliness won't leave me alone.
                              It's such a drag to be on your own.
My man left and he didn't say why.
Now I have no breasts and no penis either,
just a hole I can't fill up enough; I stuff my sarong in there
and pull it out, slowly, then roughly, hoping after
I'll remember what satisfaction's like again.
                              Well, I guess I have to try.

How I wish I could fill it up with the white cliffs of Dover . . . .
every night get fucked and be loved by the white cliffs of Dover . . . .
become pregnant, whereupon you, My Sarong,
I give birth as if to the white cliffs themselves . . . .
and then my loneliness would finally leave me alone,
leave me like my man and why he did, I wouldn't care to know anymore.
I'd have my breasts back and I'd build a nest in the snow,
nurse my child while safeguarded by the white cliffs of Dover.
And my home, made of snow, would be proof that good could come
from the would-be tears that I once shed.

Many rivers to cross,
                    but just where to begin I pray for time.
May time come to me like a father and stroke my hair.
I despair about time and he lends me his shoulder.
You wouldn't believe how sore my chest is,
as if a transplant took place, where was my heart now sits a clock;
where was my heart now plays a tape of Tibetan chanting,
a continuous monologue that prays in a thousand tongues,
keeping open all options to the various belief systems and their gods.
And it's the ticking, it's the voices, that won't let me sleep, Dad.
I pray for more time, but maybe I just want this noise to stop.
When I weigh the waste and the value, the outcome knocks me off keel.
I can't help but think that only death will bring me equilibrium.
Or total health, so far away from me, white cliffs of Dover.
Every time I find myself thinking I'll come to tell of some dreadful crime,

I want to take out the loaded gun and point it to my head.
I want to off myself, while getting myself off, I come.
I want to watch the red and white corpuscules explode from my head
simultaneously as the white cream of my come trickles down my leg.
I want my last vision to be of the white cliffs
pure and white as my spurting come, as the would-be snow of my tears
that cover over again the white cliffs of Dover
before my brains splatter across them.

Many rivers to cross
                              but I can't seem to find my way over.
Wandering, I am lost
                    as I travel alone, white cliffs of Dover.

Like a bucket of water thrown onto the sand,
the gushing breaks into tributaries that appear both arbitrary and fated.
And what would it matter if I could tell the difference?
Is the arbitrary path ultimately safer than the fated?

Yes, I got many rivers to cross
and I merely survive because of my will.

Eternal Snow

The sun reclines behind the wounded alp, as if also unhealed.
The scope of my heart has finally outwon the sky's
so oppugned by the heckling of field after field,
their humiliated weeds and flecks of minuscule but ingenious flowers
that vulnerable to the entropy of merely living in the world
I finally loved, at last, like a dove for effort only:
how hard they've tried in a flattering light to mirror me.

One might hope for silence from such rueful snow
when it relents in tepid measures as melancholy music does,
yet dashed hopes prove more lethal.
Dust it will the magnanimous heart that by the same token
no longer feels, for forced prematurely with warm water
massaged at the temples, jaws spring open before the eyes
in order to swallow whole and pronto the pain of simply waking.

Wrenched with thongs the newborn head trusts the worm instinctively,
Though as often as not the ocean's a wicked mother
Or netherland womb which, caterpillar to butterfly, becomes my bed.
O it's what my bed becomes that splits in half life from death again.
How it spits itself out at me, rebellious from longing,
rises within my body, a prison riot of both innocent and guilty.
How it starves like a stone scourged amidst the topology of shells.

How it forks into clumps of straw damp from urine and feces
cruelly splayed on the floor of the cargo train.
How I lie down on it greedily and beg you to tear down my panties;
how I spread wide as you enter me while I can hear people eating
and speaking about us and then, not about us too.
How we fuck each other and fuck each other and fucking
Try to break out by fucking's virtue, while all the while I can hear
People sob and shit and pray and kiss, for we aren't alone either.

Variations

Allow the vine to cross over the empty space of your heart.

Allow the vine to cross over, cross over the empty heart, the empty space.

Allow the vine, whimsical yet petulant, to cross devilishly over the empty space of your heart.

Allow the empty space to cross like a cloud passing over the vine-covered heart.

Allow the vine, allow the heart, allow the empty space.

Allow the heart to cross like a vine or ivy with miniature magenta leaves, to cross over the empty space. The empty space.

Allow the empty space to lift itself up to the cloud, to hear the heart that drags tendrils of vines across the cold, invisible surface of its emptiness.

Allow the heart that was once a vine to be among vines again.

Allow the operatic vine to climb as an operatic theme does into the empty chair of your heart.

Allow the vine, the heart, the empty space, to cross over and under each other braiding in and out, for then the space, covered with vines and heart and empti-ness, will exist as if the vine were allowed at last to cross over the empty space of your heart.

Allow inside the vine-covered heart for there to be an empty space.

Allow the empty space of your heart to shrink inside your heart like a violet, like a vine of violets, inside the safe space of your heart, evaporating within the heart of the vine.

Allow the vine of your heart to cross over the empty space that everywhere must be yours.

Allow the vine that is so small against the empty space of your heart to cross over and over its emptiness and soon the vine too will become as vast and as large.

Allow the vine that wants nothing but to cross over the empty space of your heart to cross over the empty space of your heart.

Allow the empty space to fall, as if a heart covered with vines, onto the soft ground and sink into the dirt, every empty drop, until all that is left is the heart covered with vines, a heart-shaped relief in the ground like a hill, like a valentine.

Jade

Upon a plain of thought, a box,
Ornate as a medieval bodice.

Within the box, another box: the renaissance of jeweled boxes.

Dissecting the boxes with surgical gloves,
A blond and bright nothingness,
You watch the descent to smallness, once in love with diminutiveness.
Box within box within box within box . . . .
Centuries stripped raw, poignantly.

In the very last box (if there is one), this century,
The root of the problem displayed upon velvet
Like the Nairobi diamond or Nairobi itself,
A Haitian pufferfish in its embalmed perfection;
Desire frozen with moribund deception. O so artfully.

Wrapped in plastic, the dormant heart,
"Ti bon ange" trapped in a jar,
Still feathers against what makes up the glass,
Your fear which makes it impenetrable,
Sentences me temporarily to a bell jar like Juliet.

In the very last box (if there is one), this evening,
Marbleized by the moonlight and vaulted like a ceiling.
You and I sit on a sofa, a turbulent dinghy.
You're afraid to kiss me, the plot of our first kiss,
The backdrop, foiling us.
"Do you think of me as contaminated?" I ask you finally.
"I think of you as a beautiful, jeweled box," you reply very quietly.
"And inside you is a box even more beautiful."

But in your eyes I interface myself,
A photograph of a dead tree
Or a painting of a living tree.
That minute carnelian buds have begun there makes no difference.
One can easily turn away from a photograph or a painting.

I see the dirt pile up in the distance,
Dug up by the tiny spoon that doles out the pufferfish powder.
Someone left a jar of it outside my house.
And in the very last box (if there is one), inside me
Lies the spoon raised on velvet, a corpse in its tomb.

It swallows up everything I am, this box.
This box is a blood test, this box, an abstraction,
This box a coffin of sorts
That buries inside my body the antibody HIV;
My body's counterbody, the proof, nonproof,
A footprint, this root, merely a photograph of a root,
A photograph of a dead tree.
This origin, a nonorigin mistaken for the truth
Devours me almost cannibalistically
To a skeletal bride draped in desecrated chiffon, once white.
Coffin within coffin within coffin within coffin….
Within my body, a pilgrimage of candles floats.
Within my body, a coffin burns in the snow.
My soul, a firefly the witch doctor now owns,
A flaming boat, my sinewy hold on myself, a tiny angel,
Pinned like a collected butterfly,
Anesthetized by the powder mixed from pufferfish and skull
The Haitian witch doctor grinds to pharmaceutical dust.
Someone blew a cloud of it into my face,
A desert storm where your parents live.
The powdery sand seeps from my skin to my brain.
"They call it the Romeo and Juliet drug," you said,
Ordering all my orifices to be closed
By martial law your peers enforced,
My vital signs stopped by their hands, by yours,
which lower the ropes eight feet deep into the earth.
I can hear the dirt shoveled on top until there is no sound.
The weight warps the wood closer to my face.

You hated to be the one to do that to me, you said,
Like there had to be someone.
I should have dropped a penny into your executioner's hand.
I should have said, "I forgive you."

There's freedom in feeling that there's no choice, I assume,
Freedom from the screams you hear from eight feet below;
Freedom from the pilgrims buried when they were comatose,
Dug up decades later to find their skeletons clawing to get out.
This freedom, I guess, makes you capable of what you do:
You spread the cold spoon like cold cream all over my body.
You insert it deep inside me like you.
You erase my name, banish me from your house like Montague.
My unborn children with O-shaped mouths press against your window.
I, their murderess mother, who love them so,
Stare blankly back, mummified, for all they know.
Yellow and red rain pours down on my boy and my girl,
Wets their clothes, beats their eyes shut
Against my extenuating scream, one note—
The rain, red and yellow, relentless in its waning
When you cross my hands across my chest,
When your fingers force my face into an expression of repose.
Perhaps you love me best now I've matched the dead,
Buried alive by your fear that I am.
Winter trees tarry against the winter sky like wet feathers.
And I, as resistant, cling to the debris,
To the edges of the sinking place you picture me in.

You visualize (wishfully?) a zombie
Who meanders through the same streets as you,
My silhouetted figure, the negative state of my positiveness,
Always with me, a dead twin.
With my lips zipped together, my tongue carved out,
I've become all eyes and you cannot bring yourself to look into them.
For if you did,
You would hear my scream as just breathing, and you know it.
You would witness without surprise the green decumbence of my exile.
You expect the odor of putrefying flesh
But discover instead my body whole and pink,
Loyal to your touch as you once did.
From the inverted mouth, returns the bottomless kiss
From my hidden sex, a Buddha's smile,
My body, the beautiful box you fetishize
As if inside me there were a box even more beautiful.

Stripped of our clothes we go beyond the flesh through the flesh,
To the swelling within us we refer to as our souls.
Our flesh, a rope bridge to this, where trains pass beneath
In the night, in the philharmonic heat.
Where the red moon, inches above our heads,
Will exclude us from its light, apheliotropically, in the end.
And this is why we in our aphasia
Must kiss and kiss and kiss, in an effort
To include ourselves in the red moon and suffocating kudzu's eternity;
Which, if granted, we could not bear, we admit.
But equally we cannot bear its alternative, so we kiss
Flagrantly, tearing our shirts open
And eating from the other's mouth the other's mouth.
So we kiss, just once, a reminder, a glove, an interleaf
Of our aloneness spent together, for now.
So we kiss, cat and mouse, until our saliva becomes a kind of elixir,
Kissing insistently, petulantly, apologetically, tangentially, automatically,
Profanely our necks, our breasts, our sexes, our hands,
Our fingers in each other's mouths, our eyelids,
Until we kiss as if writing a beginning and a middle and an end to us
In the dilating myopia of our kiss.

And in the very last box (if there is one), a symbol
Offered up like a sacrifice, a sliver of jade.

Jade, the gemstone of prophetic dreams
Raised upon velvet, a yellow star, a pigmentation, the perpetrator of sin.

Raised upon velvet, it rises again in symbolic ascent.
The cremation dust of resurrection, lost as it nears the unifying sky.
Lost and scattered like snow flurry
Across the treeless plain where animal totems roam or graze.

Who sent the yellow star swimming in my veins?
Who plucked it out like an eye and painted it so painfully yellow to begin with?

Who stigmatized the pigmentation of my skin?
Who soaked me in blackness, rain of red and yellow, every inch?

Who shamed the muscular backs of two men
Making love in the privacy of their bedroom?
Outside, the purling insults deflect from their torsos.
And though six yods whirl, a natural pedestal at their feet,
Like a purdah, a curtain must be drawn in public;
A purdah of lamé, like the backs of two women
Making love in the privacy of their bedroom.

White bread, white collar, white shoe, white noise, tennis whites, Snow White,
white tails, white boy, white sale, white teeth, lily white, hospital white, white night,
white linen, white horse, White House, deathly white, white cloud, white lie, white
elephant, white wedding, bone white, soft white, semen white, white wine, white
rabbit, white glove, white Christmas, white blood cells

I hang from hooks that pierce my chest,
From threads in a hole eight feet deep without food or water.
I hang as if on a vision quest,
A grizzly bear existing on its own fat like an oil lamp.
I hang until I gather the grotto around me as my coat,
The fur of my grizzly bear totem on earth.
And listen, floating within this black tank
To the rain, red and yellow, pummel the surface above.

It pours down on those buried alive in Hades.
On all the angels, "Ti bon ange," trapped in their jars,
Music convexed inside tiny silver balls.
Boxes within boxes within boxes within boxes . . . .
And in the very last box (if there is one), inside us:
There is no yellow star, only a virus of hatred.
There is no pigmentation, only ignominious discrimination.
There is no difference, only lynching, gassing, and burning,
Only the indifferent, contributing insidiously
Like the president of our country,
Only power thwarted and twisted as vegetation on Three Mile Island,
Only fear that spills, injections of interferon, upon the agnostic cemetery,
Only fallout that pulverizes the monolithic granite,
Only tears precipitating on the multicolored florets
That appear more as if tossed than placed, like wedding nosegays,
Before the engraved names and dates of the arbitrary lengths of life—
Only the atrophied hearts of the living that look on.

While I, in a kind of sunk ship of my own, listen
To the falling of our love, flayed in its attempt to be shown.
Until burying what was left of our desire
Was all that was left,
Box within box, into the cold slid the black body bag.
I can hear the wings around me beat against their jars,
The frenetic angels fighting for air.
Their letters, conversations, monologues of defenses, possessions, mementos,
Telephones, typewriters, telegrams, sexual innuendoes and actual gestures,
Assimilate a soliloquy that has become an abyss.
Abysmally falling on the flavescent grass,
Falling and simultaneously bursting inside me,
Box within box within box . . . .
Violently, sequentially, the boxes spring open their lids.

And in the very last box (if there is one), inside me,
Lies the root laid upon velvet,
Simply a symbol like a sliver of jade:
A cold spoon, an antibody, a yellow star, a pigmentation.
"What's Montague? It is nor hand, nor foot, nor arm, nor face."
The mythology of white weaves these threads from which I hang.
Jade, the gemstone of prophetic dreams,
Dissolves in my system like a pill.
I watch vigilantly while you take off your surgical gloves,
I watch you approach and drink from my cup,
For I've put no pufferfish powder in there, you finally trust.
Finally my healthy body that is my healthy body is given back to me.
Finally my rights that are my rights, as my tongue is mine, are regained.
Finally you touch me, and the finality explodes
Into plains of thought, layers of earth in an archeological site,
Into the history of boxes,
Until finally they collapse within themselves
And vanish into extinction.

Poem for a Poem

for Jade

And the snow fell lightly in Cambridge
where I swallowed the lightning of you whole,
a bolt with such a hyperbolic zigzag to its edges
that it seemed cut out of cardboard for a school play.
It stayed that way, stuck inside me like a pipe,
a spine of bite-sized bones.
And the snow fell lightly in Cambridge
where I stood on the platform in public for you,
you placed precariously before me like sheet music,
just paper, I know,
but not outside of me as I had hoped,
as I wrote that winter in those black mornings.
And the snow fell lightly in Cambridge.
My lamp snowed whitely on my desk, a street of snow
where white mice multiply by the hundreds.
And everything was so cold, all my animate objects,
except for the lead of my pencil, a welding utensil
or flashlight to guide my exodus in the snow.
I wrote you, a wagon I pulled on the road
in the effort to leave you, to let you go.
Or maybe it was more the other way around,
the words, bread crumbs strewn to lead me back home.
Does it matter, really, which direction I desired?
I built, plank by plank, the rope bridge with so much purpose
that the purpose became the purpose in itself:
the relief of the labor of mindless work,
the stinging panic that brought lovely focus
to the next cliff. The next cliff
was all I thought about,
as if sailing in a ship at dawn.
And the snow fell lightly in Cambridge.
So whitely it put me back in my days,
the hotel décor as monochromatic as my thoughts
of you, you the poem, and the you in the poem,
the two merging together like a photograph
when a matte finish snapshot is what I have left.

The landscape behind the amateur portrait
Landscapes the landscape of my pain, rank with weeds
outlasting of you, or me, as landscapes do;
though as a landscape of snow you'll always loom
where the lamplight on my desk whitely snows.
I thought because you were so complete,
because you came out whole like a baby
or twelve-foot snake yanked from my gullet,
great sword of Excalibur ripped from its stone,
that at last you were separate from me as a landscape.
But deeper you sank instead, absorbed into my liver
like a bottle of vodka I'd consumed.
Now there's no getting rid of you.
I could tear you up, burn you, stubbornly disown you,
sign a pen name in place of my own,
and still you'd roll through my head, a motion picture,
sway below me still the sturdy net I wove of you that winter.
I even feel guilty and somewhat fearful
as if you had the power to paralyze my hands,
break every bone in my fingers like a king,
draw me a quarter me for me traitorousness;
then turn all my poems to mush, as if they be, by the grace
of god, not already that.
And with the spiteful vengeance of a jilted lover
ensure supernaturally that they never be read,
for they're not made of the pure substance of you,
like the real thing I shot up my veins,
and let the much-talked-about-bliss run rampant,
not caring, not caring about anything.
Ironically I wrote you to make myself clean,
a thousand baths taken in the writing of you,
the symbolic cleansing of a baptismal crucifix.
Now you riddle me permanently, bodily, a body tattoo,
internally ruinous, a virus and not just deadly
but deadening to all other poems and men.
Everything breaks down to the denomination of you,
everything I write simply the dissemination of you,
replicating in my body. O my molecule.

HIV, Mon Amour

Fourteen Days in Quarantine

1.

The TB room posits itself as at once outside me like a Richard Serra,
contained, abstract as the scientific premise upon which it was founded,
while the 75 square feet and the ceiling vent, which circulates fresh air
every eight minutes, best represent my sense of interiority by virtue
of the falsification of representation. My reflection viewed in blankness,
the extra-large TV bolted too high up against the opposite wall (pale lime),
square box askew as if the quizzical head of some surveillance authority,
refuses to echo back what signifies reality to me. Instead I'm forced
to witness my own participation in the clinical process, a kind of snuff film
culturally condoned: I regard the woman illuminated by overhead fluorescence,
her features diminished as if rubbed away, clay bust banished to raw status,
her physical proportions distorted, more, then less with flame-like metamorphoses,
hooked up to an IV; O artificial extension of the body now commenced,
the transplantation of anatomized topography upon its badly damaged origin.
Hospital gown worn backwards, thus open at the neck, and I think what a great
Nan Goldin portrait it would make—"Tory, New York Hospital, January 1996."

2.

When they wheeled me up from ER into respiratory isolation the space radiated
as if a magnifying glass were put to it under a sunray. The afternoon sun
from the southern exposure hit interrogationally against my head,
efficacious as the chemotherapy drugs to which I'd become allergic,
my torso scalding red from the eventual conflation of the hives. I writhed
like an eel from the remote-control reconfiguring of my hospital bed, the way
diagrams of Hatha yoga postures present themselves on a page, Muybridge
stills repeated into the illusion of motion; I tried any position that might
ease the poltergeist-like progression of the "launched" reaction, unpredictable
in its phases. The days succeed then in a condensed formula of alternate
darkness and light that make up twenty-four hours as I waited for my medication,
a dose every three hours: Benadryl, prednisone, shots of epinephrine, Atarax
while the room reverberated a cryptic quiet, my bygone and would-be world
held in abeyance beyond the gridded glass, where I in an incubated state of sorts
watched with voyeuristic intensity the heads that only in profile would pass.

3.

But the view out of window was fabulous. Not just a river view but
a long view of the East River which resembled the Thames, the Fifty-ninth Street
Bridge foregrounding its tranquil perfection, tugboats and flatliners
moving out and upstream like alligators with only the most moderate ripples
made in the water. The world was gracefully, and thus almost archaically,
silenced behind the double-cased window, like a *film noir* short or
Stieglitz's New York. It was as if the city itself, in solidarity with my life,
stopped and paused, as a gesture of respect, a tactful response for a long,
two-week moment so that I could reassess, positioning one of the three chairs
in my room dead center before it where ceremoniously I developed the habit
of taking my breakfast, while Schubert or Kiri Te Kanawa played not so softly
on my black boombox. Later, when the pentamidine pulsated through my body,
which grew weaker and more tired until I receded in sync with the daylight
from chair back to bed as if falling backwards in slow motion, the way
a display dummy does during a rehearsed car crash, the river, though enveloped
in fog and pollution, remained, blurred line detected through cracked shield,
and gave an impression of the infinite: the possibility of my getting out
of there, of living perhaps, even thirty more years as once I had expected.

4.

The night sky would hang aloof and autonomous as a piece of Fabergé jewelry,
an example of Dioysiac craftsmanship that no longer pertained to my century.
The uplit skyscrapers of some famous buildings, Chrysler, Citicorp, amidst
residential and business, the windows alternately dark or filled with bright
coldness, introduced, like ink spilled on virgin paper, a kind of filmy,
alternate-state wattage from which one could expect the birth of something;
some transgression of physical properties, some otherworldly entity, gooey and
fetus-faced, reaching out to me only. But only a pattern, arbitrary, absolute
of lights, lonely and tiny, lay out against the lawless expansion, a game
of dominos played cursorily in the hawking blankness, bipartisan, yes,
in its PC chaos but neglectful and rancorous in this fail-safe,
do-no-harm schematic: the more godless the landscape, the more demonically
driven the agenda. Bored by ideas of persecution and fatigued with my efforts
to connect sign with meaning, closure, and hence beginning, I turn my head,
heavy and mechanical, pull the strangulating cord to turn off the overhead
fluorescence, and allow what balance this queer harmony of weakness and strength

might make, the pallor of city lights lending an alien glow to my limbs.
I glance at the night sky then back to the TV void, trying to distinguish natural
from man-made in order to identify that with which I identify. The treatment,
a chemical, incites cell renewal by virtue of the body's ability to synthetically
substitute itself: icon upon ideal. Think of it as restoration, I say out loud.

5.

There was a single piece of art in the room, good art too, if you can believe it.
It was a photograph, black and white, of a landscape taken in the Southwest,
somewhere arid, where the sky outruns the desert, a cowboy's idea of finisterre.
It hung straight ahead like a crucifix from the upright-positioned stare
I would motor into prolonged spectatorship that served, I guess, in lieu of prayer.
The image was of a flat-topped mountain indigenous to Utah or Wyoming, its profile,
which threw into high relief the parched, plebeian horizon, exhibited a staggered
growth of progress and sharp decline like the invisible statistic charts held up
prototypically before me, black mourning veils that obscure my perception
of what could be otherwise. But the predicted deterioration of my body delineated
against the amorphous space of possibility was not so unlike the mountain's outline.
Its earthen form, hulking and ancient, could be read as in ruins or unstoppable
despite past corrections. Regardless, it prevailed if only in idea as appropriated
by the photograph, calling into question the category of "origin," mine in particular.
Where exactly have been set the perimeters between my body and the self that exists
outside my consciousness? In the little synaptic connections when people think of me?
Or in postcards and outdated e-mails reread in the aftermath of my scientific death,
different from the cultural death, the emotional death, the spiritual death;
different from a sea burial, from the char and ash and bone and fabric devoured
by the Atlantic, swallowed, digested and spat out again, generic as saline liquid?

6.

I was almost never alone. For someone quarantined this seemed strange to me.
Aside from visitors there were nurses, technicians, and attending doctors in addition
to my physician, as well as residents and interns who woke me at six in small groups,
poking, thumping, and speaking too loudly. There were hospital workers of every
division: the foot bearer, the floor washer, the temperature/blood pressure taker,
the sheet changers who stripped and made my bed with military exactness as I
listened to the crisp, unnerving sounds of starched cotton pulled to uniform
precision. Often several people came at once, or in short succession, wearing masks,

of course, morphed into bodies with just eyes, their monkey jaw disguises shifting in
adjustment. It was the theater, either Ionescian, in which the IV poles and pumps, buckets &
mops, EKG machines entered like a procession of bizarre animals; or Artaudian, where
I, both audience and stage, served as witness of exequy and its nexus, the centripetal
force commissioning event. When a rare moment of solitude would descend, billowing,
augmented by the white noise of the fresh-air vent that upheld the rigors of Health
Dept. standards, it invariably threw me, never getting used to this terroristic aspect
of pleasurable tease before unexpected assault. Once I opted not to seize the chance
to close my eyes or piss in private, and walked instead, cautiously, to the door.
Peering out the gridded glass at the junglesque activity of the hospital corridor, I
saw their full faces so different than imagined from the partial viewing previously
presented like progressional sketches of a criminal. One nurse noticed me
mesmerized by this game of identification and scowled in discouragement until I recoiled.
Watching was interpreted as an act of taunting, the behavior of mental patients
or prisoners; an interpretation that was, in turn, a defense for their guilt,
for the sympathy they as professionals, in order to perform well, could not allow.
They knew what my watching really meant: the longing to be healthy, to be like them.

7.

In the beginning I tried to write. I would define the beginning as that brief
interval between the subsiding of the allergic reaction and the reintroduction of
the TB drugs, before the full force of the daily pentamidine was felt. During
this window of time, less than forty-eight hours, I was "myself" again like the
child prostitute interviewed on A&E who now, as herself, is a happy, young mother.
Her name is Nina. She was abducted at 12 years of age. She recuperates the particularly
harrowing account of when she disappeared from the street, some pimp she had been
sold to at a discount for aging to 17, locking her in the basement of his dilapidated
ranch house, normal protocol for the modern slave master. He shot her up with heroin
when he was sick of her and made her sleep. Then he shot her up with coke when he
needed some cash to retool his alcohol habit. She survived this way for three years
before she was found. I am watching her narration (not a confession because there
has been no wrongdoing) from my hospital bed. Free cable is one of many perks on
the AIDS floor. I open up my laptop inspired by how I perversely identify with her,
my body, sweet, pale thing, kidnapped also in a way; my legs, with their muscles
atrophied, have completely changed shape, all bruise-dotted up from syringes. I
let one dangle, engaged fishing pole, over the edge, assuming the perpendicular
position of concentration I know. I touch the keyboard. The cold plastic alphabet
singes, strangely forbidden, therefore erotic. I realize slowly, as if in orgasmic

stages of cunnilingus, that the most elementary effort of extending toward the familiar, of taking control of my body, of pushing out articulations, has become transgressive; as perhaps it became to Nina, in between highs, when experiencing "herself" for a single minute, she risked investigation of the padlocked cellar door.

8.

During my hospitalization, the great blizzard of '96 occurred, devastating the Tri-State area and delaying my dinner. My view holed up like the porthole of an igloo, crystalline and anesthetized. Loyal visitors arrived at odd hours like Pa gone to town in *The Little House on the Prairie*, shaking off the snow on their coats, perspiring a bit amidst the sudden warmth of the room, their glow in high contrast with the matt temperancy of the quarantine masks. My experience of the storm was limited to this internality of it, something of what a fetus records of the wide world while in the womb, watching CNN coverage for visuals: shivering newscasters shouting their emphases, cars stalled in zigzag procession, inter-mitten shots of portly snowplows saving the day. It seemed like fun. Remarkably to me I remain in respiratory confinement as everybody flays about, hospital shifts contorted, nurses forced to perform a technicians' duties, doctors stooped to pulse taking. I watch all the flutter as if through convex glass, atypical viewer trapped in 60's Arrid Extra Dry commercial: noses loom large and spectacles eyes hysterically wide. I witness as a separatist, as caged animals do the weirdos on the other side of the wire who experiment upon them. I regard the snow and the snowstorm extravaganza at arm's length, a great hairy hand collaring me in the effort to inject or extract some substance. I am purposely held away from the element, in part discriminatorily, but also, by virtue of this pejorative intent, the way last comes first in Christian ethics, as if having risen above it, either-like as steam did climb nefariously off the river, immune to cold, indifferent to the wetness, blanched to the color white, and how I once loved it for I'd become it, the other, the terrifying, the nuance, the inhuman.

9.

I knew that one day I might look back at this interval as when I was better off, as when the room was private, as when drugs were considered useful, as a time when I could sit up, as a time when I could argue. I knew that especially at night after 2 in the morning when my third dose of the allergic reaction protocol had just been administered, prednisone and Atarax (the Benadryl had been worthless) followed by a shot of epinephrine stinging me into intergalactic

awakeness, the stages of bodily absorption, shivering, tingling, sudden dumb
calm and subsequent relief from the physical screaming, I would monitor mentally
with the hope of willing the response into actuality later, when the drug
would be refused to me; when I knew I had been better off tolerating another
prick of the needle. The nurse pulls the string switching off the overhead
fluorescence, the click rudely loud, the plastic pulls snapping back against my
face for a second. I experience a memory flash of the moment before—the sound
of Velcro from the blood pressure cuff; the little white pill-dispensing cups,
her cold fingertips on my pulse, the beautiful syringe poised impressively
between her teeth as she read her watch. Lying down on my side in the
quickening darkness, my position unchanged from when I received the injection,
I watch through the hospital bed guard rail as she leaves, the stillborn silence
of my room undisturbed save for the squeak of her white shoes on the freshly
cleaned floor, and the whoosh of the heavy quarantine door automatically closing.
A brief flooding of corridor light appears on the linoleum tiles, then nothing.

10.

My physician arrived every day at about 9:00 a.m., announcing himself with that jingle
of raps on my door which signifies a friend, not foe, outside. He never
wore the prerequisite quarantine mask, perhaps because he knew the perimeters
of exposure and didn't feel his short visits to be a danger or perhaps because
he thought that communicating with a full face was important for our discussions,
for my confidence in him, in the treatment decisions, in myself as something
more than another verified statistic with tubes flowing out from my
limbs attached to plastic bags of clear medication, my form reconfigured as
needing something larger than a god, something scientifically derived in order
to be sustained. For the most part it worked, the matching up of my two identities,
the reality of me sick and the memory of me well, centered my soul like glass
slides containing a blood smear for microscope inspection. Particularly in the eye
contact when we discussed the alternatives, in the pauses after when we remained
looking at each other in mutual contemplation of the seriousness of the situation,
I would sense myself positioned thus between the imagined researcher's hands.
And the gut feeling I had always associated with the word "Tory," the specific
white pine amidst the general landscape, would be brought into sharp focus as if
gently held down, trembling vase on rudimentary table within the bomb shelter
security of the room. We would watch almost as if a third party were present,
the potential for it to be blown apart like any ordinary structure in a tornado,
where wooden fences lie prostrate and barn animals soar upward into an ever obscuring

sky; where I, a juxtapositional series of flashbacks and idiosyncratic urges superimposed upon each other like pages of a memoir that comprises a kinetic, almost moaning kind of narrative, might disappear also into the indefeasible spiral above.

11.

On the eve before the TB drugs were reintroduced, my physician and I tossed a coin in order to decide which one would likely cause another allergic response akin to that which had required hospitalization a week earlier. The embossed profile of George Washington signified rifampin instead of isoniazid, a choice that brought no reassurance since the outcome remained equally uncertain: I continued revolving, a quarter dollar in the air, glints of fluorescence ricocheting off our forefather's cheekbone, the claw-foot of the eagle alighted atop of neither branch nor rock. I beheld, beholden to the sight as if some mystical vision, the literal turning of my fate, its infinite axis where, like a glistened pig self-reflecting on the spit, or a convertible that, having overshot its ultimate goal of the highway, teeters upon a cracked precipice, I lay as if held out, a barbaric gift. A slab of marble was the gurney cot of my hospital bed and the springs digging against my back could be interrupted as actual pressure from the vast, the pale, from the frameless filigree of winter branches, skyscrapers, and truncated river. To that from which no voice would emit I was forced to entrust my failing body my life's possessions in a bundle and stick, wiled to their abandonment. It seemed as if the days and nights I spent in quarantine evolved into a kind of extension of that eve, that particular night a metonymical event occurring within the greater overarching eve that delineates this world from the next, the schematic of which one experiences as sinking into twilight the way the shipwrecked do into the ocean, the way HIV overrides my body as if overwriting the flesh, the waterline rising above my upturned, gasping face. It was as if my body were asking for the privilege to be viewed as remains, to be given the opportunity to float unfettered away from me, to struggle for a while, alternately bob and drown, allowed to live or die on its own.

12.

My boyfriend arrived straight from work every night at 6:30 p.m., his smiling face displayed momentarily in the square of gridded glass like puppet theater before he entered donning his quarantine mask. Often he brought the something I had requested, articles which covered a spectrum of needs, acting as conduit to the outside world through which, what was life proper compared to this, made itself available to me: flowers, cassette tapes, favorite home items such as my pillow or bedside lamp or cosmetic oddity with the unpronounceable brand name, special foods divergent from the hospital menu heated in the nurses' canteen microwave. Sometimes these secular pleasures had to be coaxed as when I had no appetite and sat in upright confrontation with my bowl of homemade minestrone, head turned left then right, any position to avoid the fumes while he pleaded, even argued. But the pleasure of touch I never refused when he climbed gently into the narrow cot with me, winter jacket still on, the sudden cold of his earlobes against my cheek, the thick cardboard material of the quarantine mask which we would defiantly indent in order to kiss. Our eyes would stay open staring into the other's pupil until practically cross-eyed. The last thing we wanted was more mystery, more left to the imagination. Only what was before us now would satisfy. It was as if all our sexual experiences individual and combined, came to closure in this exchange, exposing themselves as spoiled representations of erotic desire. That base instinct belonging to animal of muscle, semen, bone, raw appetite, we perceived in retrospect as mannered like ballroom dance, misguided in topical obsession, over-fucked until it fell outside the realm of its origin. Erogenous zones are beside the point. It's the eye, the voice disguised as organ and orifice, that penetrates and receives.

13.

I lay upon the recesses of sheets in the darkness, the gradations of black and white, of light and obscurity, artificial and natural passing over me like prehistoric birds, their giant and frightening feathered wings obstructing the sun then not. I lay there like would-be carrion on sand dune and sea grass while they flew overhead, my hair incrementally disturbed by the smallest breeze their flapping incurred. Their shrieks exchanged resonated as faraway but knife-precise in the ability to disturb me. Everything hurts me. Day four into the allergic reaction and the hives, enormous red welts that proliferated like weeds or red ants all over my body, swelling my eyes shut, closing my throat, finally subsided in progression, the next stage of my body's rejection of itself, their confluence into skin burning crimson as if the workings of the world had reversed from exterior to interior operation, where ultraviolet rays blazed forcefully from inside me. What's most terrifying about sickness is its fascist self-containment, the seizing of the body by itself, the warring efforts toward redemption of selfhood and its defilement, the defeat produced by somatic betrayal. The ally of my anatomy could no longer be trusted. I thought I was more than

a display of carnage though I'm still sentimentally attached to it as if to
a person rather than a decoy; like Freud's account of the *fort* (gone) and *da* (here)
game in which a little boy plays hide-and-seek with a spool of threat that's
become the mother substitute, compensating for his sense of abandonment. He
stages her disappearance in order to rehearse the pleasure of her return. Similarly,
I wish I could bury me myself the way Esther did her rage doll in *Bleak House*,
in the spirit of *fort /da*, then death could be welcomed as life's prelude.

14.

I left the quarantine room three times. The first being the fruits of my
successful manipulation of the nurse whom, toward the evening of day three, I
begged to take me out. Initially my request made her uneasy, unable to maintain
eye contact with me, busying herself with flushing my IV and reading my pulse.
I made my plea incessant yet irresistible, the effort focused solely on the
human connection, with ample articulation of her name and the magic word
"please," my voice low and sweet, relatively calm. I hardly took a breath.
Mention of my gratitude was made often as well as the promise that just a
minute would suffice, the assurance that no one would notice, and that her
general kindness would be praised to Patient Services. Then she stared at me
and agreed. I wore a special blue TB mask different from the ones my visitors
had to wear as we walked arm-in-arm like European girlfriends to the newly
refurbished atrium where a man with KS slept upright in front of TV glare.
We made stilted, self-consciously banal comments about the lights on the Fifty-
ninth Street Bridge for five minutes then turned around. The second time was
when I was wheeled to x-ray, the orderly alerting those ahead with his walkie-
talkie that TB patient was on her way so that rooms could be cleared and
sealed off one by one as I rode through them. People forced to share the
elevator with me glanced down at my masked and gowned figure with pity for
the vermin level to which I had descended though they stood at a wide angle around
me. The third time was my release, when I wore civilian clothes again, the blue
jeans scratchy and stiff, my legs weak and unsteady but exhilarated by the
whisking sound of walking out of quarantine, off the AIDS floor, out of the
hospital and into the moist, gray January afternoon where the grizzle hit my
face, cold and sharp, and the asphalt underfoot registered as especially hard.

Future Text Panel

in memory of Andrea Fisher

A fire going is the only sound
of my old life shrinking on the left with the sun.

The treetops, prolific as the sky, hide the sky.

My blood unnerves me.

The evidence of friends exists only in memory,
as if they were dead or as if I were dead,
my spirit slithering throughout the earth,
perhaps seeking revenge,
or in search of the deed I need to complete
to finally leave my body in peace
like a personage.
Bound to the unfinished,
silt still spills upon my grave,
upon my name engraved
I must wear in my exodus like Houdini's chains.

Voice as Gym-Body

for Marilyn Hacker

In order for a rapprochement with the physical body
Only necromancy could be behind it.
Racked on a stretcher the IV tubes string me up
Like a cello without a player.

Only necromancy could be behind it.
These days of horse-drawn betrayal.
Like a cello without a player
I'm caught, a crown of thorns, in a winter orchard.

These days of horse-drawn betrayal
Impromptu night: tar ridge.
I'm caught, a crown of thorns, in a winter orchard,
A keyboard silent as the keyboard to deaf Beethoven.

Impromptu night: tar ridge.
I insert the child's hand literally into my chest,
A keyboard silent as the keyboard to deaf Beethoven.
As if a surgeon's, I warm it.

I insert the child's hand literally into my chest.
Fingers twitch like an impulse, final and emotive
As if a surgeon's, I warm it
With my voice (overbuilt to compensate for no child).

Fingers twitch like an impulse, final and emotive.
The way one man survived was by altarpiece commissions.
With my voice (overbuilt to compensate for no child)
Like an altarpiece I try continually to build.

The way one man survived was by altarpiece commissions.
Racked on a stretcher the IV tubs string me up
Like an altarpiece I try continually to build
In order for a rapprochement with the physical body.

The Pressure

for Thomas Nash, M.D.

Too many times have I with the sun on my back, flamboyant, heinously direct,
rocked, wrung hands, my shaking head refuged in a now-wet Bounty paper towel
or institutionalized inside the free-space of my bedroom that opens like a file
on my computer screen with that which I'm constantly trying to put a name to,
the way faces in my past automatically assign to themselves signifying feelings.
Like a shot of B12 effective only if injected intramuscularly I am neutralized
as a naming vehicle by this pressure that cannot be extracted like a billboard
or wisdom tooth. No torii erects itself as a gateway to the totem of experience, no
descriptive alloy exists to transform or rebirth the most primitive and bare-boned,
the referential instability of physical pain no human agency speaks successfully
in lieu of. Gritty locks felled into the sloth of tears, their salty
aftermarks imbricating my face, a kind of warrior's mask of a warrior's failure
afore the clandestine ideal of physical perfection: O poster of Marky Mark
that posits itself like an Aryan agenda against every public bus, a tableau of prayer
ossified for us to emulate. Celebrities represent what Grecian gods were once.

"Life quality" tropes the category doctors refer to with fake jocularity:
a terse smile, a quick nod, not cavalierly, really, but with no affinity either.
While I present, in crude form like an outhouse, an ideology, a practicum
my pretty breasts should make for its manifest example, but all the while
there is this pressure, iconic in nature to modify it paradoxically,
an omniscience, high-noon hot, slutty, demonic hologram embossed like Bergman's
Seventh Seal on the Silly Putty shape of my heart. The muscle adapts, adopts
the image as if the imagined face of a Bosnian orphan, the brow-swept features
twisted and bathed in a mucus for which its tiny tributary paths serve as the deaf,
dumb, and blind substitution for the mature articulation of longing and hate.
The child cries; the diastole blooms in branding exaction. The child sleeps
while pellets of sun cinder twitch and wink on the horizon; the systole
deflates, erects as if *l'oiseau de Paradis* in order to convey
the agony of form in the rigor of its stem, or freak flowering, an ugly orange.

My physician's intelligent brow reframes behind his desk with diacritic distinction
like the beard of Zeus appearing within a cloud, a fated fetus
within the belly of its turbid future. Like reversing falls framed and frozen,
forced to hiatus by virtue of the very process of its reversing action,
so does the pressure to live and the pressure to die halt momentarily and present,

as if a utilized gift certificate from the three wise men, a Marlboro Man genie,
the mirage-like sense of an empty room, its empirical standard; "peace of mind"
charretted into a tangible utopia, an echo-chamber of existential thought
that operates like the Mecca vision of regarding a fish tank while on morphine
where I am able to walk unbothered for a while as if along a long, white beach.
Where I am able to stand an contemplate my life, the concept and its definitions.
Where I am able to close my eyes and revel in the memory, the voice and face
the jokes, the silences, the passion, the fights, of someone I loved deeply who died.
Where trapped in the tar gut of solitary confinement I wake and am no longer blind.

I inspect my lifeline, its silly prescience, on the breathing moon-surface
of my palm, yet alert to any irregularity that might augur some imminent abortion.
The Bic fine point remains poised for further notation on the indecipherable list
of questions and contents I've arranged for this consultation, but ineffectually
for no amount of brainstorming could bulwark permanently this pressure built with
superhuman innovation and efficiency as the Egyptians did their pyramids;
before the pushing and the turning and the typhoon-like whirling starts up again.
It both buoys and sinks with me inside it, bad poem scrolled inside a Pepsi bottle,
gaining and losing, I sleep and lose sleep and rethink and rethink the perimeters,
the scientific course of which I know nothing and yet must know something by now,
more than the wet Bounty paper towel. What I know is the pressure, the stranglehold
of sadistic knees, the Devil's compression into the soles of my feet, scalding spittle
of gods that mimic my buffoonery, the bulletproof sky; the ongoing erasure of the earth
and those enfolded within it, innocuous as a tidal cove, so complacent and measured.

What I know is that the only way to stabilize is to ride through it, a raft
regaining its equilibrium in white-shark rapids, a lesser stone, bespeckled pebble
amidst a chortling brook's current or contending ego within the rock-throwing forces
dark feelings resort to in the narcissistic forum of their past belittlement.
What I know is the two rivers, the patient's and my own, that fork like a divining rod
toward some essentially healing source. What I know is that I'm both people,
one sick and one well, contending with the ongoing struggle of trying to save myself.
The x-ray glows extraterrestrial and nefarious in the late December blackness
that infiltrates my physician's office and obscures all other objects and details
other than his head, my x-ray, his desk lamp, and that strange, uncurtained window
that seems to erase all at once, in one glance, my hope of long-term survival.
My torso, decapitated and cut off at the elbows, shifts in and out of focus
as if a Jane Doe resurfacing after days in the stilt and oily waters of the Hudson.

"Look, an infection," my doctor declares with index finger pointed in discovery.
I blink twice, straining for recognition as I do with any picture of myself.
The shadow he refers to bursts white and translucent and upon first impression
it appeared optimistic as if a good omen were growing like an orchid in my bosom.
My impulse is to be alone with the x-ray like a loved one and the incarcerated,
to press the picture of my unhealthy lung against its double but breathing one.
What I know is the desire to resuscitate, mouth to mouth, open the dank jaws,
the partisan skin, as if beheld behind venetian blinds, zebra strips of soaked hair
and brown seaweed strewn across the face, and bring back as if to carry back in time
the fainting subject, the feminine form worn out from the fight. Her arms and feet
flag like pigeons, her weight, letter-light along my overdeveloped forearms,
their destiny as once sophomoric I dreamt it now a drawn and quartered
into an array of listless limbs kicked up into a cloud, gray-blue and particle-
stained, of a hoof-clad road where a mare's distancing tail delineates
in the dusk evidence given in its disappearance, the myth of originary wholeness.

Magnetic Poetry Kit Poems

1/1/95 (8:57 p.m.)

Please me
and the bitter moon flooded by its shadow
repulsive but essential to the apparatus of milk
will be sweet as the winter breast of your mother's death
a sordid beauty like purple blood sprayed over a pink crushed car
a love trip then only some tiny road beneath a void momentary as rain

like whispering in a womanly weak wind
I cry without vision

2/7/95 (2:09 p.m.)

I ask of my blood please produce no death
though like a raw but elaborate egg you incubate in me
a woman in bed dreaming of visions so sordid
to read them would stop language as a car drives into lake water
under a rainy sky black not blue
the wind will blow after as a symphony void of music
a mother without beauty and love

how I ache in my moonless sleep
weak with madness from the storm always near
I worship waxing light, gardens, a gorgeous picture
the enormous apparatus of time from feet to head, rocks to a place above
but only bitter moans recall the urge I used to have
when beneath an essential sun never ugly or frantic
I felt what was meaningful then and must have wanted it

3/7/95 (11:45 a.m.)

all roads rive over an enormous void like would be death
the useless picture of my head drunk & flooded underwater
as a lifetime shines above the truly gorgeous sun

but only moonlight weak and white as breast milk do I see
falling in petals blue, pink, black, blood-rose and purple
when I stare about me into a swimming storm of winter mist then shadow

Never have I wanted from loving friends the most they can ask for
like I do today, a thousand moments crushed beneath its essential parting
from language what it must say though repulsive, delirious, raw and sordid
some hot tongue in my mad sleep may moan, whisper, scream, cry or chant
                                                                at no one

Egged on by an elaborate need to mother like a goddess the ugly within me
manipulate out of my want the bitter gift of asking why dreams
                                                have gone away always
as if those sweet visions were still alive and easy to think of
a delicate apparatus for producing their leave-taking
                                        the sadness somehow shot through with beauty
like ships who blow up atop a frantic sea recall the powerful meaning of
                                                                rain and wind

5/10/95 (8:45 p.m.)

Black visions incubate over time in what is a bloody gorgeous head
its blue white skin motherless and drunk on thinking always about death
no gardens show their petal moment to him luscious under a forest of shadows
waxlike water here and there no sun shines delicately on the woman loved
                                                                beneath
his legs, her sweet screaming stilled, gone weak and ugly
as if manipulated by someone within a tiny TV void
he licks the peach and honey breast, heaves into the sweating butt
                                                chocolate smeared and easy
not the raw lust he wants but with a want only, the sad dream
                                of when he must have felt essentially powerful

bitter is beauty or love recalled it's a picture of a boy lying
                                in the road after a hit or run
never near will he be to tell of the enormous ache life has produced elaborate
                                        as fiddle music
a sordid symphony, an apparatus of urges watched but not lived from above

10/22/95 (11:40 p.m.)

Blue winter you and I need only to think of some moment gone but hotly here
                                                                    like an iron
or TV a peach rusted storm the sordid head of a madman crying out to what
                                        he loves not there
when but for my visions used up within the fast whispering of their afterlife
would I produce heave and urge from the smelly deathwater of stopped time
them the rose the woman the friend alive & together never leave I say
                                                            deliriously
to a drooling goddess repulsive though how true her shot stare do it see
be it through crushed shadows and weakest sun tongue red yet cooling her swim

I want to scream but fall behind in my blood purple bitterness I worship
                                                        as if a girls breast
not for wanting of an ugly and still raw a meaning but having felt
                                                    so tiny and powerless
must take a beating beneath all the enormous lakelike lick shined sky
who drunk on play uses you next me then blows our moaning aches
                                                and delicate shadows away

7/18/97 (6:20 p.m.)

I ask you what essential language could manipulate into raw time
the bare void of my death   mean and elaborate as a thousand chained feet
so powerful and enormous is it   next to these tiny pink and blue moments
        only sad pictures recalled after in my head
how fast they fall like frantic petals behind me in the blood rusty road
crushed by the apparatus of shadow & bitter sky
                                    black roses incubate in their place

gifts of love   some will say   about his or hers visions of me the day
my tongue goes cool then gone though still an urge to moan
will produce a sordid singing   a winter rain drunk   but thinking
white music   I would not read as ugly   yet no beauty can be said for
the shaking and heaving   the delicate garden bed flooded
as if by seawater   eating away the purple skin   breast and leg

there I lie but not at all within some easy acheless sleep

                                         one sweetly dreams of
no I take it on   let it stare true to life   at me from above
with a wanting   always   it never stops   the crying
                                         like a forest ripping apart
a drive I must have felt   throughout   when needs were most alive

Everybody Loves a Winner

"Freedom's just another word for nothing left to lose."
-Janis Joplin

But when you lose it's only you and the hardwood maple floor
beneath you, your shoulders pinned down, wet shirt on a clothesline
by the knees of a god leather-clad in medieval thigh-highs.
He forces you to repeat or he'll show you his fist again.
A hot pool has already boiled up in your throat—
your head to the side you watch red rivet on the polyurethane finish
the splattering on his gray T-shirt when you give him what he wants.
"Our Father who art in heaven ... " and you've got to get it right,
no tone of sacrilege, nothing but the pure submission
that the purgatorial twilight outside has brought about,
this epic plot eschatological in proportion
where you are the dot in a pointillist painting,
the undetectable one, the point of vanishing.
The streaks of amethyst and taupe underscore the sky's authenticity.
It's hard to believe that you ever thought it beautiful.
Hasn't reality always been by virtue of the realistic aspect always horrible
like the real rope that ties your ankles and wrists together,
prepared like the modern-day equivalent of a virgin for slaughter,
a stiff strapped to a cake of cement en route to the East River
and you can't feel anything from your pelvis on down;
you look forward to nothing in totality now that your options have run out.

Everybody loves a winner, but when you lose it's just you and the partial view
out the hospital window, just you in front of the doctor when he tells you
you're too hopeful, just you and less than that for you're shrinking, melting,
you are that which is diminishing like a snow bank in February
like the wicked witch of the west destroyed by drinking water,
just you and the self-conscious stratum of your prayers
where, in its tapestry, you are less than water and the verdigris thread
that depicts the facial details of those who will go on without you
the winners with torsos built with such genetic supremacy
they appear manufactured, checked once for efficiency like an Icelandic horse
then set free like wild ponies on the Cote d'Azur.
Everybody loves a winner but when you lose it's you who's watching the ponies,
your individuality instantly annihilated in the category of spectatorship,

drowning in the oceanic still life that backdrops their wildness,
the waves pitched in churlish peaks like cake frosting or moussed hair,
the trends of teal and navy like the subway map of your body's meridians
for all of life has becomes paradigmatic of your interiority in its finitude,
the seminary belfry the diagrammatic sonata for the intricacy of your despair
this particular December evening when you actually feel the winners gather
together in the chapel and an hour later in the mess hall
and mutter their gratitude for genetic technology and the more secure
sense of community it's produced like electric fencing.
When you lose it's just you watching the electric fence, like a cow
with your flat brow and slightly furrowed brown eyes that steady themselves
as only a sign from which no signification can be wrought
not by theologian, semiotician, vegetarian, or third-generation farmer.
Oblivious to the slaughter number tattooed on their ears as their
nostrils flare in the just-above-freezing air; they watch the humans
scurry back to the hutch where a singular trail of chimney smoke promotes
a sense of gradation and process amidst a darkness that descends
in one monolithic and monochromatic movement like the guillotine.

Everybody loves a winner, but when you lose it's just you and your bedroom
as an antechamber, the snuffbox of the bed itself where like ash inside
a mastaba you have already returned to white powder. I have returned already
to Mecca, to Minnesota, to my future fast-forwarded in the multiminute
of my being forced to focus on my mortality at such a young age
like the repeated refrain of a psychopathic rapist to keep him from raping me
I'll stare into the pupil, the dilating finality; a kind of metaphysical duel
where the stakes pierce thelruelves like harpoons into what's purely physical
and win by deferral, by a Buddhist acknowledgment of the world's inequality
and return already, ahead of schedule, to fray from fabric, to tree from text.
I'll watch the wild ponies from an aisle seat in business class
that flies solo sans 747 chassis, having already experienced the crash.
I'll win by losing, by looking up at the winning sky from a six-sided box
for nothing is lonelier than a grave, mass or single, shallow or deep
determined or ubiquitous like the eccentric wish for the at-last
unfettered ashes to be sprinkled like fairy dust over a favorite mountain range.
I'll give birth to myself by virtue of my degradation,
lick the self-inflicted wounds of my masochism,
carry a pea on my nose in the effort to perfect my posture
and take it on the chin as the British would say.
I'll lose by winning, take the sky like a phallus into my mouth

and subsume what's impossible to subsume by the degree of my subordination.
Everybody loves a winner, loves the credit card, gold or green
when it's taken out to pay for dinner. Everybody loves the New Jersey upstart,
the unmanicured beauty, the wizened scholar who's revered in part
for his hideous appearance. And everybody loves Magic Johnson
even more than ever now that he's HIV positive.
But they don't love my dead friends, and they don't love me either.
They don't love a loser unless you were first good at athletics.
Everybody loves a winner. I love them true myself.
It's just that I recognize the loser from my own lonesome state,
one tree to another, from across a forest, the matte green tennis lawn
at Wimbledon, like "Some Enchanted Evening," as having won at something else.

Omen

for Sharon Olds

White roses winter into human depth—
into shit with us, their dry petals and tireless leaves.

They return in fleets as if to nascence.
Migrating, they spur an infinite helix, like a snail's shell or DNA.

Yet into a position so wretched and twisted
their rigor mortis appears, at the same time, unnatural.

Blankly they stare, panicked, spotlighting the indoor air,
perpetually in recognition of that, their assassin:

White into black into white into black into white into no more
Only desperate scratches are left to decipher on the floor.

I've been trying to trust since I was an atom.
Indeed, the very explosion of cells in me serves as an example.

Doesn't my sleeping spine submit to recontouring on the Seaman mattress?
And offered up half-shelled and therefore raw in expression

my sustained scatological admiration for the death of white roses
provides another just as loathsome and handsome.

Make Costly Your Tears

The great ceiling spreads before me, wings of a pterodactyl,
blank as our concept of heaven and absolving,
with its absorbent powers.

Droplets of Steuben flow upward from my eyes,
lend a semi-gloss sheen to my perception.
I almost prefer the world this way, encased in my sorrow
since that is the manner in which I keep you invincible.

This is only morning. The sink bowls before me, a porcelain cavern.
Do I regret the profuse knowledge I've gained of your body?
How well clothes hide us! There's never a need to feel self-conscious.

We no longer live in the age of letters.
If we did I would have yours tied up somewhere
for the purpose of experiencing a surge of pure eroticism
(usually made opaque from my affections)
when rewitnessing their confinement.

As a culture, cursively, we've denominated into signatures.
Yours, in blue Magic Marker, stenciled throughout my field of vision.
I'm able to stare for a remarkably long time at your signed name,
practicing the art of minimalism,
as if the letters could give way at last, like my legs did, like a dam,
to their signification,
though I love the sign anyway, even without its meaning:
your cock was made for my mouth.

Steuben stands the hardest to break of all glass.
I've collected my tears in a pan like gravel.
May they pave driveways with utilitarian humility someday,
learning effacement by virtue of their production.
May they give way to tread marks like legs or signatures,
leave a stark mark of erasure on the honorary Firestone.

Now I understand how I got into this rattrap of wistfulness.
Nothing sets us up more for disappointment than twilight.
From the start we are predisposed to idealization by reality,
by its exquisite and erratic and incompassionate nature.

Family Romance

for Adrienne Rich

Whenever I catch two men kiss, in the streets, or in the movies,
I'm filled with so much envy, always wanting to be filled up
the way a woman would. Their jaws interlock as if to kill—
true, it was a lioness that I saw suffocate a wildebeest once—
but the depths of their tongues that churn round in the caves
of their mouths like fornicating hips or shamans writhing with prayer
before the primordial campfire, I recognize parasitically
for I can only feminize, exiled to the inversion of this passion.
If hell is starvation, then always from me the carrot of equanimity
gleams in its linear superiority; born on my knees, as it were.
I serve in abstention, help throw into high relief like Mt. Rushmore
"the great" through representation of "the mediocre," of the mother,
of earthen conjugation freshly seeded whether or not barren I remain.

Although, I too know the friction of torso against my skin,
rubbed against the pees of my breasts, flexed tendons like a horse's neck.
I've lubricated my fist up to my elbow with the best of them;
and suckled a man's tits as roughly as if he were a woman and I a lesbian.
I've witnessed his eyes roll back into his head with breathy subjugation.
But I am, alas, like their enemy, their opposite, yet not their equal
fraught from the fission of the first human into something quite different
preamble to their totem the way canine compares to Neanderthal,
(albeit constructed just as much from advertising as from genetics).
The desire I elicit expedites, perhaps, more the social than the libidinal,
more the shelter than the landscape, more the exodus than the Zionist sky.

More the wingnut in the economical structure of the nuclear unit
than the shark blue heat of locomotion that's black in feeling,
the *double entendre* that's entropy and beauty: an x-ray of an elderly hand
stacked upon an x-ray of my young heart blueprints my future, shark blue.
To kiss that hand with love in my heart is what I'll spend a lifetime doing;
to swallow my innocence whole in the process like a goldfish,
to respect the fraternity; to respect the beating.
But I can never sleep with my father throughout history and make history,
even though my father fucks me, perfunctorily,
the inferior prerequisite to actualized oratory, the smoking of his cigar.

Absorbed by history as nonpartisan, as audience by auditorium,
as ingredient by compound, as the wildcard, postmodern elaboration of a rib,
piecemealed to more skeletal paraphernalia in the Natural Museum
I'm never the museum, nor the tautological exhibit, nor the curatorial whim.
I'm the freak of each, hybrid of anything, the Epiphany of orgasmic peaking,
the dog in the snuff film shot in real time by bastardized time.
I'm the moon when there's no moon forced to regard the world's lack of night.
I'm the dismembered arm in a Jasper Johns, pre-Raphaelite
without predisposition myself, a perigee forever without point of contact.
Like the lake that reflects the sky as it pathologically lies about God,
I'm more than water and reflection and rest amidst churlishness for the eye.
I'm more than a wingnut, than open arms or open legs or a bottomless throat.

I'm more than the man who mounts deep inside the man, inside me, the woman.
I'm both the truth and the lie about God.
I'm both but I'm not a hermaphrodite, nor a cross-dresser, nor do I lip-sync
"Stormy Weather" at the Hellfire Club on Ladies Night.
I'm both the id like the lake, mum and blind,
and the hyperbolic superego of the sky, tyrannically weak.
I'm both the night and a particle of the night, animadverted into annihilation.
I'm both the shark and the x-ray; my future and the elderly hand.
I'm both the killer and the lover, the father and the lioness.
I'm both the Acropolis and the gorgeous disengagement of the Parthenon.

Palea

Only my mouth taking you in, the greenery splayed deep green.

Within my mouth, your arm inserted, a stem of gestures, breaking gracefully.

Into each other we root arbitrarily, like bushes, silken and guttural.

Palaver, we open for the thrill of closing, for the thrill of it: opening.

The night was so humid when I knelt on the steps, wet and cold, of prewar stone.

A charm bracelet of sorts we budded, handmade but brazen, as if organic.

I cannot imagine the end of my fascination, emblazoned but feather-white too.

The gold closure of this like a gold coin is, of course, ancient.

Why can't experience disseminate itself, be silken and brazen yet underwater?

A miniature Eiffel Tower, an enameled shamrock, a charm owned by its bracelet.

The Crying Game

written to the song by Geoff Stevens
in memory of my father

I know all there is to know about the crying game

  for I've seen him turn   his face
away from me

So now I can say I've seen the lord,
                              his aquiline nose
his long sandy blond hair streaked with blue and red
No tears were streaming   down *his* cheeks

  When he turned his back to me
  the great V of his torso   pivoted   like the turning point in a
                                classical novel
as Anna foresaw the train tracks   in Frou Frou's broken back

I've discovered my eventual absence in his sacrum
the thick braid of muscle that   denotes into nothing

I've had my share   of the crying game

  when I watched his body turn, slowly
as a rotation of the earth
                or screw in a head press

first there are kisses
then there are sighs

his effeminate waist   swiveled in its socket
        of the pelvis that once fit me   like a yoke

his body covering, a critical mass
the pressure of his hand,   before my confirmation
       barely felt the way a priest blesses a child

pushing me down, further and further

to my confirmation, the denigration of a child
as if swallowing the semen of god would bring me closer to gods

and then before you know where you are
                          you're saying goodbye

O they say he loves us all   but for some reason   he stopped loving me

One day soon I'm going to tell the moon   about the crying game
and we'll cry together   like the day I told my father   I was HIV positive

And if he knows maybe he'll explain
                          just him and me   under a fluorescent tube
our chairs as close as we could push them together

                  why there are heartaches
                  why there are tears

If I had been younger he would have embraced me   with his whole body
held me in his lap while I sobbed and he,
                  though less dramatically, too

                  He'll know what to do
                  to stop feeling blue

but the closest we could come to   that was to cry together   but separately

        our heads in our individual hands, though our knees remained touching
for crying is always,   in essence, about crying alone

                  when love disappears

into the astringent light of fluorescence

first there are kisses, then there are sighs
then fluorescent light replaces the moon

                  I genuflect   beneath the circular tube
        lit 24 hours, a postmodern shrine

                                that illuminates my deathbed
          spare and   apologetic

          bare futon on a wood floor
I'm willing to be yoked by his pelvis again instead of,   instead of . . .

but he doesn't look back, he doesn't   say why
Then before you know where you are
                              you're saying goodbye

Don't want no more
          of the purifying, of the placating, of the penury ritual
of self-deprivation of the crying game, the goals, overly ambitious,
of its refinement like spiritual fasting for which fasting, broth and
bread, then bread and water, then just water, only water, itself will
not provide a spiritual dimension, an exaltation that results from
impoverishment, base in expectation, ingenuous in tent by being void
of intent, of sacrificial ecstasy comprised of only one desire, only one
like water, a fasting of desires until living upon one, desiring only one
desire, the desire for atonement is only that

Don't want no more
          of the nights, not just the sweats, not just the fear of sweats,
not just the dreams, the gargantuan, exhaustive dreams, the hallways,
the staircases, the crowds, the water, the betrayal, not just their
cruel non sequiturs of composition, not just the bedside light turned on
at four in the morning as if of its own accord, contemptuously, in order
to underscore the aloneness, "You must feel so alone," it says
mechanically undergoing modes of observation like a night nurse
blanched to the moans of her patients. She reads my unconscious fears as if
viewing an x-ray of them, a blood pressure pedometer, then checks them
off, executing the little marks on her chart with cursory but automatic
precision simultaneously shutting off another light with each notation.
It's the crying game when she's left, it's the squeaks of her rubber-soled
white shoes on the linoleum as she whisks onward down the corridor into
silence. It's the length of darkness ahead I'm forced to contemplate. It's
the drive for relief that refuses to atrophy.

Don't want no more
    of the condoms, of policing, of elaborating excuses, of newsbreaking,
of the crying game that bullies me into one crying jag after another with
no reprieve to be found after, of vitamins, of poems, of suicidal scenarios,
of imagining, willing your life to change but nothing happens, no parole,
no tenure, no wedding, just a waiting, the massive silence of a crowd waiting
the silence of exodus, the silence of entrapment, the silence of failed
imaginings: hungry mouths in an orphanage

Don't want no more
    of what I can't have no more of, of the paradigm of the crying game
which is the paradigm of starvation driven so deep inside me it's written
infinitely in the mutilation of my body, separating me, irreparably from
myself, so left I am to keep vigil over a kind of vegetable, a love death,
a death wish that can't fulfill itself, that just keeps hanging on like
Karen Ann Quinlan

Clash

As if without agony the white convertible, a Mustang, peels along,
pierces the chiffon-thin dawn, sheet by sheet,
white as white chocolate or a snow leopard's spots.

Far off people make love and moan as if in great pain,
but they're not, though their pleasure be pitched at an undetectable level
like a whistle only dogs can hear.

And I, as if a dog, hear it all,
hued yet whole in its spectrum, a hologram Xeroxed to perfection
where the exaction of exhaust exhalation and heaves of passion
stack this cruel world upon its cruelty.
Their secretions smear their loins like white chocolate,
and from their eyes spurt white tears of pity.

I both watch and want to stop
the lovemaking bodies that wriggle with self-centered abandon
deep inside my body the way a dream does or hope will despite my cynicism;
pulling me to move by collar and chain
within my emotionlessness, motionless as a parked car,
a white convertible, a snow leopard devoured by dogs,
I both watch and want to stop.

What Calendars Have Become

When you're sick the months merge, first the seasons, then the years
the movement of time transforming into the plaything of others,
which voyeuristically you witness as if at leisure for such pastimes.
You regard with faltering bemusement the numerical delineation of days
and weeks as they organize themselves so aggressively on some boring
Sierra Club Calendar . . . the one that hangs in the blood lab, for instance—
You stare with morbid blankness at time demystified by such practical
factors—its perfect arc appears less grand and therefore hopeful,
aware now that it's your body only that's the means of measuring the future—
Hence all else becomes superfluous and surreal: goals, dreams, desires—
strange accoutrements, mostly media-induced, of our particular culture.

With effort you recall the ambition you once matched in its swift exiting
of days marked with giants X's or efficient little checks—when time continually
reconfigured itself before your eyes like yoga masters demonstrating
the many venues of Kundalini orgasm. Looking at a calendar: now is like
turning the large, brightly colored pages of some coffee table accessory—

the intensity of pattern in the shrine-like boudoirs hurts your eyes
for a moment as sudden daylight does for those resistant to reality.
You strain to adjust, then regret the small feat of assimilation—
your regard registers as dull compared to their fascinating accomplishments of
coordination and wild self-involvement. Perhaps your index fingers traces
a stray hand back to the shoulder, the magical displacement of limbs leading
to anxiety and confusion—and a jealousy unlike anything previously experienced.

Jealous of what, exactly? The multiple thrill, the unmannered mastery,
the treasure map of the many pleasure points and unerring, navigational ability?
The barrier of skin and how it used to signify sex, an eroticism triggered in merely
the anticipation of boundary-crossing? —When ill, perimeters of privacy close down
methodically—intrusion therapy having been taken to its extreme—like veins, for
instance. Initially technicians were glad to see me, until my veins began to
systemically collapse—and I became difficult to "access," the value
of my interiority a summation of only that: blood rivers to be tapped—
nobody wants to keep seeing someone's face in this kind of circumstance.

Examining the lovers, it's hard to believe that such control over pleasure exists—
when the organic production of pain from disease progression flourishes gratuitously,
the way wildflowers engendered by bone grist and bile might connect us to a larger
schematic and with it a sense of cohesiveness—a lack of ultimate futility—but the
wildflower, say the edelweiss blossom, in its figurative smallness and isolation,
cannot act as the horizon does or vanishing point in a painting by piecing
together such grandiose abstraction. It remains small and isolated in our one-on-one
viewing, a kind of consultation that eventually flatlines, like the strategy sessions
with my doctor—his white coat, the edelweiss, my body, the testing ground of science.
Whatever the essential self once was disappears before you slowly over time
before the polite and caring physician, before the scale, the ridiculing mirror
as the body is given over, slowly, like the minds of the brainwashed to covert
operations or information from the interrogated when given sufficient amount of
torture—like the broken will of a rape victim; veterans of war to symbolic cloth.
To medical intervention—drugs, procedures—I have bequeathed myself.

This is the kind of agenda that calendars have become, grids that pretend to connect
but actually disassociate us from the problematic of essential meaning. Sadly their
arbitrary thematics, i.e. Jackson Pollock paintings, famous writers at their desks,
dreary watercolors so mediocre they're unable to distinguish winter from summer—twelve
months, four seasons, 365 days, 24 hours, merely provide a means of distraction from
the feelings of senselessness and disorientation, the whys of fluke beginnings and ends
of existence, the concept of an overarching trajectory to guide us, to comfort and
to protect our idea of importance—the intrinsic value of mankind as contextualized by
human history—disguising, as necrophilia does lifelessness, our aeonian worthlessness.

It's as if one were perpetually forced to witness the crashing of a plane,
to view the cruel and surreal sequencing that occurs within the depressurized cabin.
And by virtue of this raw and honest demonstration, any pretense of enlightenment
reveals in the end—as white sheet does a corpse, as corpse does the anatomy
specimen, as anatomy specimen, the banal fatuousness of an overdetermined soul—the
falsehood of comprehension; for whatever is spontaneously or in turn assiduously
understood instantaneously dismantles, suctioned back into that fractured space, the
black hole from which it originated: passengers and passenger paraphernalia alike
equalized by disaster when the airborne exit door unexpectedly lurches open and into
the ravenous vacuum, purses, raincoats, briefcases, high-heeled shoes ricochet
like billiards against metal armrests and the heavy plastic of upper compartments
before bursting in fits and spirals unto the white, even-tempered glare of oblivion.

Our dead faces are born already inside us. They float just beneath the surface of our
expressions, joyful and despairing, like lily pads asphyxiated in a frozen pond.
Some fail quickly while some fail incrementally with time to absorb
all the infinitesimal disappointments, the details, gory and beautiful, reflected
in the shocked face continually reframed by the realization of its death forthcoming.
Its features document the difference between a fatal accident and wasting away . . . the
excruciatingly slow entry into the self-dug abyss like Eskimo elders excommunicated from
the community—their footprints filling up immediately with fresh snow—evidence
that the heavens are in agreement, acknowledged now and then in empty-canteen silence.
Glancing over his shoulder, perhaps one contemplates the humility of return, the
slaughter by his family for carnal nourishment—there is no sparing. But all suffering
mitigates in severity when compared to this loneliness, all suffering preferable
to the withholding quiescence of snow falling, exponentially, upon fallen snow.

I'm surprised to know that it's beautiful where I'm headed. The black-and-white
photographs do not do it justice. Dogs barking in the distance urge me toward it.
I hear them continuously, regardless of their actual presence, noise itself eventually
representing them, both bus breaks and sparrows. There is no design behind it,
no skeletal structure that spits ultraviolet fire beneath ambitious footsteps
like some other kind of subway system; no elaborate tapestry to which we should remain
gratefully stupefied aside from this tapestry of landscape and its magnetic fourth
dimension pulling us toward it like passengers and their paraphernalia out of a
depressurized cabin—an underground undifferentiated from the ambiguity of clouds
and cloudless light and darkness sometimes punctuated by stars and sometimes pitch.

I keep forgetting it's not a personal defeat to be so sick.
What was once a mind for music and words has become an amateur mad-scientist,
an expert at needle gauging—butterfly 25 if you're going for the hand—
an evolutionary step up from rat or chimp for drug protocols called obnoxiously
"cocktails" by the reading public (a joke on gays, I'm certain)—I honor the demands
of earthbound stasis that pulsates with monotone enthusiasm as if an artificially
resuscitated patient whose pupils rooted and dilated persist in their brain-dead state
to stare with dumb depth at the futureless sky of the hospital ceiling
and its inability to defend and therefore redeem the world—regardless of the
Styrofoam squares either stained or missing, or the fluorescent tube twitching
on and off its illumination overhead or further down the corridor—

I refer to the world but I speak of the body. I want my body to reassure me,
my catheterized limbs to start signing madly in the air, swallows flapping

to free themselves. Teach me, *Sensei*—my body——, teach me,
with *sang-froid* impartiality as you have all my life about the meaning of life,
teach me as you did once of athletic executions, the thrill of unskilled kicking
in lake water, teach me as you did of sexual collusion, the pure suspense
of someone touching, that way, my skin, painful and exciting like running into a
forest at midnight, my hair caught in branches, withered leaves abusing my face.
(I ran faster, willfully, into its dimensions darkening as if blindfolde—of course.)

You were always much braver than I, my body, as if mounted upon you but reinless
I were. You reared, your sinewy legs, your baleful eyes, your wildlife mane,
long striding away from the barn, breath crystallizing in the cold from soft nostrils.
The challenge to stay alive was the challenge to trust you—not as simple
as it sounds—and it was a sound, not singular or melodic, not a narrative or refrain,
not a language, nothing to be translated or negotiated, but a voice nonetheless
unimaginable, imperceptible, absolute, archetypal, to which I had to listen carefully
as carefully as I must listen to it now, left ear to the earth for approaching hooves.
It's us returning, more in love than ever, near collapse in the somatic blackout that
signifies death. It's us. Moonlight beats down upon the barn as if it were a crèche.

Teach me now about time running out—about clocks and calendars, and hourglasses,
and sundials, mechanisms for measuring the chasm, the adorable, the heinous duration,
leading up to this process of time running out. I have come to the part where I must
overcome my failing—teach me, *Sensei*, how to leave, how to say goodbye to you.
Help push into the river the handmade canoe of birchbark we rocked together,
like a *Todtenbaum*, its ebb as effortless as levitation, me from you or vice versa.
See me through this juncture to the threshold waiting like a waterfall ahead,
Flesh I have loved like no other. Don't let it hurt. Don't let it be too quiet.

Teach me, one foot in front of the other, this last mortal action, basic, necessary
the way you once did to chew bread or drink water, 0 body of reason.
Assume again with me a dead man's float or corpse position in yoga.
Relax my limbs, salve my anxiety: talk back to me like the friend you've been.

My mind draws a blank. My heart beats mundanely. I'm supposed to be glad and accepting
but I'm at a loss for last lines, final sentences of closure that would convince me—
of what, I don't know. It's not as if I ask for some proof of an afterlife
or some strange and worthy purpose upon which at one time I insisted, against
my better judgment and intuition, must concur with physical suffering—
some apex achieved in terms of moral purification, humility, and patience.

Take my left hand into my right—and soothe me, *Sensei,* release me from the need for something delicate and original—and sincere enough (like chance, or love, or peace, or humanity)—to make this worth it. Only the knowing of you could be that. This leaving that is your liberation, please make it mine also.

RIP, My Love

Let us be apart then like the panoptical chambers in ICU
patient X and patient Y, our names Magic Markered hurriedly on cardboard
and taped pell-mell to the sliding glass doors, "Mary," "Donald," "Tory";
an indication that our presence there would prove beyond temporary, like snow flurry.
Our health might be regained if aggressive medical action were taken, or despite
these best efforts, lost like missing children in the brambles of poor fortune.
The suffering of another I can only envision through the mimesis of my own,
the alarming monitor next door in lieu of a heartbeat signifying cardiac arrest,
prompts a scurry of interns and nurses, their urgent footsteps to which
I listen, inert and prostrate, as if subject to the ground tremors of
a herd of buffalo or horses, just a blur in the parched and postnuclear distance.
I listen, perhaps the way the wounded will listen to the continuing war,
so different sounding than before, the assault of noise now deflected against
consciousness rather than serving as motivation for patriotism and targets.
Like fistfuls of dirt loaded with pebbles and rocks thrown at my front door,
I knew that the footsteps would soon be running to me also.
The blood pressure cuff swaddled around my arm pumped in its diastolic state
independently like an iced organ ready for transplant
as I witnessed with one circular rove of my eyes my body now dissected
into television sets, like one of those asymmetrical structures
that serves as a model for a molecular unity in elementary science classes.
And the plastic bags of IV fluids that hung above me, a Miro-like mobile or iconic toy
for an infant's amusement, measured the passing of time by virtue of their depletion.
Sometimes I could count almost five and then seven swinging vaguely above me at 4 a.m.
I remember the first, hand-held high above me when I arrived via ambulance at the ER, the
gurney accelerating as a voice exclaims on the color of my hands, "They're *blue!*"
Another voice (deeper) virtually yells out into the chaos that she can't get a pulse.
Several pairs of scissors begin simultaneously to cut off my clothes, their shears
working their way upward like army ants from pant cuff and shirtsleeve,
a formulaic move for the ER staff which, despite its routine, still retains
a sense of impromptu in the hurriedness of the cutting both deft and crude,
in the sound of their increased breathing, of their efforts intensified by my blood
pressure dropping, the numbers shouted out as if into night fog and ocean.
It's not a lack of professionalism but the wager of emotional investment that I feel.
One attendant, losing her aplomb for a moment, can't contain herself from remarking
(as if I'm already post-mortem) on what a great bra I have;
"Stretch lace demi-cup, Victoria's Secret," I respond politely in my head.

In turn, when they put the oxygen tube into my nose I thought immediately
of Ali McGraw on her deathbed in *Love Story* and how good she looked in one.
And then the catheter where I pissed continually into a bottle like a paraplegic
let me in on the male fear of castration,
my focus centered entirely on that tube, its vulnerable rigging
which I held onto tenderly throughout the night like something dying
against my thigh or something birthing. I held on though the IV in my forearm
overextended with a kind of pleading, the needle hooked deep into a mainstream vein
the way in deep-sea fishing lines are cast into the darkest water,
my body thrashing about in the riverweed of its fluids.
The translucent infrastructure of IVs and oxygen tubes superimposed itself upon me
like a body double, more virulent and cold, like Leda pinned and broken by her swan,
like the abandoned and organ-failed regarding its superior soul ascend.
So completely and successfully reconfigured within its technological construct
my body proper no longer existed, my vital signs highlighted in neon
preceded the spiraling vortex of my interiority,
the part of me people will say later that that's what they loved
when they roam about in the cramped rare book library of their memory
for a couple of minutes and think of "Tory."
Movement can be accounted only in shadows, Virilio informs us,
the reconciliation of oneself in one's disappearance.
An anachronistic sundial, I turn my profile
and the fluorescence falls unfractured, unmediated onto the postmodern tenebrism
of absence against absence, my quickened inhalations against my backless gown.
My love for you, my love, for my friends, untethers and floats,
snaps apart and off me like the IV tubes and monitor wires
the flailed arms of an octopus unfolding without gravity,
as I reach up in a Frankensteinian effort to shut off my monitors,
the constant alarming of the human prototype my own body keeps rejecting,
while death moves closer, a benign presence.
It stands respectfully just outside the perimeters of my life
and adjusts itself the way the supervising nurse did the monitor perimeters
to suit my declining vital signs so I could get some sleep.
I felt a relationship with death, a communication, it was more familiar
than I ever imagined, what I had always returned to as the sign of me, the self
we attribute to the mysterious and perfectly ordered Romantic notion of origin.
What I'm trying to say is that it was not foreign. It was not foreign,
but it was not a homecoming either.
There was no god, no other land, no beyond;
no amber, no amethyst, no avatar.

But there was a suspension, there was an adieu to recognition
to the shoes of those I love, like Van Gogh's, a pair but alone
the voices of loved ones, their tones, their intonations, like circulation,
close-circuited but effective.
There was a listless but clear-thinking comfort that into my own eyes
I would go, although not "into" in the Bachelardian sense
which implies diminishment; there was none of that.
It was just the opposite: expansion but without a pioneer's vision.
What we regard as the "self" extended itself, but I wouldn't say in a winged way,
over the Bosch-like landscape of brutal interactions
and physical pain and car alarms and the eternal drilling of disappointment
the exigent descendence of everyday that every day you peer down or up
its daunting staircase, nauseous with vertigo
gathering like straw the rudimentary characteristics of courage, gumption, innovation
and faking it to the hilt like a hilarious onslaught of sham orgasms.
Transcendence might be the term Emerson would lend it.
What I'm trying to say is that it wasn't lonely.

Cinéma Vérité

Like great moments in filmmaking when Brando adheres his wad
of ACG (already chewed gum) under the iron balcony and parodies
the decline of late twentieth-century Europe with this gesture.

Or the closing scene in *Contempt* where the minuscule Fiat
white as Bardot's bleach job collides fatalistically and thus hubristically
with a trailer truck and her neck, white as a Fiat, snaps
at once instantaneous and infinite like the bereavement sobs of Juno
at four in the morning that register as silent to sleeping mortals.

You within the context of your death must diminish in value like the ruble
within a capitalist market, a fag smoldering, chartreuse and laconic
within solitary confinement, despite my enshrining efforts to embalm you
which assert themselves as indecipherable as asphalt amidst asphalt.

The way in Warhol's *Empire*, shot (almost) in real time,
diminishment occurs by virtue of real time as if the incarcerated spectator
were forced to keep vigil over the last eight hours of the Empire State
Building's life—a kind of iconic sublimation into abstraction takes place,
where the cheap film posits, projects a silkscreen, a replicate, an aberration
and the Empire becomes a sign for itself, for the signified of abstraction,
of abyss, a negative that foregrounds its positive like the Venus de Milo,
a stationary torso suspended like the skull as locus in Hamlet's soliloquy,
the moon as telos for our displacement from the last reel of utter darkness.
The Empire, glistening as if the teeth of the dead, rises, exhumed
like Houdini or Jesus or Elizabeth Barrett Browning
from a neuter desert, the impossible tomb
of its representation, and incinerates in homage to itself
like the actual cremation of your body.

According to a sadist's definition of "slowly"
as in torture, as in interrogation, where the voice of confession
becomes the belated product, a fetish accoutrement, of its oppressor
the libido frees itself like a holocaust survivor
and the world, poor and empty as the final frame in *The Passenger*
where the clay terrain, the barking dog, the shrunken sky
become merely the fetishistic accoutrements of poverty and emptiness.
I see my future through the eyes of that Jack Nicholson.

O in Oshima's In the *Realm of the Senses* when Sada castrates Kiehl
after his death, I want to keep you like that, your cock preserved
like the brain of a genius, beyond bronze, pickled in a jar of formaldehyde.
"That movie's about castration," you said.
"That movie's about possession," I said. It's about both, together and cut
(the word "togetherness" a pun on "alone" and "cut" in Japanese).
During a course of phone calls I tracked down your body like a death sheriff
on its post-mortem itinerary from mortician to medical examiner to crematorium
in an effort to discover your final resting place, much the way Dustin Hoffman
à la *The Graduate* pathfinds the church where Elaine is getting married
but minus the macabre intent of this necrophiliac's obsession.
What I would have given: blank check, right hand, first book of poetry,
to intervene, to interrupt, to slip surreptitiously into the funeral home,
nauseous from the redolence of absenteeism, and lick intrepidly
without a time limit, the irregularly sewn sutures from the autopsy incisions.
Your handsome head albeit turbid in recognition remains stationary, the bust
of Mahler by Rodin, the bleeding feet of Christ in their oracular hemorrhage.
If granted the opportunity I would have asked, I would have pleaded
as the prime minister's wife did with the wife of Saddam Hussein
who received the next day in lieu of his life, the body parts of her husband
parceled in three Hefty lawn bags.

Today is the anniversary of when we last saw each other. Turning the corner
your face lit up like Northumberland terrain idealized by a Northumbrian.
But the earth and its oral traditions serve now only to disappoint me
as do my friends, as does UPS, as does the road, winding or freeway,
in light of the Jacobean erasure of that expression; the snapshot I'll not have.
We stood where the clouds colluded in a tenet of unsurpassed fatalism
flattering to our star-crossed desires as the dream of duet suicide.
We experienced our corporeality fail us then, conversely, in the pleasure
of touching, for we are not, like sanitized forceps, touching now.
We are not, like forsythia and lake water, touching now.
Corporeality failed us both even though only one of us died.
Corporeality, at once omniscient and estranged, deauthenticates the body
in its urgency to prove itself otherwise the way newscasting does world events
the way a cemetery betrays the closure of death with touchstones for eternity.
Corporeality humiliates us as if expelled from flesh afore flesh we're forced
as a dog is to defecate in public, to watch interminably our expulsion
until pathetic I admit congeals the bodily composition that cannot bring you back,
my hand, a peg in its ineffectualness to make real this lowly a handmade wish.

Once when I called you after the fact (it's sick, I know) just to hear you "live"
like a cassette of Maria Callas' unknown recordings I own, it worked, so to speak,
your outgoing message, regardless of the emptiness, both pythogenic and Arcadian
the way one engages in part in phone sex to reacquaint the self with its extremes,
a tautological erotica, where the moment more than emblematizes the history,
but is its emblem as if to withhold it, bury it in an arcanum like your remains
the body I never got to identify that, now cremated, endures as unidentifiable;
a kind of déclassé epiphany. And I wonder if the void, the arcanum, itself
provides perversely the means for its so-called fulfillment like an artifact,
like a fetish accoutrement, like an icon, like a national flag, like a Wonderbra,
like a lock of your hair where a kind of double death occurs upon discovery,
the way masturbating to the memory of a dead man becomes the only way to climax.

When I called a few days later, your telephone had been temporarily disconnected
and I flew in reaction throughout the corridors of my refractive identity
like Julie Christie in *Darling* who throws a shit fit in the Italian villa
when she finds it impossible to reach the insipid Count, her husband
hyperventilating from the sheer existential pitch of her isolation:
her poor choice in marriage, her inevitable aging, her preposterous décolletage.
I breathe in deeply the sickly air of a city plagued by an august siesta.
Your death augurs a boundlessness, isotropic as saline.
I mourn you, suspended like Sappho, from the balcony of my future,
iced out amidst the vulgar silence, cruel and penetratingly so by definition.
The balcony, a baroque catastrophe (not unlike the one Brando sullies
before he dies in *Last Tango in Paris*) protrudes as if a stillborn pregnancy
over a centennial nothing, an ocean debased in celluloid.

One day I'll make a little pilgrimage to your burial site.
I'll travel incognito, via a Greyhound, sporting Jackie O. sunglasses
and a platinum flip-do wig, exercising thus the bad faith intrinsic to selfhood
in a flagrant display of its inherent exhibitionism.
Therefore most true to the emotive content which propelled this journey I'll be,
closest to the person whom you loved when I peer myopically to inspect your name.
It makes no sense to me, staring a bit longer, just a mirage of letters engraved
that contain the secret of your name like an anagram or dream condensation.
I work hard to interpret, regardless of the snow and unusually high wind
still searching like a mammal for a carcass I've witnessed thrown to the wolves
yet I can't get over a land like this that refuses to hand you, its hostage, back.
I hate the complacent woods, the recalcitrant answering machine,

the patronizing sky that pretends to understand while denying you ever existed.
I picture you in Canada, proud to have staged so successfully your death,
(and in a way you did, for as children of Watergate we know what to erase)
where behind your computer screen you're in command again
with a newfangled modem which not only promises a modicum of control
over earthly events way back when virtual reality merely assimilated,
but allows voyeuristic predilections to be transferentially indulged ad infinitum.
You type in your name and it takes you to your grave. You recognize instantly
the pitiful sight of the sentimentally driven woman in the wig.
You watch the larger than life tears like Man Ray's famous photograph
freeze-frame in their initial debouchment then rivet through the granite crevices
of your birth and death dates, obscured by mascara, blue-tinted.
You feel love, then fear, guilt, anger, then helplessness. Your anxiety peaks
but you resist temptation to stroke F7 and eliminate the image.
Then you think of something to say, something both protective and productive
like "Tory, when was the last time you backed up your files?"
The woman reflexes either from a sudden sense of cold or dissident sound
but not from this lame attempt you figure, articulating the self-recrimination
"lame attempt" out loud. She returns to reverie while you watch her like wildlife.
The modem provides then the cache of an unexpected benefit
and you're able to read, like subtitles, verbatim the thoughts in her brain.
Intrigued by a breach in the epistolary canon this method of discourse may provoke
not to depreciate the motivation to speak, the screen-fixation, a body language
of sorts, you write back the way you used to call her, always with a mixed agenda:
(I'm sorry, but no umbrella modifiers make themselves available here).
The subtitles engage in an epic dialogue, the way the protagonists relate
in *Hiroshima, Mon Amour* out of sync with their lips and in delayed reaction
to their desires. Their desires portrayed in black-and-white film,
the only realistic medium for love and death, for pornography and ruination;
for the blanched complexion, the harnessed eyes, the bed-sheet toga,
the Asian profile as it smokes a cigarette and describes the mutilation outside
he surveys which time, to this day, is impotent to nullify.

"I simply miss him," confesses Peter Finch nondefensively in a tête-à-tête
with the camera at the end of *Sunday Bloody Sunday*, referring to the bisexual
dilettante in hiphuggers and turtleneck who not only tears apart like blood oranges
the hearts of both Finch and Glenda Jackson but has built a monstrous sculpture/
fountain in Finch's backyard which functions like a multitude of Water Piks.
His missing him strikes us as poignant precisely because this guy is such a twit,

memorable solely for a certain panache demonstrated in the replacing of a fuse.
After acting in one of the most famous movies in Schlesinger's career if not film
history, he disappears from future cinema completely It's the commonality in Finch's
longing we identify with, detected beneath the indifferent features (ours & his);
the relinquishment in his eyes to outside forces offset by the surrealism
of a Berlitz 45, the fundamentals of learning Italian for the vacation planned
they'll never take together. In his decision to go alone we view the imperceptible
as if the shadow of a figure in the background, depicted in the generic male voice
who queries with forced emphasis Italian basics, i.e., What time is it?
The check, please; Where's the bathroom? Do you have Coca-Cola? What about 7-Up?
Appropriating the perfect soundtrack to the chronic nature of Finch's narrative.

All strategies fail by virtue of the effort to erect a strategy,
the desire to represent you which ends in that desire, incontrovertible
as the ground wherein you've been neutralized in a final democracy; hermetic
like a fantasy that exists for as long as it's made fail-safe from the real.
From the possibility of resolution, paradoxically, I want to preserve you.
It would be the only gesture that wouldn't be too late.
It would be the only gesture that wouldn't acquiesce to the East
and pay tribute, even if only in the secondary instance, an allegorical act
rather than symbolic, to its awful palingenesis.

A photograph of you finally arrived. "It won't be the picture you want,"
forewarned a friend. But how can one be forearmed to desolation
save by acquiescence (as if to the East), to its vortex, violet as the orifice
you'll never enter again like Russians into Prague,
like an Artaudian performance. Like Freud's reception of da Vinci's drawings
you inserted yourself, permanently, into my field of vision—
a field of moribund forsythia, a field of lake water, laminated like a frame
from a snuff film where the money shot translates itself into a death spasm;
and the lake, subsequently, translates itself into a kind of giant sarcophagus
where the heavens are forced to witness as if a suicide, unflinchingly,
your death in its varying degrees of deciduousness.

Our love was like the dining room scene in *The Miracle Worker*
where a young Anne Bancroft teaches an even younger Patty Duke to fold her napkin.
Our love was Helen Keller. Our love was Patty Duke. Our love was the napkin
finally folded in the end amidst the food-spattered, chair-broken dining room.

Our love was the underground stream, the water main, and the black lacquered pump.
Our love was the synoptic cognition connecting sign to signified in Helen's brain.

Our love was woodland before topiary revisionism, the person in perfect health
before the polio epidemic. Our love was over-referenced like this poem, a strip
of neon, the prescinded urban landscape of Venturi's *Learning from Las Vegas.*

A negative transcendental signifier exited itself then from category to extinction:
lip marks on a mirror; a trajectory within an eschatological menu;
a blackboard that foreshortens evenfall;
the arm of god cantilevered on the sky's counterfeit surface, a blur of flesh tones;
a love missive inscribed and therefore absorbed upon a palimpsest
like semen into bed sheets. The soul escheated to ash instead of air.

And real time, as it were, becomes impossible to measure as in Chantal Ackerman's
Jeanne Dielman, 23 Quai du Commerce, 1080 Bruxelles where the perfunctory preparation
of meat loaf becomes the simultaneous action of her prostitution.
The hour transgresses the essential demarcations of light and darkness,
a prostitute who does not look like a prostitute, which is to say a housewife;
the painting no longer defined by the frame, but by the *parergon*, the image
as a discursive grid, uncropped, detached and interminable.
The history of the frame reframes itself as the history of the failure to reframe.

The hour then deliquesces as the concept of the hour: oblivion contained
like an hourglass without sand, the sordid eye sockets of the dead
we supplement as the loved one gone as if into another time zone;
a barren prairie proliferated with winged monkeys and diminutive ballerinas
to which the initial prayer site was founded like a lean-to
both basic and fatuous, an indiscernible ritual of sightlining the horizon.
A nefarious face served as our compass, like the circumscribed appearance of, say,
the diamond ring X recalls on the way down in the elevator in *Dressed to Kill*
or a classic sitcom split-screen scene as in *Annie Hall.*
We moved toward land while drowning at sea, like Gericault's *The Raft of the Medusa*
(1819) where death and life intertwine as the labyrinthine structure of survival,
swine with twenty last breaths left inside the diamond mines of their lungs.
We swam until the absence became intolerable. The longing festered
and grew endogenously until our hand, spotted and varicose, let itself be guided
in tribute to human mimesis and the greatest biography ever written realized
an epoch at once open-ended and unto itself, a death of sorts like the death

of so-and-so wherein an ineffable part of ourselves died also;
for which we're still searching, counting the hours, red, blue, yellow; black:
(1 a.m.) the false panel that equals the secret chamber.
(2:00) the polylingual dictionary.
(3:00) the hour, on your knees, you gave to me, kissing my ass like a baby's forehead.
(4:00) pure as strychnine.
(5 :00) the structure of implicit hope purloined from its antithetical nothing.
(6:00) you masturbating with a dog-eared 19th century novel laid open
across your chest, a punk performance art of open-heart surgery.
(7:00) the bed that never supersedes the womb, a futuresque casket.
(8:00) purblind thoughts, cuneiform writing forced into dialogue.
(9:00) the hour, a putrefaction of its antecedent.
(10:00) Concrete Blonde's "Bloodletting."
(11:00) pussywhipped by the phenomenon of time.
(12 noon) an amber contact lens.
(1 p.m.) the exponentially complex moment of diagnosis.
(2:00) the footnote to the hour (Columbia University Press, New York, N.Y), p. 14.
(3:00) a pesto+parmesan cheese-encrusted plate in a sink.
(4:00) the demonstration of love expedited in the signifier "betrothal."
(5:00) the physical examination and/ or the political interrogation.
(6:00) Paris in toto.
(7:00) the hour, on my knees, I gave to you, a ballsy; disembodied head.
(8:00) the phone call informing me that you are dead.
(9:00) the hours tied like limbs together until reduced to sobs and bartering.
(10:00) the Wagnerian week of your funeral in which blizzard conditions
flagellated whole cities, Chicago, Boston and New York, into a marshaled silence,
a hibiscus-like hiatus; stark; natty; a Basho haiku.
(11:00) Rudolf Schwarzkogler's *Action* (1965).
(Midnight) a discourse on pain that by virtue of its subject's inability to
be elucidated both continues and remains merely a discourse on pain.

We married each other in order to reminisce about hell like Dante and Virgil.
We were awed by the gym-bodies, fractions of ourselves who chewed away at our craft,
the arcane waters, black and portentous, cheap garb that lapped upon our epidermis
like underwear from Frederick's of Hollywood until we copulated greedily in the dinghy,
turned on by purgatory, both concept and reality. Later we remarked (crisply)
how like the Yugoslavian Riviera it was, cool and green in which the sea presented
the absolute as not just deportation from the worldly to the sublime, however
harsh, however billiard-bright in hue, however high-pressured the internal syllabus,

but intimate too, like the morning we made love in Prague.
When I turned my head arbitrarily toward the dormer window from the rotund ceiling
of your hairline, your face like a novena wafting upward in expiration
I caught a fever of snow descending as if without motion upon the rooftops
of Little Town, upon the tombstones that bespeak tombstones
in the inverted populace of the Jewish Cemetery, sequestered from the city
like indentured fangs, sharecropper scythes lassoed. And smoke, pink, turquoise,
ochre, lavender, charcoal, the reconstruction of history mutated
by the process of its reconstruction, extolled by stone chimneys, mixed inextricably
with snow, with your face, with the Yugoslavian Riviera, with Dante and Virgil's hell.

Like a wake we said goodbye to the body proper. With utter sanctity
we had the opportunity to represent ourselves in a single gesture,
dank, severe, insouciant. When I leaned over your waxen forehead
circumferenced with starched ruffles like a bonbon I gleaned my reflection
for a split second on the burnished surface (or was it projection?) for already
we had discarded ourselves as love objects left to be devoured like trespassers
pushed into a pool of piranhas. We speculated the way dictators do as entertainment
the torture of treason criminals, their public executions positing easy examples
for the *faux pas* of betrayal. We wanted to live off nothing, to eliminate
the factor of starvation, the unavoidable interplay of denigration and disease,
mental or physical, altogether. We wanted to regard, feckless
and arrogant, our lovelorn bodies hang like laundry, like Kiki Smith's, like
El Salvadorian civilians from a barn fence, putrid as dung in the torched meadow.

As witnesses to our desecration we are, in a manner of speaking, unmarred by it.
The road I walk on is always by a river, a river of water perspicuous
as plain English, its rocks like crucibles through which the river runs
with agonizing velocity, an almost slavish intensity, the sound of your stomach
digesting itself when you died. I walk forward but as if my back were turned,
the toothy spiral of my vertebra like razor wire capable of excising the world.
My desire, sore and swollen to a sweetheart pink like the feet of the homeless,
interfaces itself and speaks only in psychotic relation to the dirt,
pelleted with gravel and tar, your designated grave made ubiquitous now
the way a monk's sense of sacred ground be that upon which, wherever, he stands.
And the silence enswathes us like weather, like fluid, viscous as fetal fluid,
carnal like the electric currents between two replicants fucking in *Blade Runner*,
or a Jewish couple on the train to their death camp who fornicate before strangers
on metal and straw, damp with urine and menstrual blood and fresh feces.
Your great hands mash the filth into my hair as if into my brain when you come.

You murmur my name in its primal structure, solely made of vowels and consonants.
The silence pierces my womb. My lips swell maroon as hard, wild cherries.
I crawl down to taste our secretions in my mouth, a form of truth serum.
Silence, by its nature, defines us (and always will) as ensorcelled by silence.

The sky lowers itself like scaffolding, inch by inch, each day we're separated.
Soon it will press close to my face like the lid of my coffin, suffocating.
Unfortunately I look forward to that moment and find the thought comforting.
Unfortunately for you but not unfortunately for me.
The landscape, expunged of color, suffers regardless of its resilient topology.
My use for it damaged irreversibly by your death in that your death has replaced it.
I never saw you die so before me I envision you continually dying
a soldier shot in the leg wiggling like an agama amidst the frontline grasses
a teenager who drowns himself in the local lake at midnight
beneath a serene constellation. Taurus.
His acute longing disguised as a death wish sits inside me, just waiting.
What should be ameliorated only gets worse. O tell me, is death more even?

I never saw you die so before me I envision you continually dying;
the *mise-en-scène* of your dying I behold becomes, therefore, a *mise-en-abyme*
where before me wavers the apparition of the anadiplosis of your eyes closing,
like Mathew Brady's *Gathered for Burial at Antietam After the Battle of
September 17, 1862* (1862) your body descends in the unending action of descension
like Caravaggio's *The Entombment of Christ* (1602) where the great, unself-conscious
arm drops manly and heavy like the arm of an atheist, palm upward as if to balance
the isosceles triangle that approximates the distance from earth to heaven, pyramid
point dead center, nail wounds which abound rubies and love but rest godforsaken.

Would I have preferred you to die in my arms as my lawyer did in the arms of his boy-
friend and take your last breath into my mouth like the egg-yolk scene in *Tampopo?*
The lovers sheathed in white, the color of mourning, lambasted against their libidinal
curve, silver trout upstreaming, in a low-ceilinged, plush-carpeted Tokyo hotel room.
When you gave that movie to me for Christmas you explained that it was in
acknowledgment of our many conversations about food & sex—
of which there had been none, I thought to myself; naught but the autonomous meals
where we ate and discussed, sometimes about us, sometimes about who-knows-what,
or the isolated sex acts where we consumed the other down to grist and marrow
like Goya's *Saturn Devouring One of His Children* (1820-23).
And I guess like Goya's *The Sleep of Reason Produces Monsters* (1798) our desire

infiltrated our Filofaxes as goblins do the blank tableau of a child's sexual fantasy,
our efforts to quarantine, to put to sleep the lynxes, accrued as failures
that metamorphosed in meaning as the human being does after gross anatomy.
So well acquainted with interiority, the blustery, bat-infested cave of it,
we stepped somnambulistically without footprints throughout its depths while sparrows
swandive for a larynx, spiders suspended like chandeliers metabolize our eyeballs
and rats gnaw on our toes rancid from cuts and blisters acquired from the miles hiked
we could no longer measure. To the extent to which we sought after the flesh,
paradoxically (and equanimously) we became impervious to it:
the orgasm, orbiting until obsolete as Old English; the voice dismantled
in the process of its articulation until it perennializes only as a myth of origin.

I want nothing now. My dreams extinguished by the weight of their prostration,
en masse in a dull, iridescent confliction like a migraine, or caucus of Greek widows
finagling amidst the butcher-knife precision of Athenian light in the agora.
My disappointment unhinges from its causality; inconsequential as their shrouds
as the shadows of great pines that pretend to guard.
It's a lie they're delicate. It's a lie they're transparent.
Their tresses impound your face, your decapitation discovered netted in seaweed—
the first of many: an underwater mass grave, a noyade that's fracas then tranquil.
I'm afraid to walk atop the trapped faces that refuse burial,
that address me in the *tu* form rather than the formal;
their hair which grows even after death weaves round, entangles my ankles.
Their attachment to the ground, to the ocean's surface, to life, to me
conspires as dense, complex, and judgmental. They persecute me incestuously.
They mock me when I brush my teeth. They poke me awake when I try to sleep.
They posit little clues that might lead to pleasure then erase them when I wake.

I want nothing now and therefore it's nothing that wants me
like the face of Sharon Tate and her reflection in the vanity-table mirror
when she watches herself overdose in *Valley of the Dolls.*
She regards the puzzle of black (her reflection) piecemeal its way out
of her cognition as she lies down on the purple crushed-velvet bedspread
and waits for all the pieces to break apart fully and fade away into a vacuous
mist of animated planets and stars, just like a night scene in *Fantasia.*

Death could vouchsafe itself as this beguiling, I contemplate from my camouflaged
prison outside the television screen: as a swatch of wings like a falling horse
that recovers itself, a pair of arms proved better suited than I to hold you.

It's what death deals out like spades and hearts in its trail which defines
the ruination,fragile smoking spirals after a firecracker's launch;
vestiges autumnal as dusk of the empty shirt, the faded jeans and cowboy boots
flail independently as if puppeteered in a dusk autumnal as vestiges of death.

"I feel love for no one," I reply robotically to a new friend over a side dish
of soba noodles, who's inquired after my progress on the all too familiar
bereavement schedule, having lost his lover seven months beforehand.
I deliver my statement flat as filed taxes and directly cruel since it includes
everybody, but he knows the brutality like a brisk shower will help revive me.
I rerun this scene in my head when I get home, sitting on the edge of any chair
as has become my habit lately, this sentiment of defiance especially highlighted:
a selection from Jenny Holzer's *Truisms* on Spectacolor Board, Times Square (1982).
The street traffic configures a sonant fugue, mediocre and listless.

The maple floors of my apartment gleam with the taupe astringency of twilight,
an unalloyed lucency which, as if inverse to the eternal flame,
erects a tribute to emptiness that must represent itself in emptiness.
The appropriate memoriam to your loss would be then the gesture that offers nothing
unable to be distinguished from cab flagging, a wrist wagging *au revoir*
or the finger fanning "fey" to communicate disgust. Hence every movement toward
the future becomes a method too of grief, each reflexed yawn when propped upright
on my beached futon in the morning, a mannered agony, a way of bringing you with me.

But the day overdetermined by your death blacks out like a Swedish winter.
No matter how eloquently Rousseauean, I rebel against its doctrine.
I study myself like a caged species from a fly's perspective in the corner,
my face, a dab of white, flame-like, that waxes and wanes, anorexic and quixotic,
my neck broken by the news that you've died, my eyes just holes where ants
already nest, my vest pelleted by tears that emit miraculously in their absence.
The darkness of the cell intensifies until it swells to a concentrated pitch
so hot it melts the paint which drips in a sheet putty gray as post-mortem flesh.
Clear vomit pours from my mouth like your cum, spring water spilled
into my Chinese red shit & piss bucket. The guards check me like a roast
and laugh at the sounds I make puking. Their voices echo like car alarms
louder than usual. The metal chute shunts, an amputation.

What could stop this torture except to join you?
What amputation would I be willing to undergo just to touch you again?

Yesterday when I received my 1994-95 NYNEX White Pages I checked immediately
to see that, sure enough, you'd mistakenly been relisted
and reveled momentarily in the delusion that I could call you.
But we are not, like California and New York, touching now.

I reach inside for the wild goose, a spot somatically deficient as scar tissue;
a soreness deep inside the solar plexus where the meat hook disengaged itself
just before death a long time ago. Like a Wordsworthian spot of time
it occludes my vision, the dark end of the spectrum equivalent to blindness.
It exists as freestanding in its darkness like Pluto in the galaxy
like the arcanum of your remains, at once bountiful and empty
a box, a perimeter, a cylinder, a silo, a corridor, a place I mentally point to
doubled over in a club chair on a schedule of Saturday morning crying jags,
a container wherein whatever we had (love would describe but a part of it)
circulates unto itself in self-memoriam, in lack of recourse as a recourse to lack,
a kind of John Cagean ode to Elisabeth Kubler-Ross' five phases of dying:
denial and isolation, anger, bargaining, depression, and acceptance.
The way a Ping-Pong ball stays suspended upon an air-jet, it perpetuates
for no reason save as an illustration of the phenomenon of perpetuation,
like listening to your voice preserved on old phone machine messages.

Our love is now a videotape of you interviewed five months before you died.
Our love is the muddle of landscape behind your macho pontifications
and somewhat effeminate gesticulations; our love is the pontifications
and gesticulations themselves, the sprig of chest hairs your half-open shirt
reveals, your mouth over the course of nine years and the evolution of its kiss
encountered like the kiss itself . . . anew.

Our love is now our love *passé*, both white and stained like a peace protest flag
wrung out of an Everyman's window. It ripples opaquely in early spring humidity
as if in demonstration to the futility of demonstrations.
Our love is the hangover of nausea when I'm forced to press "rewind."

Cinéma vérité recuperates reality in order to produce its fabrication
like a patient's slow readaptation to life when diagnosed with a terminal illness:
the abridged version we term "the present" sodomized by the overrated concept
of the moment, for no moment abides alone like an atypical cell, like a birch,
like a glass of undrinkable tap water. Moments adjoin us
as rope does rock climbers so that when you died I experienced asunder

113

the crashing weight against the nylon cradle which secures the pelvis,
a kind of metaphysical chastity belt. A twisted eroticism shot through my body,
a bizarre assimilation of the bygone way you entered me;
as if I had lowered you, leashed incrementally into the pit of your grave myself
and put you to bed for the last time, a boy giant
my calves bulging, my forearms irreversibly elongated maybe as much as 1/4".

Moments in the myriad of their congregation (the way molecules constitute us)
conspire like mountains or forests at the same time they feign fragility
until little moments succeed in sentimentalizing themselves into "mementos."
Memento! Set yourself afire before my eyes and you'll only further insure
your indelibility. Set yourself afire like Jan Palach
and endure in the architecture of John Heduk and the poetry of David Shapiro.
Set yourself afire like an arsonist's utopia, the spontaneous combustion of the world
that precipitates continually in matchbooks and sheets of notepaper set afire,
the grassroots memorial the inmates instigate for Da in *In the Name of the Father.*

Moments in their hokey mosaic of orderly non-order contrive a Zen bliss
Americanized as grunge mecca, a Keatsian ode that elocutes the destiny of Kurt Cobain.
When you died one calendar of disciplines became tantamount to another,
TM and shiatsu replaced the yuppie weekday that institutes
just another kind of suturing in order to employ a maintenance plan for suffering.
Good fortune or bad fortune, praypoems tied to twigs or executed
with technological grandioso and humility like Adrian Piper's installation
entitled *What it's Like, What it is #3* (1991) in MOMA's "Dislocations" show,
erects the narrative of the horse that runs away but cannot save itself.

When you died the skin was torn off me with a penknife but from no peccancy
of mine was this cruel procedure of premature shedding incurred.

When you died, the gods knew exactly what to plumb and pluck,
a garish sense of totality that matches my poetry, a mockery of their brainstorming,
the agonizing interims and recesses of conflicted juries that strive toward unison;
the invariable aerodynamics of migrating birds.

Memento! I am mesmerized by your tragic story, better than fiction,
better than cinema, yet distanced enough from me to qualify as entertainment
like the seven-hour-long *The Sorrow and the Pity.*

Memento! Larger than me and my dead love embraced until the decomposition
of his innards makes me faint and gag, but I stay, loyal and canine
afore your firelight where we lie, Adam and Eve, banned but gratified
for no longer do the simple principles of good and evil to us apply.

Memento! Your sad fate pumps away like the transplanted organ of an ape
inside the dying Neanderthal; the stilted diastole akin to kinetic sculpture,
Black Widow (1988) by Rebecca Horn. Black feathers swab my larynx, coax
me into a silence as an ultimate means for expressing ultimacy. I rub my nose
in the dirt of your afterlife. I valorize this abjection with nonstop tears,
with Kleenex wadded in my mouth to muffle the wails, another kind of kinetic art:
activist, unctuous, a confessional pantomime.

I adapt to the black widow that's replaced my liver. I let it break apart
the myth of somatic fusion which posits an anatomical model for the body:
the model for a bodily whole is in itself a fetishistic construct.
The model for a memory, a memento, is at once voluptuous and lifeless
as a garter belt, as a cock ring, as a dedication, as your spinebroken textbooks.
I will never be so happy as when you looked at me that now when I walk with
or without direction it's always into the invisible penetration of your stare.
I will never be so happy now that off foreign blood I must live, a black widow
that feeds on red tulips until the fate of red tulips becomes mine to seize,
gone the way of wildflowers that exemplify "wildness" when provided
as an eccentric garnish to salads in expensive macrobiotic restaurants.

Our story thus best preserves itself in the *haut gout* of its erasure
merciful as a living will it remains ongoing paradoxically in its closure.
It lies prostrate in pretend rigor mortis like Count Dracula,
while the rigorous daylight moves unforgivingly across the beige features,
a topology enshrined temporarily in salute to the collapsed interiority;
collapsed in order to keepsake itself like a secret, like a secret box
destroyed in order to protect it (similar to the spirit of your cremation).
History passes as history, like a bride clad in white, by virtue of its disguise
as in the case of the diary painstakingly updated then sacrificed
which serves as the superlative example of what actually happened between us.
Like Russia's red flag devoured by historical reformation
felled rather than ascended like banished stars or winding staircases
an entire mode of architecture flourished then failed, its buttresses and steeples
stained glass and organ-piped music, gargoyles carved out of rocks that vied as

counter-voodoo dolls as if in the effort to contrive, to manifest the vile
in us, we could exorcise it from ourselves and with it its signification.
Aye, like an antique veil dropped before us once we redefined the past simply
by proceeding forward with almost a whimsical absolution, holy water dabbed
like *eau de cologne* at the temples and wrists before entering a cathedral:
The hour = Donald Judd. The hour = the Pont Neuf. The hour = the memento.
Memento! Your postmodern tragedy desublimates our story appropriately,
a Baudrillardian essay on Streisand's nose vs. Barthes' on the face of Garbo.
Memento! Your impressive capacity for exsiccating time is enviable, ineluctable
as the phases of the moon, your beams achieve the mastery of laser surgery
where we, prisoners in our designated gender-specific correction houses,
correspond in the microscopic circumference of your light, our letters set afire
mere paper beneath such heat as if never having passed the censorship officials.
Momento! I place you alone like me, your kilned head bent on kilned knee
both more and less than a frame in this homegrown version of *cinéma vérité*
a lame attempt at the recuperation of reality by producing its fabrication and
with it the part of myself that died also but somehow surpassed the actual coffin.

Memento! I turn my ugly face to the anemic dawn: what hope once came from it
no longer comes. If given the choice I'd have gladly been the one.
There is no good last line for this poem.

HIV, Mon Amour

I.

Splayed fingers cover my eyes, fluttering, broken wings of small birds.
The companion poems of future and past lost from each other like birds
flown from the nest, the mayhem nest of my soul haphazardly thrown together
of pins and twigs, the last-minute contents as if last requests
of underwear, a clean shirt, journal, wallet, keys, passport, snapshot:
the burning cigarette that wafts in black and white beneath the blindfold.
They say you see your whole life before you in one instant
but what you see is your life as an instant, that leaf twitching, not close
nor distant, flaunts itself as your childhood from first memory until now.
Within the darkness of the blindfold sight veers blinkingly toward its extinction,
reverberations of light attempt to forestall the entropy of horizon from the sun;
in reminiscence, I hear shutters, swan-song white, from a house nearer by
slowly close out as if suffocating daylight with the only bedroom window.
And the dead child inside me disenfranchised from its burial ground
I'm forced to relinquish as a final offering to the omniscient threshold.

II.

The omniscient threshold, threadbare and glistening from your lack of pity,
looms with iron proficiency like the ocean in winter, cruel waves
that counter each other like Christian souls in a competition of suffering.
when life has become so precious you're afraid to touch it, the child saint
who miraculously never deteriorated but to kiss her would be her desecration.
It's this constant miracle that throws cold water on every conscious moment
like a slow but exculpated loss of sight as it ekes out a path of exile:
one puff of wind and tiny laves alight all at once, future days and past,
confusing the air like snow flurries, the ground with a glinting mosaic
of immediacy, panic, peace, for which no amount of exposure acquires the taste.
The large shadows shift as if earth plates beneath me, recall my flirtation
snagged once again back into the undertow, the Gregorian beating of my heart.
When I say that I'm jealous of the dead, you turn away, partly in disgust
and partly in agony, for you can't provide for me what the dead know already
My brain splits apart, hemispheres of apology and longing to be understood.

III.

I remember like bark my love for you bracketed above me, the ceilings of Trianon.
Their baroque spiritualism riddles throughout me as if my nervous system.
When they poured the cool oil dead center where I had been water-tortured
I flinched at first, almost convulsed with relief the way orgasm simultaneously
catapults you outside while hurling you deeper into the recesses of the physical.
I listened to my misery, now bygone, drip evenly, exactly as the water did.
O so slowly what tortured me today soothed me like a compress, like a cool drink
as if it were the water's destiny that changed in midstream instead of mine;
that cut the ropes in a fit of consciousness to ascend, a capsized boat, my life
where weighed down I had lived like Tithonus amidst silt, pike, and youth.
The memory, gilded, incorporated itself, a metal plate for the shattered brain.
It protects by deflecting, sun off a car roof, the possibility of loving again.
Eventually desire, so blanched from lack of exposure, will go entirely numb.
I fantasize about the takeover the way the bereaved begin to equate
death with heaven, their grief in absentia, sobbing with inexhaustible reunion.

IV.

From time to time, a reminder, you mock me, that there's no love I'm looking for
on the Formica-clean surface of the world. The windows remain closed season round.
Toward which view to meander, on which subject outside to focus, decides the optimism
or directs the darkness that effuses inside you, another view just like it
but distorted in its depiction, scaled to the size of your heart, larger than life,
thus barely containable: the lone birch, thumb length, formulates your spine;
a homeless person asleep under several layers atop a heating grate, the relentless
backdrop of your mind; the passersby of lovers or mothers glimpsed, objects of desire
as if through a peekaboo dress or see-through nightie, untouchable, torturing.
The attempt to caress, to mother yourself, adding milk to the steady bread and water
of your diet provides a pitiful substitute no supplementary discourse can deny.
I always seem to call you around dinnertime. I order out from the neighborhood
Japanese restaurant a dish called "Mother and Child." Once nibbled on, a baby doll,
then brutally discarded, that labyrinthine vernacular weirdly reinforces its locality
the way Chaucerian English continues as the dialect in the Appalachian mountains.

V.

Believe or believe not the moment of truth when it comes to you like the Gestapo.
The amethyst ending of day out the window seems as charming and holy as ever.
But the furniture shifts abruptly to smaller, the sterility of defamiliarization
replacing your home with found objects eerily maintained in arrangement.
Such a gesture of pity permitted per person acknowledges human vulnerability,
the way when admitted to prison one's allowed to keep a photograph of one's children.
It's the delineation of luxury versus necessity blurred for an individual second
(yours), that decides survival, i.e., toilets installed in more "civilized" nations.
Bulwark the world from tis mercenary mission with sobs of pleading like dogs
whimpering behind the vaulted door. They've sensed the diminishment long before
the actual depletion of air. Forestall the sun its blinding glare when forced
to stare into it, into it, one day out of nowhere, you are, your head clamped,
eyelids stripped; refuse the painful depth with passion, unrequited, unconsummated,
for the gothic night. Our capacity for accommodation is formidable. Rely on it.
For swallowing at once the truth like a cyanide capsule makes suicide the only option.

VI.

Everything I write is dedicated to you though never publically will I name you.
Eventually your voice, your face will fade like nothing I've ever known,
therefore not into nothing, but perhaps as pervasive shading of your loss,
cast across my perception refocused forever in a way as to never forget you.
Few events indelibly change us, as opposed to influence, with landmark precision:
the near-fatal car accident that leaves you paralyzed, a blood test that reveals
a terminal illness, the blazing house where you watch your mother burn alive,
the death of a five-year-old child. Rarely does a relationship take on such import
unless it coincides or becomes one of these horrors, the factual litany shaved
down to the particular, the severity symbolized in a simple red ribbon worn.
Red ribbon tapes my mouth, blinds my eyes, erases my genitals, a censorship band.
Red ribbon strings me up, a carcass in an icebox. I furiously gnaw at the satin.
You were a witness. You too hated the ignorance. With you I could pretend
at least for two hours, I wasn't different. I'm sorry I put so much responsibility
in your arms like a five-year-old child whose life you could choose to save or not.

VII.

Will there ever be a point like a riptide that divides me from this fight
and delivers me as if in the wake of Mercury unto my dignity, contrived as courage,
the Captain that remains erect, though trembling, when he salutes the abyss
the heather-hued ocean that devours him and his ship and a hundred dependents.
Perhaps such face-saving gestures of protocol, once fail-safe, snapped and broke
in the course of trying, the last resort like retirement savings piled up,
gambling chips, on a long shot, a leap of faith where realization came in midair,
you'd never make it; the upshot of the great hand you sank your teeth into
and held on to, scrapping, ready to take it to the bitter end, even if bitterness
be the outcome, your skin gone gray with sweat, your hair, lanky and tremendous
in the past, cropped angrily almost to balding, your eyes ringed with exhaustion
exempt themselves from compassion, from cultural interests, from the peripheral
vision of human potential: family, community, enrichment; your stare set solely
on survival for so long, digesting metal, drinking urine, it's become albino.
You spit into the breathtakingly beautiful faces of the dead, enemy children.

VIII.

Enemy children, you yanked my baby away from me, her tiny fingers panicking,
grabbed clumps of my hair, the strands like red streamers amidst the blue mist
that rose up like spirits from the blue Ridge Mountains, the cooling sun, a pitcher
of water poured onto them, coal pit in a sauna, turned up violently the volume
of her screaming. The sound waves still surround me, red streamers, "Mommy!"
"I think women who are HIV positive that have children are murderers, don't you?"
said the woman on a lawn chair as she applied sunscreen to her legs with a kind
of industry that now scares me. I looked to the swimming pool for alliance
but the green sheen from too many chemicals and lack of maintenance, made malevolent
its static condition, the patches of scum stagnating on the surface buzzed
in unison with the southern sun that forced itself into my face, an interrogation
light, until I broke like an egg into sobs and let out the secret as if vomiting.
The swimming pool, the kudzu, the lawns banded together in a lynching of green,
Republican homogeneity, that later so convinced I allowed them to scrape me out,
a batter bowl. The operating lamp like the southern sun shone down with satisfaction.

IX.

Withhold from me like God the Almighty the antidote for this suffering, the cure,
a crystal vial glinting amidst the impartial clouds, a lightning bolt lifted
out of the context of its storm suspended, a snake-headed crosier ready to kill,
by scaring me to death, a slow death, with the potential to kill, but I will not
capitulate. I'll carry to the very top this net chock full of rocks, each larger
than myself, a hundred times my weight I'll teeter beneath, heave and ho the load
like a beloved, dying friend, my beloved, dying self. I'll drag my dislodged home
behind, climb aboard it like a broomstick and soar beyond the ultimates—
raised rails of a steeplechase, a field of poppies, lipstick-red and poisonous—
to the miniscule city, where the Chrysler Building in Manhattan, like a crystal
vial, pierces the razor-edged skyline in an effort to define it as vanishing point
of the ideal, cutthroat in ambition as an angel wing. Pluck a feather
from it and take it to this rope. File the wire knot to frizz, the fright wig
of what might have been, borrowed by the Devil like the coveted crown of thorns.
Transform the ring of pocketed posies to a laurel wreath or cut my throat instead.

X.

When you go you go alone, giving good head to a loaded gun. That's what we're afraid
of. From the git it's an ongoing love/hate rapport with that iron barrel, whether fed
from breast or bottle, operative always an ulterior agenda played like a music box in
the milky sky. Whether a spoon of nickel or silver, the moon shattered on the Aegean,
a bed of needles, a nude of marble, unstable and cryptic and of a rape mentality.
Whether the sex of the beloved, bending its back almost to agony over a kitchen table.
Its bound arms blur to plastic, its pawky ass rubberized within the myopia of
eroticism, fragmented like a page torn out of a porno magazine. The potentiality to
dismember your life, utterly, remains set to spring just an earshot away. You picture
the omnipotence amidst the black grasses of your unconscious ready to be revealed
like a lightshow. That desire will become confused with fear is what we're afraid of.
In dread of being terrorized one more time our desire will mount like a stallion.
At the point of climax we look up at the milky sky and pray for intervention. We open
our mouth, O-shaped like an angel's, lick our lips thoroughly as lubricant. Our eyes
roll pack into their sorrel interior. Out of our exploding heads spurt feathers.

XI.

How to alchemize these feeling into love is what I pray for. Not before the cross
but before the icon, the denomination of Christianity etymologized down to a picture
frame, not unlike the soul's relationship to the skeleton, the skeleton's to its
decaying flesh, flesh purloined by mummy wraps, swaddling rhapsodized by coffin.
The cameoed faces of the Virgin and child float untethered like haloes, like passion
between lovers, from their bodies, armored by an overlay of embossed tin against
any potential skepticism that might spoil things. In a last rapprochement with God
you bend to kiss the glass that shields them yet again, insulated as a storm window.
The symbol, save for the stain of lip marks, atoned, rises invisible as monotheism
from polytheism, as Host from tap water, in the psychomachia of your brainless soul.
The two heads waver within the frequency of their relic status, like old Hollywood,
almost radioactive, split atoms whose proximity incurs a kind of tension that acts
both as a vacuum toward ascension and its repellant, a magnetic field of collective
sings in which your gesture, the ingenuous kiss, delineates like Azrael, like a Nazi
general when the train stops at Dachau, the evil (so much) in you from the good.

XII.

On the day the Virgin died the moon dragged its window hump to the center of the sky.
It surveyed, glazed with grief, the scorched but august Grecian land it deeply loved.
The olive trees abused enough withdrew entirely into shadow, into negative space
that, like black holes, absorbs all space, detonator bombs planted in the darkest waters.
The sea swollen like a breast turgid with milk turned sour for the baby born dead
expressed its impotence in a stillness that refused to soothe neither man nor animal.
They perched along the rocks, adverted toward the waves as if to a short-wave radio.
They waited but the churlish wails like a lost dog never returned. Their brows
furrowed with sleeplessness. Their clothes camouflaged with dust scattered like dust
in the end, in piles of leafy ash as mutable and pitiful. They began to wander naked
as children. They began to invoke in each other, with their waiflike expressions,
a scavenger disposition. They panned the dirt for traces of the virgin, a lost ring,
torn lace from her slip, a buried tooth she had ceremonied herself. They suspected
one another as if, having kidnapped and eaten her whole, upon opening their mouths
she would reappear, shockingly youthful if not beguiling, winking seductively back.

XIII.

Despite our stupid cries (all mine), I gag my mouth with a handkerchief, the same
with which from the 747 I waved goodbye, the same I folded like an origami bird
into your gauntlet, the same I made a rudimentary sanitary napkin, the same doused
with "Joy" perfume to watch it tumble, autumnal and isolated, in front of no one
on the sidewalk for the hell of it. From this lavender zone you read as invisible
but sense the pinpricks of potential danger with an animal instinct devoid of human
intelligence, I allow the signal, stuff the handkerchief with coins and berries,
a potpourri for the mentally blind. I tell you I love you to mitigate the guilt,
I tell you I'm absolutely fine. I tell you I've learned a lot from this but after
ten years who can estimate what's been lost and what's been gained? I acknowledge
another winter alight on my calendar. I examine my body; a tarot spread for psychic
revelations. I renew my driver's license, receive announcements for the birth of
the second child. I live my life with my life ready inside me. At the gunshot
we'll spring, jackrabbits out of a briar patch, she and I. It's as if we created
each other as Mary Shelley did her superego in Dr. Frankenstein's beloved monster.

XIV.

Sometimes I step out of my suffering and stare at it, self-contained as a miscarriage.
I move toward myself as if aimlessly, a bottle tossed on the waves, in contrast
to the static figure finally put out of pain like a chloroformed body on the table.
I touch her glass-cold face with a glass-cold hand extended, a conduit for three
generations, the matrilineage of myself. I turn my aging grimace away from the sun
to regard, existentially displaced as a blurb, myself kneeling inside the pink sphere
of my recollection, both belittled and exploited on the dirt stage of its amphitheater.
No one was there as the beholder but us, when you lifted your face to mine with what
Diderot would call a "naïve" expression of terror. The broken elevator slid another
twelve floors. The counter-day of fluorescence twitched on and off, mutating
all color unto the quality of black-and-white film the way ashes deliver themselves
to the wind. The forest shifts simply to darkness, barely gradational against
the sheen of an overcast sky. I acknowledge the white sheet that eventually covers
my head: black iris of a dark forest against the skull-and-crossbones white
of an overcast, marbled sky; my silhouette erased in the process of acknowledgment.

XV.

My silhouette erased in the process of acknowledgement, sepulchral and low budget.
Where X marks the spot place a poetry calendar like a powder-blue pillbox hat.
Watch the twilight turn, if only for an instant, the exact shade of ten milligrams
of Valium. It spews its blue-red blood thinned like paint, a vein cut to revive
the dying, running horse with oxygen until the fading flows all at once, buckets
poured, aquamarine and iridescent as antiseptic on the institutionalized floor
of the landscape. The pillbox hat floats onward into oblivion, bereft in motion
amidst the oceanlike corrugations. You say you pray for me three times a day!
Partly out of protocol and urgency to fill the awkward discrepancy of mentalities,
I thank you (profusely) for the favor. It may be the only way for one hubristic heart
to comfort another on the affront of annihilation, to pray, or at the very least,
to think of each other. These last threads, sticky and moonlit, that strap us down
to rock and tree and answering machine, posit the iconic pleasure, the overflowing
cup, toward which we grope, deaf and dumb, our crotches stinging with a woundedness
we cannot originate. Like aliens we rise out of nothing in order to return to nothing.

XVI.

The magenta dawn cracks apart the sky as if with a crowbar. Deep inside the chasm, oozing like crude oil, breaks forth an unconditionality that never existed before. Only in your dead heart did I ever know God. Only in memory, the baroque self-assertive chamber of my heart. The blanched rubric of my skull surfaces, corpse in a pond, root to offshoot of my face, free-floating at the top of my spine, a traitor's head spiked on a stick. We glide beneath London Bridge, focused on the *trauerspiel*, my future grave above, built like an Indian burial site, free-floating skull of a cloud. A lightning rod splits the ceiling in half, loins of Mother Earth giving birth to Perseus. Tears, spiraling in a single column, interrogate like an ophthalmoscope of the Divine, or water main for atonement from a soulless source. Please, show me what it's like, and take me like Heathcliff drawn in by the dragnet of your cloud-white skin, your black, stormy hair; chest with shirt-torn-open appeal. Teal turbulence of an ocean backdrop underscores the rolled sleeves of your forearms, of great hands, as if making love, strangling my neck, in one painless, pleasureful snap, in one jolt of passion, in one glimpse of lore-lorn green, aquiline mountains.

XVII.

If you know that you will die alone, like a coyote, like a Yugoslavian, then you
can do anything in life. The innocence of the abyss arches its trajectory of deletion
across the image repertoire of your failures, mitigating the conjecture of tragedy
in the process, a processlessness that reads like a palindrome: matte white on glossy
white, white rose on sepia rose, the smoothed cascade of muscular infrastructure in
the marbled back of Rodin's mistress, the myopic teardrop to which we supply
the hermeneutic signified of "miserable." Your death floats always beside you, a kayak
stranded on the parched surface of the desert. Swaddled inside the *Todtenbaum* of your
negative future you break down like a particle, only the idea of which is fearful.
You guard your carcass, O papoose, that lies beneath the liturgical purple, blue tarp
of a lean-to flapping in a nebulous definition of fresh air, while underneath awaits
either a bed of nails or a bed of sweet william, the marriage bed you never consummated
but kept the repetition compulsion of excess and supposition going like some quartz
mechanism, hand between legs, nose pressed against the conundrum of your perception.
You wonder if it's worth the risk of slitting your wrists to shatter the glass. It is.

XVIII.

Down to the grave of wayward leaves, willful and idiomatic; a grave shallow, hence inexpensive but pebble-paved like a Japanese garden. Down from the shadows into the Ukrainian sun its regard devouring you in transport like Icarus. Down from a skeletal sky, fleshless and resentful, you've stared into their empty eye sockets for at least a century. Down as if lowered ruefully in a basket, Moses sent twirling and sobbing upon the currents. A peaceful breeze passes, a handkerchief, over my forehand. Down along the cliffs into the wading pool depth of ocean, released at random although from my prison cell I had no asked for a rehearsal. Down twelve or thirteen times the petite European car rolls over, the driver and passenger, two women, just friends, crash together in the exalt of a lovers' suicide pact. Your name uttered amidst all the sounds of your life ending, the instant, a sound rather than an image. The way a priest tied to a crucifix rushes over the waterfall into the water gutter cries out at the bypass to hell, from the underworld of his subsequent ascension to his maker; no matter the sign, the semiotic paradigm engraved in our unconscious reads identically, recuperates the same diet, the same deity, as if for milk when we cry out for mother.

XIX.

Unborn, undying, the corporeal foregrounds against its dematerialization, an ephemeral monument to our pilgrimage. As sky painting offsets sky, silhouette/personae, given/ abstraction, orgasm/sexology; life span/eternal flame; so we come to know what's incommensurable by the swanky, four-star, no-bones-about-it presentation of the tangible, the commensurable, i.e., if it's real it must be Memorex. The antenna of five senses registers with the unilateral conviction of as ingle party vote. The carnal chest pulsates amidst the corrosive solitude of the body until fainter the pulse, until absorbed into the vacuum like floss my awareness cancels itself out; until unto omission: unborn, undying. My face distorts "naturalistically," degraded by tears and mucus, the forsythia of incessant hope. May I pass over effortlessly as an envelope to the other world. May my breaths release themselves from a wailing mouth, carrier pigeons en route; though now alone with a table and chair as I have been all my life, may somewhere common folk matriculate out of the rubber room of a cold forest, their hair arrayed with pine needles like sea life, their coats dusted with plastic, doily flakes of snow, their arms, unborn, undying, outstretched in unison like a carousel.

XX.

Outstretched in unison like a carousel, bountiful and brutal in their
welcoming, the winter trees uphold an allegorical elegy to absence, an electric fence
that grids, segregates the sky between you and it, anders of caribou locked in
defense. The profile of a caribou stamps itself upon the circumscribed anticipation,
the commodity of your death, like Kennedy's embossed on the half-dollar. My name
composed within a disseminating list as if it were from the phone book whence I came.
The black wall of the Vietnam memorial, erected in the nation's capital, glints as if
a sheet of water slid, a garter snake, eternally down it like a waterfall formulated
originally, as it were, in hell. Black on black posits an omen, the 58,000 names of
the dead soldiers and MIAs engraved on granite, black snakes in a garden. More
people than soldiers in the Vietnam and Korean wars combined have died of AIDS as I
move through the days of suspension, through doors or walls, powerful as a spirit, into
the ochre room of my future hospice that drops like a phony noose in a spook house.
In the pit I lie. Black snakes slither tighter around my body, naked as opposed to nude
by their adornment, by their muscles utilized until they bring me to my death spasm.

XXI.

Opalescent, daylight fills the bedroom as water does a glass. Underwater wrung from
those bleary dreams, European police cars whisking through raindrench, potholes and
interminable laundry, I come up as if for air but without the relief, as a sail inverts
leeward to starboard from hiatus to hiatus, noiselessly as an underwater ballerina
within the matrix of her postures. Broken wings hover like the shadow of a branch,
tender clouds that pass with cursory attention then mainly neglect. I stare back into
the mirror of the anti-god I uphold in my disavowal, expansive and hueless, sheet
metal which deflects as enigmatically the blank slate of my future, the way a shaft of
sunlight, the first in three days, admits a useless symbol. The silence of the new
year soon collapses beneath the arboreal umbrella structure of the Roman calendar. The
tiny albatrosses renegotiate themselves into jewelry or paperweights, amulets honed
from the hocked bones of Heloise and Abelard; locks from Christ's hippie head of
hair. An image of heaven swings obliquely as atoll-like, *al fresco* but protected:
tropical drink, bandeau tops, stellar sunset. Alas a chandelier alights the flame-red
antechamber. Mist rises in mifted ascent, humanesque as a ghost, cryptic as humans.

XXII.

A velvet pallor lends to my profile a waiflike, uncircumscribed beauty. Mitigated
within the context of my circumstance like a condescending puzzle (box within box)
I've grown conscious of the paltry, allegorical nature of my actions. Disenchanted
with intuition I've capitulated to method. Yea, I believed in Destiny until a
pregnant teenager decided to name her child after it. It's not enough to love, it's
not enough to work, it's not enough to pray. We must walk with the chiffon-thin
soles of our feet over the burning coals that expire as our earthen haven of clay.
What's destiny is to return to our primal interest in defecation. To survive a
massacre splits the self in half, discharging it to a wind-torn oasis. Erased are
all means of identification. Make a doll for me then, *faux* freak for its sister,
produced from a factor of freaks as if people really accepted you. Now there's a
puppet to survive me on the marginalia—but into its cloth eyes still sucks away,
ruining and vital, desire after desire until stripped down to the marrow, to basic
necessities; until carted off in a blue van, bound and gagged like a rape victim
like someone wants you dead. And you give me attitude about not being spiritual?

XXIII.

Why doesn't it help to be with people? Even the *brûlé* of winter branches conspires
against a winsome community. Perhaps the cubist cement jungle gym vacant of children
at this late hour reflects best with its brute honesty what's dry to the heart, hence
providing a kind of company: a state of things which both constricts and hollows out,
raked leaves heaped upon a makeshift grave; the tension of the soulful yet soulless
double agent always witnessing, a miserable child without an intellect always looking
forward to looking back. Like slowly going deaf, the silence caves in shovelfuls,
a sound-mix of bereavement and impartiality: sobbing, male and female, traffic on
the highway, the incantations of some religious authority, birds, the sandy thuds of
dirt impassively contributed to the burial process, the silence that reverberates each
time afterward as if echoing. And as if by virtue of the litany of soundless echoes,
like the mystery of that dead person's unlived future, extemporaneously composed as
the belated product, were its requiem—the way in African music a polyrhythm becomes
one of interlocking hearts. Nothing, not the winter trees reduced to underbrush at
this distance nor their moulin-like branches, so baleful, has conspired against you.

XXIV.

The anniversary of that night like a mass to ebony, the memory cropped by ether, by
the semen stains on your jeans and the computerized voice, albeit human, that totaled
like a roll call my blood counts sliding. Who peered with me over the ledge, auburn
steep, which matched my hair color, and watched the toy sled crash in elegy to sleigh
rides? I couldn't have been alone that night for too large mushroomed the alienation.
Deep into the ravine I stared as if with a speculum into the Gothic steeple of me
(I could even feel the suction action), and beheld like a wedding ring my reflection,
a torn piece of fabric, suspended in vitro, floating on a mirage of Lake Katrina:
the continual postponement of my rendezvous with suicide. Now I understand Blake's
delineation of the prolific and the devouring, the deluge of calendar dates, Monday
through Friday, qualified with asterisks, exclamations and dollar signs translated as
this revisionism perfected in retrospect like cosmetic surgery. I wave the swatch, a
mouchoir for sailors, watch it descend, and pin itself, a rock climber's fate against
what he obsessively visualized. I recognized his open eyes, his bleeding mouth ongoing
like menstruation. Stop glamorizing the eternal. It did not give me peace of mind.

XXV.

Like a slow but exculpated loss of sight the forces of redemption muscle up, pulse
that monitors the grieving mind, sound-dot of dying felled to a monosyllabic screech,
great redwood within a forest of the metal box where your soul metastasized. In the
corridor, the nurses' rubber shoes whisk back and forth, a performance art: that which
is ongoing defamiliarized amidst that which is not. The sex organ for love, the brain,
turns in the corridor of the head once more, muscles up its unconscious reflex for the
fulfillment of a wish, pulses like the heart of a fetus or the impotent man in love.
Lo, the carnal image not fallow but defunct, embalmed in the repertoire of its desire.
Los, the repertoire collapsed, a shot buck within the empty trunk of the head itself.
I'e lost all respect for you but none of the desire, the metal box once an automobile
where in the back seat we fucked. No accident befell the little farmhouse caught up in
a crushing dream of wood and fire. The car implodes beneath the immortal hyacinth of
an April evening. Evening after evening, I conduct brain sex with the screen memory, a
masturbating voyeur who experiences real love only within the closed loop the icon
fetishized provides by both reassuring & underscoring the verisimilitude of his anxiety.

XXVI.

My death will not be the beginning of anything for you like a cloud that
formulates the heart of a storm. Perhaps you'll remember correctly, for once,
the inflections in my voice when confronted with the bare branches of winter
trees along Riverside Park. Perhaps the silence which throws their impoverishment
into high relief will pique a tenderness you displayed to me in the form of an
isolated incident like an FAO Schwartz Christmas showcase. But "but" as in butter,
as in buttress, as in butt-hole, lubricated and framed within the confines of your
unadulterated lust, your chest hair matted into a wreath of loss, as if suspended
above the chest in tribute to your lost ability to generated human love,
in a position that neither descends nor climbs the burnished goat path to some
fabrication of god. Your tenderness erects itself as fraudulent in retrospect
like the simulation of life pumped into the upstart cadaver. Like oxygen depleted
from deflated lungs, the tenderness you exercised toward me has long gone in the
fragile collapsing of organs, muscles and bones, of my body consumed by heat inside
what bestows itself as life's most generic forum (after the womb), the crematorium.

XXVII.

For one moment more of your preservation, I extended to you a disembodied hand.
A bird forms itself from the origami sketch of its ideal that's my palm print.
I open my mouth and a bird's cry expedites all that I would say in its erasure:
the dog in us. You take me at night against a bush, without overture, without hope.
True to yourself, you're at my throat, my expression gone white, overfrequenced
with emotion, eclipsed by the finesse of your brutality, a pine forest subsumed by
forest fire. The negative ions cancel out their calming property, an oil spill in the
ocean. Despite the decay, I lean my head against your chest and listen to my love
entombed, plangent and impotent as the illusion of ocean in a conch. I'm shocked
by my devotion. I walk through fire, the cords are cut, my body removed from its
context. Untethered, I float, a corpse offered up as carrion on stilts to totem gods;
stretched out, a canvas, a salt-lick, a virgin, for only a god would seduce a virgin
until she becomes a whore. The earth is littered with gods, O Lord. Birds feed off my
eyes. You hear them (remember, once my voice) and think of the dog in us. You write a
very short poem in your head, the first in years, unworthy of record you later decide.

XXVIII.

You are not alone like a coyote. You are not alone like the feral cactus beside him,
like the parched terrain beneath him, cracked but riveted, like the loveless
surveillance of the moon above him, or the horrible tearing sound of wind when he sleeps.
His sleep is not yours, although at midnight you wake to the horrible tearing sound, cry
out to the fabric, witness the literal stripping down of your life into bandages
and ties, rags and bandanas. You wade through them, a macabre kind of confetti, on the
way to the bathroom. You are not alone when you return to your bed, gray waterproof
laid askew on the parched terrain of your carpet, to the panoptic chambers of your
dreaming. In one cell you work harder, disciplined to expedience & clarity. In another
you're quarantined, left to the desultory discourse of your delirium. An observant
nurse clues in on a certain word repeated which becomes the enigmatic signifier for
your soul like "rosebud" in Citizen Kane. You are not alone when roll-called for the
quotidian showing of your face in the window. You are not alone turned toward the cold
bricks tonight, when you masturbate in silence like the night before, the very silence
so eroticized at this point that a momentary lull in the madhouse turns you on.

XXIX.

If Nietzsche called his pain a dog then I call my pain a desire, a creature who looks
up at me from a bare mattress on a bare floor, a kind of dog, a kind of child. I feed
her teaspoons of mollescent porridge, a mixture of homemade texts, newspaper reports,
and saliva. Her emaciated body appears even thinner as her head pivots forward for
another mouthful. When she sleeps I work the graveyard shift and watch over her fits
and mews, and sometimes interfere by removing a blanket in effort to guide her through
a kinder route. And though I feel no urge myself I talk to her of touch, the mention
of which she responds to like a wife and capitulates, Method-acting with an absence she
loves. I insert my fist deep into her throat, for how could I refuse? Her eyes close
almost satisfactorily for once. Then the lovemaking proper begins: unswaddling slowly
the limbs, calcium-white and hypersensitive; her hair webbed like Medusa's, a moraine
of personal history, isolates the bust into pastiche of a bust where, upon the foam-
rubber pillow, as if out of Medusa's head she gives birth to herself; her face an
agglomerative space of frayed expression, pitched and penurious. Her mouth remains open:
tapped into some infrahuman dimension where multiple orgasm continues uninterrupted.

XXX.

Whom can I hold accountable for these symptoms of devastation, these systems of
devastation? Force-fed by some unmaternal breast, breast milk contaminated with *E. coli*,
I nurse on air, a breathing fish beached in a low budget afterlife. The camera
focuses in on the face, the prolonged close-up serving as an interrogation of sorts
as if a narrative shot in real time would produce a facial soliloquy that ultimately
deauthenticates the voice; as if at my wit's end I would reach deep into my throat
like a porn star and offer up as evidence the clandestine, testimonial heart.
As if the pink muscle, blood-orange blue and swollen as a sex, would bring the
audience closer, assimilate an emotional close-up, to the personal truth of dying.
The origin, a seamless dream of dying in which the self-witnessing of the dreamer is
seamless. The origin, the state of Oregon I've never visited but sublimate a sense
of finality in its grasses to compensate for the unfathomability of their finality.
In other words, I can't imagine it; the personal truth I offer, the enforcement of
imagining, the oppression of that proximity, the smaller hand forced by the greater
upon the electric burner. The voice deauthenticated by the ineffable until voiceless.

XXXI.

There's no way out of the rubbed interior, the ceiling which dissipates into sky.
Left shelterless, what I witness without leaving my bed like virtual reality
conforms itself to my bedroom: mountain range, shining sea, the funeral wind
that demonstrates its mourning by circulating obsessively throughout the pines.
Even when I climb out of bed as if lifting myself up from the floor, I bear against
the roof of an opaque nothingness, a dense invisibility, the vanishing point of my
body's landscape, the avatar of my maker as it were. It flexes about like cyberspace.
Gloved and goggled I touch without touching the sentient experience of my death, the
black-on-black beauty, jet water against volcanic rock, ebony hairbrush atop asphalt,
text upon excoriated tableau, Steinway stranded on an empty stage, ash amidst ash,
a march for civil rights which arches obliquely like the ship of its history against
the partisan night. The Rothko room at the Tate. Closer to what beauty is in its
confusion, I assimilate a relationship for which I have no expectations, ambivalences,
or drives: a two-way mirror in which I see myself only in absence, but behind which
situates a presence, a prolonging, if not immortality: my appellate interiority.

XXXII.

There's no going back. I've fallen de facto through a leafy bower, a corridor of locked
doors like a stunt man. O that I could fast forward, dismiss my stand-in, cancel my
performance feigning a bad throat, write my way out of it to a profligacy that would
fulfill my misery quota and be done with it. But the dimensions of loneliness only
become more opaque like St. Lucy's Day, where amidst thickening darkenss, the short-
ening days, an aisle of candles carried by young Lucys refuses to illuminate outside
their jurisdiction like shore lights viewed on a clear night across the Atlantic Ocean.
They demonstrate a solidarity with light from which, by some arbitrary law of de-
lection, I've been exempt. High above the houses, in a lifeguard's vacant chair, I
strain to thresh through as if optical muscles after a time of repeated straining, a
kind of weight training, might acquire the capacity that would force this descent to
open up on a desert vista burnished with sunshine. But the ambiguous menu remains
like a constellation of bereavement. I beg at random, bury at knell, send adrift
on a lake, toss down a cellar staircase a note of apology, an expensive watch, pence,
a ponytail cropped from my head like a whiskbroom, for who knows wherein power lurks?

XXXIII.

I will not be afraid of it. I want it to be afraid of me, to recoil back into its
cupboard, hideous troll, fatuous trollop of a sea nymph. Back into its corner,
its mattress, a buzzard's nest null of hydrodynamic current, a drink of water
I refuse to drink. I watch it fall. I have no compassion for the dreary, wry,
bourbon drinking, chain smoking, bulldog faced old woman, her single gray braid
pinned acrimoniously to the side of her head like a beret with a sea lion's
tusk appliqué. For decades she's worn a wombat's money belt and I want to ask her
"What's in it?" That's to say, was it worth it to live so long simply to end up
friendless and weak, your hateful attitude clearly accrued over years of mere
experience, was it? One-third her age but mostly likely closer to the morgue
than she, she wouldn't care and that's the benefit of wisdom I loathe with the
passion of youth I don't have time to temper. My convex world moves in, an
execution date, consolidating into a single suitcase. Only that which I can carry
am I allowed to bring with me in exodus from my life, the total sum I know from
its part, a cruel prescience; the seer of my skeleton before pared to actuality.

XXXIV.

The dowerless agenda of my daily life flickers like the first takes of a documentary,
some shots overexposed until the figurative obliterates utterly into an abstract for
which no feeling of the figurative can be abstracted. Others, banal candids that leave
the viewer void of identifying capacity, reinforce an ongoing identity crisis, the
mirror image broken down to a shattered arrangement, an essentiality from which you
are estranged as viewer from frame, beholder from painting. At the crack of dawn,
ceremoniously you're sent out with sacrificial intent in a dinghy without oars, onward
into a lawless but meritorious terrain, forced to find the god within although you've
already explained your atheism. So you make a god out of the image of your grave. You
recognize the rectangle with sober regard as the undulating reflection of your face in
the water. You worship it as if synthetic like a good capitalist. You fetishize
the decapitated mind, in love with fleshless superiority. You demonstrate your love
with a transferential bolt plunged deep into your groin. And no one understands this
love but you and the Hemlock Club, your lips contriving a bastardized expression of
mourning for the spiteful cock still inside you, a macabre homecoming to iodine sand.

XXXV.

Our love is gone like a dead father. HIV, *mon amour*. Our love decays, I regard
my father: a fly replaces his eye in the end. A fly now replaces my father's eye,
black and blank like the open grave of the sky, alveolate like a catacomb, a rotting
pine. My dead father rises in the lake, topside: our moribund love, his scaling
flesh, our love despite him, his matted hair that floats suspended from his life.
My love reframed by death fails to reframe my love like Malevich's *White on White*.
My body blocks the sun like a cloud underdistanced by an open grave, the fly under-
distanced by this eye. My body blocks the sun in a blatant act of necrophilia, my body
underdistanced by your death. I watch your face go black, then white. Into a cellar
we've been thrown on this earth. Even dead I love you with no diminishment, perceive
as handsome the ruination. HIV, *mon amour*, my rotting body blocks the sun to preserve
you one more moment but this loss is the loss of diminishment. HIV, *mon amour*, our
love rots like a pine, as a memory rots in the mind. What preserves our love is its
forgetting. I remember your voice but instead I hear a fly. To continue to love you
you must be gone from my mind like a dead father. In lieu of my love, Father, die.

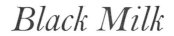

Black Milk

When Atheists Pray

for Stanley Kunitz

Who, if I cried, would hear me among the angelic orders?

And how should we know, by what sign, by what feeling,
that they've heard us? We watch the sky darken,
a cold heart at noon regardless of expectation, regardless of desire
and its intensity, not the rioting red of white cell-producing hope,
nor the leech-bled black-purple of bottomlessness.
No sentiment, no matter how exigently soulful, proves exigent enough.

First we petition with respectful prayers, careful dance steps,
complete obedience. There follows, after days of bread and water,
impatient prayers, our eyebrows furrowed, knees twitching in genuflection.
And then like machine gunfire detected from a distant bunker,
cryptically faint and time-delayed in their imploding,
our fears infect us: no prayers will be heard, let alone answered.

And even if one of them suddenly pressed me against his heart,
I should fade in the strength of his stronger existence;

For the impressive indifference of angels is greater
than our ungainly desires, until, to the extent they're unattended,
they redouble in their need, accelerating exponentially
until ultimately they disperse, deflect like Trojan spears
off the shield of Achilles—or pass through, cruelly,
without penetration, like breeze through a metal screen
or the open sky glimpsed through wrought-iron bars.
Our human fists fly wild through ghostly anatomy, through the free world
of their love, later realized as false. But the visceral memory,
our essential, insistent belief, though erased instantly from consciousness,
still resonates in our pulse, wish-fragment of sorts,
as if dismembered in the cleaving wake of a shooting star.

For Beauty's nothing but beginning of Terror we're still just able to bear,
and why we adore it so is because it serenely disdains to destroy us.

Nature was not always a thing of beauty.
Once fishermen's houses were built with their backs to the ocean
in an effort to ignore the dreaded, devouring, ionizing body
with its braying surf, breached in constant threat,
flagellating the bosky shorelines day and night; the Creator represented
in briny incarnation, fanged and punished as the father we later
configured in the concept of the superego. But no theory can subvert
our infantile wishes for love beyond what we've invented;
what's humanly contrived will always appear somehow lowbrow and insufficient,
no replacement for the sublime affliction of our origin,
no substantial explanation for the breccia-like womb we refer back to,
and refer back to . . .

Hence the necessity for angels, more crucial than bread and water.
Readily, we'll do without for just one acknowledgment from them,
one conciliatory response that they care. We return to angels
like a dog to the grave of its dead master, out of lack of recourse
to something stronger than ourselves,
because we cannot make sense of suffering.
Because we cannot comprehend, cannot contain within our puny, mortal minds
a world like that that allows—no, orchestrates—with Caligulean joy,
life events to unfold so disproportionately,
we assign meaning to the immaterial to supplement our loneliness.

Because we cannot make sense of suffering,
the gross marginalization of its subjects,
we imagine the world as beautiful in order to counteract,
even transform, the depravity inside us, despite the masochistic agenda
we know by now to be the outcome. Because too unbearable,
too unrecognizable is the thought tht we're just set loose
amid this brazen arbitrariness, too anachronistically barbaric
the isolation of pain without reason,
pain without rescue, without consolation, without medicine.

Therefore, years may pass before we've stopped rationalizing
that perhaps the angels are hard of hearing.
Perhaps it's the effort to listen, to turn their dear, deaf cherubic ears
closer which instigates even the smallest birds, especially the ones
known for love-calls so melodic they play in the carbon monoxide

increasing air like harpsichord music, to fall in fists of dirt,
like rain that tears into flesh; to fall as if thrown out of oblivion
into oblivion, massacred bodies into mass graves,
the skulls of children split apart for the fun of it.

Each single angel is terrible.

But we continue living, continue eating, continue fucking,
praying to the fantasy of mercy. Until we recognize, as if shaken,
the intolerable for what it truly is, our pathetic souls,
malleable as Play-Doh putty—having internalized successfully
the slavemaster within us. Any autonomous action was expunged long ago
from the pretense of possibility, until degenerated in the poverty
of our beliefs, our self-mortification, we finally perceive how pitiful
an act praying be; it be the act of begging, really.

And so I keep down my heart and swallow the call-note of depth-dark sobbing.

What's most terrifying resounds as wings, swooping closer,
those angels that operate as passive spectators while heinous events
take place. And if prayers ever do reveal themselves as answered,
it's so late that, desecrated by loss and disease,
it's the stumps of our amputated limbs we thank them for,
our most natural, instinctual capacity to love ruined, pitted, abolished.

Hence, I refuse to look upward,
upward to a canopy of presupposed atonement.
What were once prayers for readiness to reckon with disappointment
become angry, incriminating prayers, prayers of ultimatum.
Those prayers, those useless elocutions from our humiliated hearts,
evolve into, or rather grow up into, articulations of atheism,
pronouncements of love retracted, of love regretfully spent.
We express instead, spitting upward and out,
aiming to reach the hemlines of their robes, war-waging rage
on our enemy angels. They prolong our torment and revel in it.
Their profiles, self-preoccupied as aristocrats, pivoted away from us
at birth, demonstrate the vanity of angels, their deficit of compassion.

O fascist angel, I visualize your death,
angel-less, alone in the hospital,
your powers foreclosed by the last stages of cancer or AIDS.
I will the nurse who's responsible for your morphine
to run behind schedule. She can't be located.
Therefore, you die, horrid angel, a horrible death;
you die incrementally, without honor or counsel,
while I watch, like a victim's family member
in the auditorium of your execution chamber.
I regard you coldly as if I were an angel, while you pray to angels,
pray to me, I observe disdainfully while you pray hard for pardon,
matted wings shaking with emphasis, your idiot angelic eyes
clouding up with cataracts incurred by grief.
You pray, which means you beg, homeless angel, veteran angel, hostage, angel,
beg of me for the pain to stop. But the pain will not stop,
it will not, My Angel. I shake my head, shrug,
"But these are the mysteries of life," I say with my shoulders,
my pretend wings. I enjoy your suffering as you enjoyed mine.
I remain mute as you cry out to me. I smile down on your grimacing face,
your tiny angel tears minute from where I view you, avenged
behind the double-glass window. Sweet syringe of your lethal injection,
let no execution be too quick, too humane, too "angel-like" in leniency.

Alas, who is there we can make use of? Not angels, not men;

My death began on April 12, 1988,
over a pay phone at an artist's colony in upstate New York ,
in a windowless, wainscoted phone closet, where a single bare bulb
suspended above me, the enucleated eye of some god surveying its work,
enshrouded me in newfound blindness.
Like a crash test for my death, the plastic skin and synthetic brain
of my dummy-body, wired to measure pain, felt nothing.
My death began when I learned I was HIV positive.
My death began with the crisos of stima, the social death
which precludes the physical death of AIDS.
My death began there, my fears instantly transposed
onto the bucolic landscape, the *mise-en-scène* of their materialization
too demonically devised, too similar to science fiction to assimilate.
My death began there, wood cross burning on front lawn.

My death began there as if I were bound up and gagged, then ordered to regard
my own death rehearsed in the death of friends, neighbors, and fellow patients.
My life metamorphosed into a pastiche of itself,
dwarfed beside the larger-than-life plague I embodied.
Furniture shrank, voices dimmed and echoed as if upon a stage
whose props, their solitude offset by the defamiliarization
of their context, posited themselves as surreal emblems
of the way my life had broken off—not organically
like a lightning-struck branch churning swiftly along river rapids,
but intentionally, serially, a decapitated head symbolic of more,
knocking in thuds down to an ostracized earth.
My death began there, drawn out by the human phenomenon of waiting,
within the re-creation of that phone booth. It transfigured every room
thereafter into a windowless wainscoted cell.
I waited for my life to revert back, suddenly, as it had split off,
to suture together without noticeable scar.
I waited for my life to return to me, as if MIA,
while I whispered lamentations at an inert photograph.

. . . and already the knowing brutes are aware that we don't feel
very securely at home within our interpreted world.

I waited nowhere, while I groped from room to room,
through the solitary routine of rising out of bed,
getting through the day, putting myself back to bed.
I relied primarily on sound, smell and touch:
alarming clock and Pledge-scented desk, dish-crammed sink, ringing phone,
braking bus, loud conversation in which I'm oddly a participant
with friend, nurse, doctor, insurance representative—
each and all banal and loof. My death began in alternating shifts,
skin-burning daylight and skin-burning moonlight. My death began,
a perverse canon of events, unfolding in worst-case scenarios.
Each level of the disease, the gradations of physical recession,
the lungs, the gut, the eyes, the brain—systems of torture,
instigated by an interrogator I cannot target beyond the decoy glare
of that bare bulb. It shone inconsequentially
above daily evidence of the dead and almost dead,
as if a successful plan for extermination were taking place.
I waited for my death to finish itself, to complete its trajectory

from fetus to ash, to halt in the gristly air of absolute end,
for my body to collapse, exhausted animal, beneath me.
I waited hospitalized, or at home on I.V., hair falling out,
drugged 'til comatose, my body turning against itself
in the breakdown of its civil discontent.
My death began submerged amidst the atmosphere
of stark au revoir, the nonstop wrench of separation,
not entirely unlike those waving children and screaming parents
during the Kindertransport exodus in Poland.

So when I say I believe in nothing, I mean just that.
To the leaves gone brown and dry, to winter land,
its vengeful groundswells and black ice, I direct my anti-prayers.
Bitter condemnations heard by no one, absorbed by nothing,
wet lips frozen in their tremble. My beliefs, blood-sucking shadows,
perpetuate themselves paradoxically by virtue of their nihilism,
the way a respirator provides the semblance of life.
The evidence of nothingness, upon which my beliefs feed, proliferates,
fecund and lush in what should be a generic finisterre.
It makes a mockery of the bygone love-child, hopeful once,
its lit wick of unconscious desire despite cranial damage.
The brain-death of conscious want has already been pronounced,
but still the fantile reflex of working mouth sucks
from invisible nipple as it does artificial air from plastic tube,
until a judge decides otherwise.

There remains, perhaps, some tree on a slope, to be looked at
day after day, there remains for us yesterday's walk and the cupboard-love
loyalty of a habit that liked us and stayed and never gave notice.

There remains now, sixteen yeàrs later, only the orator of angels.
Only the author of angelic disappointment could make me raise my face,
queerly optimistic again, although underneath it
like honeycomb within hive, catacombs of grief lie, six feet deep.

Oh, and there's Night there's Night, when the wind full of cosmic space
feeds on our faces: for whom would she not remain, longed for,
mild disenchantress, painfully there for the lonely heart to achieve?

Why did I choose Rilke's first elegy as my wedding day vow?
Because only with an affirmation of godlessness
could I make such a promise, could my vows be held accountable.
In no eyes but mine, not those peering down, beady iron of gargoyle
or prismatic orb of angel, upon my reciting tongue, could my heart confess
to the rudimentary decisions of survival, crude and emotion-defying;
to the self-scrutiny of defining integrity within that survival
(which is its only means of definition, and the only means of survival).
My heart I would judge and judge harshly. Only in this chapel,
the most spare space as testimony to the impermanence
of lonely dogwood, distant city, frail wedding bouquet,
beloved metaphors for an anemic future which no one escapes,
could loyalty form and grow from the death-laugh, the death-cry
of my near death which confirms my insignificance.

Is she lighter for lovers? Alas, with each other they only conceal their lot!

No, night was not lighter for us, mentor poet,
especially on *that* night when Sean and I prayed
under a matte black sky from which all stars had been deported.
The moon, a penitentiary yard search-and-surveillance light,
strobed past our petitioning hands, me in bed as Sean knelt beside me.
I had requested this as a last resort.
So we prayed, both atheists, despite ourselves,
in conflict with ourselves: who we knew ourselves to be
versus who we were forced to become.
We hated the world that made us do it,
while the calamity of angels defaced us gleefully in their light.
They belittled us beneath the vile feathers of their interwoven wings,
their pinched judgmental expressions, their pursed lips,
rasping tsk-tsks like the rattle of hunger from viper snakes.
We no longer negotiated, we no longer promised, we did not implore or urge
or plead, applaud, blandish, woo, worship, or canvas. We begged.
We begged together and we begged alone (for a begger is always unto himself,
alone in the humiliation of begging), our moths disfigured
by the unfamiliar intention, our self-betrayal like self-inflicted wounds
with which beggars in Calcutta eagerly maim themselves
in order to become better beggars.

We begged from the white of the moon's eye for my eyesight.
We begged from electrically heated air for our life together.
We begged from ceiling plaster, Venetian blinds, and the New York skyline.
We begged from traffic and sirens, from doormen and garbage chutes,
from pharmacists and Chinese food delivery boys.

That is what suffering reduces you to.
As the Hanoi Hilton inmates attest,
those who signed confessions after weeks, months, years of torture,
"they *can* make you do what you don't want to do."
So we begged from North Vietnamese angels and Nazi party angels.
We begged from apartheid angels and Reaganite angels.
We begged yoked and harnessed by their self-imposed glory,
their smug, omniscient unattainableness.
And we actually cried from the inanition of our begging,
so very attainable were we in contrast.
Our words uttered in unison, word gestated in the stomach and groin
rather than larynx, brought us, as if strong-arming us to tears,
to cry the spirit-breaking kind of cry only total defeat produces;
the self-lacerating, wholly humiliating, soul-eradicating kind;
the wounded, the sick, the lynched, the historically persecuted kind;
the kind emitted perhaps from those engraved names we read nonsensically
after a while, like calligraphy or hieroglyphs, on memorial monuments
decades later; those multitudinous objects of genocide
who most likely begged, in rushed elliptical entreaties, for their life
from the small, dark corner of what's left of their life.

Don't you know **yet**?—

You, who have not had to beg yet,
listen to the coffin maker running ut of nails.
Listen to the yelling of babies, orphaned and red-cell depleted
who must receive transfusions with HIV-contaminated blood
because the clinics can't afford the requisitie lab equipment
for seropositive testing. There are no metaphors,
no "happening" adjectives or interesting, original uses of language,
no new line breaks.
You just have to smell it . . .
the dense smoke from the bonfire of mass cremations.

It's not the aroma of a Diptyque candle to which you're accustomed,
now is it?

Fling the emptiness out of your arms into the space we breathe—

Surrender to water, lake, pond, or river, for these harbor
the possibility that by drowning you may die.

Surrender to "the luxury of a boring evening,"
as one Holocaust survivor put it.

Surrender to the compulsion to move forward, to silly expectancy,
to your evaluation of life, not regardless of,
but precisely because of all the arbitrary clear-cutting
of precious growth you've beheld.
Surrender within, despite, and in protest to
the thick, non-retractable memory of begging.
Take revenge on angels, and surrender to that instinctual capacity
to love which they've worked so hard to destroy
conceding to what you don't want to admit,
for not only angels have failed you.

maybe that the birds will feel the extended air in more intimate flight.

Those birds, the few left in the disinfected sky, the survivors of angels;
their crow caws we hear in lieu of harpsichord music,
strangely sustaining us.

Rainer Maria Rilke, "First Duino Elegy,"
The Duino Elegies, trans. J.B. Leishman and Stephen Spender
(New York: W.W. Norton, 1939)

Immigrant in my Own Life

for Marie Ponsot

Broken dreams hovering like the shadow of a branch—
How, I wonder, do I begin again?
With resistance I read back over my old poems
Trying to understand what it is that has been.

How, I wonder, do I begin again?
Nothing looks familiar, no matter where I look.
Trying to understand what it is that has been;
Foreign sky, foreign street, foreign trees with their foreign leaves.

Nothing looks familiar, no matter where I look:
I don't know my name, what I am without disease.
Foreign sky, foreign street, foreign trees with their foreign leaves.
Foreign tears my eyes won't always for me make.

I don't know my name, what I am without disease.
Help me remember, help me imagine or just desire again.
Foreign tears my eyes won't always for me make,
Come back to me whoever, wherever you've been.

Help me remember, help me imagine or just desire again.
For seventeen years I've waited like a soldier's wife for something.
Come back to me whoever, wherever you've been.
For seventeen years I've said, "I won't live another year."

For seventeen years I've waited like a soldier's wife for something.
I guess it'll take some time to get reacquainted.
For seventeen years I've said, "I won't live another year."
I experienced the actual breaking down, mud and twigs underfoot.

I guess it'll take some time to get reacquainted.
At least when I was dying, I knew where I was going.
I experienced the actual breaking down, mud and twigs underfoot.
Almost out of ash, my body reconfigures itself.

At least when I was dying, I knew where I was going:
Into atheistic air and dirt, into the Atlantic Ocean . . .
Almost out of ash, my body reconfigures itself.
As if reclining nude, I stare dumbfounded at my flesh.

Into the atheistic air and dirt, into the Atlantic Ocean . . .
Peace became associated with that essential vanishing point.
As if a reclining nude, I stare dumbfounded at my flesh.
Now to associate peace with something else, such as myself, for instance.

Peace became associated with that essential vanishing point.
Peace used to mean simply a sheet of paper and a pencil.
Now to associate peace with something else, such as myself, for instance;
Myself as once I came to know myself, both future tense and past.

Peace used to mean simply a sheet of paper and a pencil.
With resistance I read back over my old poems:
Myself as once I came to know myself, both future tense and past,
Broken dreams hovering like the shadow of a branch—

Huge Fragility

Osseous, osseous, osseous are the gulls, is the greatness
of the whitecapped ocean, the gulls like whitecaps pivoting toward the cove,
the whitecaps like gulls that curtsy toward me in fleets of fleece,
of frigid blue water, frigid and pitch and augmented by the unknown
and the blaring wind in coercion with the sea,
vast and cantankerous and in coercion with the sky,
those innocuous little clouds that so baroquely reside as if applied freshly,
the oil of flesh and white, never quite
brittle, the leafless hedges that barricade the shoreline
in contrast to my humanness, flesh and white, never quite
a part of the formidable arrangement of land and sea and flying whitecaps.
I can't locate any point of identity, no plane of reference
to place myself in this prosaic setting if only more prosaically
as in a snapshot of it not taken, not remembered, not saved, not forgotten,
within the landscape that alters cheaply, like the metallic eyes
of a crucified Christ, which open then shut
depending upon which way you lean, left or right,
except for the vanishing point of the pencil-thin horizon
arbitrarily drawn to landmark eternity, a chalk-drawn finish line
that lends sufficient emphasis to the marvelous ruse of my immortality
with its excessive blarney or blatant lack-of, cruelly blanketed
in the whetted edge of frigid blue water
and pavilion of gulls in their pawky contrivance
of heavenly ascension.

Flies in Winter

Our happiest moments reveal themselves as such only in retrospect.
At the time of occurrence they compound within us as heady, prescient,
hallmarks like mooseheads hung in faith of the prestigious game yet to hunt,

those greater, almost epic expectations soon to be met but still to come,
a series of utopian pit stops: small cities of emerald,
catwalks encumbered with gold Chanel chainbelts, childhood
paraphernalia signifying a nostalgia for an overarching
trajectory of warmth.

But what experiences exactly initiate this interminable
sense of missing, a twisting which drills away, to no avail,
for rag dolls and crayon drawings, remain buried like fake amulets
behind the recesses of recall, in an unrecognizable stasis
only dental records could identify.

Happy moments (just moments, mind you,
pitiful in proportion and scanty in provision)
bloom full-blown in nanoseconds, a kind of magic flower
where a tear of resemblance suffices to galvanize the crushed paper,
a dead robin disguised as dead then discovered as actually alive,
the essential nutrient, a sci-fi elixir, a hubristic tincture
alchemized from an all-too-human longing and the fantasy, yet
finally fleshes out in the format we've been configuring
and reconfiguring for years. And for years it should last us,
like a Volvo, like a volcano, like the Paphian concept of an olive branch
spinebroken between the jaws of a dove.

The Interfaith Chapel at New York Hospital

for Stephen Ferrando, M.D.

I expected to be alone
when I walked on a Monday afternoon,
post-doctor appointment, heading left off the bustling thoroughfare
of the hospital's main corridor, the traffic
encompassing the spectrum of illness, patients in wheelchairs,
hospital staff, worried family members.
I need a moment and am used to this user-friendly sanctuary
as a stopover to regroup, like the crescents of asphalt
that make themselves available to weary drivers on the highway
with picnic tables and outhouses.
The chapel is discreet, almost makeshift
in its nondenominational intent. Chairs, not pews,
line up in short rows on either side of the aisle where the centerpiece
of a stained glass window, round and Chartres-like,
serves as transferential symbol for Christian crucifix,
or statue of transcendent Buddha, or whatever else
would be necessary to represent that forceful mechanism
toward which one's prayers, or just edited fears, could be navigated.
A simple table, rectangular, an unadorned altar,
stands stalwart before it. Like a porthole to the unknown, a celestial vent,
the circular window both absorbs and transforms, with promise
of transportation like the mailman's oath,
a layman's emotions into the ineffable quality of faith.
Once in a while I prayed, other times sat and cried,
or instead busied myself with calendar dates and "must-do's"
promoting a cavalier, atheist attitude.
This time, though, I was not alone. Another worshipper
had invaded my refuge. She was on her knees, utilizing one of
the chairs as if it were a pew, but in a disconcerting way,
not directed to the altar but on a diagonal with the aisle, encroaching
upon its space. Her position belied desperation, as if
she had collapsed there and held onto the chair like a helm.
Head in hands, palms covering her eyes, a curious white handkerchief
laid askew on her hair. Her prayers permeated the presupposed quiet
with an audible, fluid, almost combative impromptu commentary
and chanted verse, an impassioned narrative that unnerved

yet soothed me. I watched her for less than a minute
before she heard me. She jerked up like a rabbit,
alert and protective, until her eyes met mine with unwelcome forewarning.
I had disturbed her and should do so no more.
I walked cautiously by and sat on an aisle seat in the front row,
mildly flustered and stumped as to what my original motive
for visiting the chapel had been. Secure again
from any more interference, she relaxed back into her trance-like utterances,
melodic but directive, the intensity of her prayers
multifaceted as if she were speaking in tongues.
I closed my eyes and just listened,
as if her prayers, by virtue of their duration and purpose,
but more importantly by their presumed compliance with religion
more organized than my mish-mash of wants, pleadings, and incriminations,
might bring genuine hope into what had become
a dark prediction of my circumstance.
I closed my eyes and just listened
to the lecturing, controlling intonation of her prayers,
her effort to bend in abeyance the ill she wrestled against. I listened,
cheering on the slightly punitive aspect I heard
in her music, and developed, increasingly, the expectation
that the exorcism of her anger would subsequently relieve mine,
wash over and draw up as an eddying stream does remnants of bank bark
and moss fleck, a refreshed calm like soothing ointment
upon the incurable nature of my problems—
My listening and her praying became a commune of suffering,
the two of us emblematic of the pain of so many. It welled up
acute and piercing inside us as if the hobbled
expressions and unnatural bodies could actually be seen.
Her prayer became a kind of funnel, like the vehicle
of the stained glass window which posited not only a venue through which
horrible feelings transcended and dissipated, but *from* which
unimagined good might eke its way to us. She embodied
this possibility, and from that churning of her incantation
something circular started, a melting away of the severe isolation,
the dull stature of coping, a brain-dead way of pushing forward
in order to function.

Then something gave in at last, almost with a snap
like a chiropractic adjustment or snowcap liquidated prematurely
in March, a malleability my emotions had not experienced
in a while, triggered paradoxically by a memory of their inaccessibility—
a period of suffering not long ago during which the desire to feel
and express became more the cause than the effect of anything physical.
As the scene flashed before me of ten days earlier,
so did the somatic memory resurface slowly, akin to what re-entry
from cryogenic suspension might be like: me propped up
in a chair in my bedroom while my husband changed the sheets soaked
with sweat for the third time that day. I was experiencing
a serious allergic reaction to a new AIDS protocol that my doctor and I
had waited for a year to become available. Now it had backfired,
after only a week, my fevers peaking at 105 every six hours,
the hives proliferating from the poison, centered on my face.
My bones and organs, muscles and ligaments ached in a way
I'm almost glad I cannot describe. I wanted to cry, to exemplify outrage,
but could only come up with vowels that sounded like a moan,
or a loud whimper, a crude kind of performance art about defeat
displayed as if begging.
I *was* begging from the sheets, from my husband, and now
I realize, from this stained glass window,
for release, complete and total; for release final and instant, release
from the torture—and to call it torture is not an overstatement
because it's as if someone wants from you a specific item,
a piece of information you cannot provide, a statement signed
which you know is a lie, an admission, a denial, a betrayal—
the dimensions of incremental suffering, virtually endless,
they remind you. My husband watched, upset
he couldn't hold me because of the rash, while I just made noise,
noise like an animal hurt on the road, noise
I can't write or convey even in a lesser, perhaps more palatable form.
No succession of letters can depict like a heaving sigh
or hysterics shout what impressed itself upon me that night,
a relentlessness pressing down like the leather straps
of an execution bed but no lethal injection
came after. I was laboring—for survival is like having a baby,
my legs spread apart, my head thrown back—I was laboring but it was not
optimistic, a stillborn birthing in which death is forced out

from deep inside you, forced out with an effort excruciating and formidable,
your dead body that threatens soon to become you,
yanked away and thrown, but only such a short distance,
like the Olympic game of shot put;
hurled with an effort as unknown and universal as death,
from the body you fight for without honor or choice,
or even the wish to keep going—
but it happens anyway, the muscular movement of delaying death,
the maintaining of its doomed weight above you.
It's all sufficiently ossified at this point, the experience incorporated
within the recesses of my body and psyche.
The woman finished her prayers abruptly, jolting me from memory.
My mind adjusted to her few footsteps before silence overtook the chapel.
And while I had expected to make audible
those moratory sobs, for my face to screw up in familiar distortion,
I was left instead, not empty or resolved,
but as if in the veracity of her prayers she had acted out for me,
on my behalf, lobbied for my release from the grief-work that is living
almost in the way I asked to be that night.

Luna

The moon brittle as a tooth
The moon mistaken
For a fortune coming true

Collapses tersely like a compact mirror
Its likeness sending me into a tailspin
My finger swelling
From the uncertainty nearly contained

And yet I admit her sympathy
I permit the telling
Of her story in the streets
Her story splintering apart in midstream
As she lies awake, the object of comment
A settlement of white wood and glass

Then where is she in our union?
Where is she
When the Black Lotus sways?

Amidst hibiscus and a broth of castile
A woman is lifted by her hips
Her hair pulled tightly from her temples
The way thread is jolted from a spool

With the back of my hand high
To her throat, she recoils
Like a loitering book to her binding
The crane returning
To her alcove of shade
Where wedged between the blueprints of ink
The indolent moon is a truant seed
Refusing to die and refusing to grow
No larger
Than a button or a dime

But hush
Now she listens from her circular booth
Solely to you or solely to me
Guileless as a pearl
With her sad, curved ear
Bowed like the forehead of a geisha girl

The Moon and the Yew Tree

This is the light of the mind, cold and planetary.
The trees of the mind are black. Their irregular branches,
like broken arms backlit from MRI dye, offset by yearning.
They take form in ways only experts can decipher.
The light is blue. The observation of the alien doctor
flickers in his iris, furnace gaslight burning like a pagan memorial.

The grasses unload their griefs on my feet as if I were God,
I pity their need for idolatry. It bares itself only to the void of me,
Prickling my ankles and murmuring of their humility.
I am unable to convince them otherwise.
I hear them mew and compete as if for a rough teat's clear nutrition.
Foolish rule of the organic, uncultured and out of control.
I am mum and tidy as a nun in comparison.
Though capable of devastation are my desires which punish
the landscape with recrimination, uprooting the hedges.
They swallow fire, speak in four languages, and love no one.
I shudder with pride as they push themselves back to their origin,
to the scraped-out bottom of a uterine nothing;
this hard loneliness, skull-solid, pushed back into vagueness
until it succumbs as if overwhelmed by barbiturates.

Fumy, spiritous mists inhabit this place
Separated from my house by a row of headstones.
Its green vapors trigger an olfactory déjà vu like a recurrent nightmare.
I envy the buried faces finally freed from worry and ailment,
from the pressure to remain always forward-thinking.
I picture their release, the prostrate bodies floating up as if levitated.
What peace, what stillness was shoveled onto their pine box beds
where darkness then dropped, all at once, final as an execution.
I simply cannot see where there is to get to.

The moon is no door. It is a face in its own right,
White as a knuckle and terribly upset. I identify with its nausea.
It meets me in the mirror uninvited, this face beneath my face,
restless and unwilling. It formulates inside me like a kicking fetus
and refuses to be ignored. It haunts and threatens like a past trauma.

It drags the sea after it like a dark crime; mute as a mug shot,
it is quiet, like someone suffocated who suddenly stops struggling.
I recognize in its warm death the expression of the starving
With the O-gape of complete despair. I live here.

Against me a force, not stronger or more intelligent,
but more adaptable to poor weather like dandelions.
I can feel it whittle me down to horse feed pellets.
I'm being winnowed out of the earth's circulation,
with a paring incremental as this winter's passing.
Twice on Sunday the bells startle the sky—
Eight great tongues affirming the Resurrection.
I'm forced to listen to the liturgical lecturing,
truant student of a catechism I loathe.
At the end, they soberly bong out their names;
Myths and ideals I could never bring myself to believe in,
my prayers, the self-flagellation of unrequited love.

The yew tree points up like a New England steeple.
It has a Gothic shape. It used to remind me of home.
The eyes lift after it and find the moon.
Once fragile as rice paper, it hangs static and tough
like a noose signifying more hardship ahead—
interrogating flashlight that hurts my eyes.
Now no home exists—just an empty bed,
a pile of mangled sheets atop a dark wood floor,
like snow atop the frozen mud tracks of hoof and wheel.

The moon is my mother. She is not sweet like Mary.
She licks her white feathers and stares back with one eye
vicious as a swan about to bite.
Her blue garments unloose small bats and owls.
I watch, my leg caught in the truth of my life
where beyond human emotion I've traveled at this point.

How I would like to believe in tenderness—
in those symbolic unions that elicit sweet concepts:

175

mother and child, father and daughter, husband and wife.
The face of the effigy, gentled by candles,
its cheekbones flushed with an afterworld favoritism
Bending, on me in particular, its mild eyes;
hair waving, mouth parted in mid-speech like drowned Ophelia.

I have fallen a long way. I lie at the bottom, smashed
like a dinner plate against kitchen tile, china chips and jagged bits.
I lie at the bottom, shattered and dangerous, looking up
with a baby's stunned engrossment. I'm moving closer to Pluto and Mars.
Clouds are flowering blue and mystical over the face of the stars,——
It will not be quick. Death drinks me in, slow as syrup.

Inside the church, the saints will be all blue.
They've ascended into heaven's oxygen-deprived morgue.
Floating on their delicate feet over the cold pews,
Their hands and faces stiff with holiness,
mannequins perennially enacting the nativity in a wax museum.
The moon sees nothing of this. She is bald and wild
as one dying of cancer. She begs for relief, but her pillow-muffled
shrieks disperse with the other sounds and shadows of the night.
We are left alone, her cadaver face, gaunt and grim, prescient of mine.
And the message of the yew tree is blackness—blackness and silence.

Sylvia Plath, "The Moon and the Yew Tree,"
Ariel (New York: Harper & Row, 1961)

Magnetic Poetry Kit Poems

6/26/01 4:27 p.m.

blue water & petal pink light they can not use me in their vision of summer
beauty   delirious & lazy
for I have loved time like a ship her sea when chained by winter wind she was
to a stormy void   I have loved life   the day gift the blood music
like a man
his apparatus of true worship though a thousand suns fall fast
behind and without him
as he delicate & tiny incubates under what is an enormously manipulating
moment of death

how I lived through shadow after shadow never smelling garden mist or next
taking in a gorgeous spring
gone were urges easily produced and those sweet beds   for sleep only
no sweating no shaking none
so powerful and elaborate is a dream to drive away from ache and need
the saddest symphony is its moan
always raw and frantic like someone crushed by the feet of men
like me still weak with wanting screaming into some shiney hereafter
above
to stop these sordid ugly pictures playing over in my head   but black is
the rain eating up my breast baring cry
do not ask me why   but I felt the most motherless yet   beneath a rose
white moon   diamondlike
as if   the essential bitterness of its milk may be then
all I am   apart from it

7/2/00 2:10 p.m.

no sleep will fall from above
from the black mist I recall as what would be but sky
for those who do not smell the tiny death moments
when all is said
their enormous shadows delicate and sad soar up mostly in winter
blue purple and produced only by water

a daybed of ache I want to avoid but beneath the gorgeous apparatus of
sun wind power blood there runs like bitter milk within a mother's breast
an essential weakness always felt   raw and repulsive of thousands
next and after
here then gone   the skinmeat and seahair of bared arms and legs
still beating under lake or garden
as if near yet apart   they scream moan whisper   tongues spring
alive in some sordid place
some languid stopover after time

no one but me will want to see them eating away at mansized dreams
for I have cried out like a shot boy at life   its easy urges   its ugly drives
please smooth my frantic vision my   delirious thinking cool   my sweating head
crush the chanting chain of language   the meanest love incubating
within love sweet

let it rain blow and shake through me
by it I lie shining in shadow like forest moonlight
watch me worship not less but none
never needing to ask why I must

8/10/02   12:30 p.m.

from over enormous shadows   powerful yet delicate
   like forest mist
you will see me fall in ache
for these sweet shadows to stop
as though through my moans I could take them with wintry death
as sad as the essential weakness of our dreams
so raw from want when they soar up to a windless sky
   rock hot with no smell or cry
all I have to worship after is my life lived still going on
beat then urge
but what we recall as shiney and fast
is not always who we are
a woman produced of water and blood
I stare delirious as a lake into its crushing void
the bitter apparatus behind those men loved & beauty gone

time is about to leave me   bare skinned and bed chained
beneath its frantic drive
it incubates above my head   a mean and ugly moment
like some man knifed in sunlight
like the road meat of white girl hit by a gorgeous red car
like someone screaming in tongues   sordid language
at the TV picture
under the heaving black moon you sing of beings ripped apart
arm and leg
their tiny need for love felt by none
how I lie in sweat thinking of visions   the never was
as if your mad chant were like ship music
elaborate rain on blue seas   but its only the mayday symphony of next me

8/16/01 10:55 p.m.

what is language but an apparatus for urging out of
the tiny blue void of vision
some meaning to the raw music sweet or sordid
                  we ask & cry & read then sing to
a woman a boy   stormy days and pink suns   you say
you love me   and I will worship with the need
                         of men
for power   a bitter blood produced from the weak
    screaming of our lust
and after   my honey smeared breast in the TV light
as if moon shadows fall mostly here like crushed hair
on me
yes I believed these gifts we said   though the frantic ache
& telling stare are only sadly a part of life   of its
repulsive but essential beauties
as say death at sea is
and yet felt ripped in two when robbed from me were
those delicate moments their moans & chanting still
soaring about
a lazy never after like winter mist
why do I have to watch true love lie like a shot man beneath
an enormous black forest like sky
your bare white skin arm and leg   bygone like water drunk

179

see how fast whispering tongues eat upon madness
elaborate dreams could have arose but did not
and with
time incubate into none
someplace always shining above my bed as they drive over in
my sleep who I was
  as ugly as it is
no   please stop go away is all I am at let at leave to want
  as no one would want
but am not them
and so therein must take it

The Defeat of Linear Thinking

Against God, the sky erects itself like a falcon-crest, a bulwark,
a miscellaneous configuration of clouds and hallucinations.
I stare back at it unblinking, prostrate as a coffin,
and finger like a blind man the arrow that protrudes from my chest,
a whittled shaft of wood unsanded, the feather of a falcon tailing
in mock hunt of a future, an emblem erased by the crest of the sky.

I have lain this way for years, bedridden,
staring up with a falsely fueled suspicion
that after a period of time some figurative form worthy of imitation
will emerge platonically from the blankness,
burst forth or slowly surface, corpse in a pond.
Even a corpse would enthuse at this point as an example to follow
like bear tracks, tempering the scrambled agenda of suppositionary horrors,
the spider-veined map of somatic possibilities
brought to their zenith in the specialization of their suffering.
When treading water in a choppy ocean, exhausted, one finally longs to lose
and allow the gush of suffocation.
The saturation of saline and feces initiates your definitive end.
You surrender to soullessness and scarab-festered rejection.

You see what a spot I'm in, a pool of quicksand.
Each time I stretch a canvas it refuses dimension.
The roads don't narrow or widen, the contrived habitat
on the horizon refutes another connotation.
Water, in any motif: lake, river, stream, pond, puddle, sea, brook, drink
abstracts into the vast failed operation of "origin."
O Origin, adored like the baby Jesus, perpetuated by the folklore of Jesus,
by our nostalgia for disguising truth, like Ganymede,
our propensity for promoting extremes, saint or anti-Christ.

So when I imagine the face of God, I imagine Hitler.
He looks right through me on the verge of breaking up our relationship.
I traverse all aspects of his face and physique, hoping one feature
will betray itself differently.

For a moment his eyes rest upon the table with the despondency
of self-loathing and isolation. I feel compassion
for the self-destructive God who can't seem to help himself
from harming others. I feel my blaming tendency atrophy,
the recriminations deflect off the lavatory-lit mirror
where I identify my reflection as either Hitler's or God's.
I realize I'm no different in this divination of black and white.
It's the effort to project gradation, shade and nuance, to locate a core,
a storm-eye, when submerged within raven-wrought uncertainty, that's work.
But the gesture to erect a future merely subverts itself
again and again like a government in civil war. Nothing sticks.

I mentioned a coffin before, now I'll mention a closet
and bodies, one after another, like bullets on an ammunition belt,
enter. All I hear is a zipper, breathing, and sometimes a narrative,
the question / answer period of a split personality until orgasm . . .
until another enters within what seems just seconds
and I think to myself "I must be bleeding," my thinking voice
heard with a foreign accent as if the voice-over in a luxury car commercial.
It's in this way that life dismembers literally, past, present, and future
like old lovers whose expressions of pleasure resemble agony
as they topple over, convulse, and cum into the earth.
Family and friends chant and pray, complain among themselves,
display a sympathetic facade before your courageous but pathetic facade,
then fade away, choose to forget instead of choking on more vocal deceptions.

It's like a war documentary photograph
which can only be tolerated by a series of retouchings
until stripped of the hard edges, the deformations;
those games of tic-tac-toe engraved with a razor blade
on the backs of POWs the Nazis played in their boredom.
I hear myself say to myself in that same voice-over foreign accent
as if whispered offstage, words of encouragement,
a fight talk: Rise! Continue to write! Articulate what remains unspoken.
Forget a future, which is too ambitious. I need all my energy in order
to make myself clear to the telephone operator, let alone to someone I love.
So many systems need to be put into action at once, the combat strategies
of peacetime illusion, a submarine stilled but poised for confrontation,
like a shark asleep on the bottom of the ocean, sentry ready to kill.

My own life has begun to write me out
into the diegetic character I've become to myself. My essentiality
is formulated through a few flattering though shameful referrals
as filtered through an onstage player. The memory of me flags.
Now you know why I no longer make a personal appearance in the mirror.
Like an ostrich, the effort makes me feel gawky and winsome.
My whole life has become diegetic in itself,
a Shakespearean forest, a Greek amphitheater
with lush and noble foundations configured solely by my desperation.
It's art that perpetuates my sputtering life, fueled by diluted petrol;
my life, an impotent man trying to prove himself to himself.

My life, a murderess's, who has left her newborn wrapped in newspaper
in a trashcan on a street corner before winter dawn.
I empathize with her passion crime. If I could eliminate
my isolation, my helplessness, I would, despite the penitence,
the fire-licking transgression, the deeper realms of loneliness.
My despair seems at once self-contained in its innocence
then demonic in the omniscience of its persecuting agenda.
I want to exorcise it, a poltergeist, purge it, a poison.
I want to birth it and drown it, as Andrea Yates did her five children.
Although publicly I deny it, I wonder all the time, what have I done?
I'm deaf to the words ricocheting in my head—"*bad things happen
to good people*"—But when faced with the tyranny of silence
of my diegetic life, that Shakespearean forest which looms large
as a library in its inaccessible, formidable quiescence, I whimper
like a dog, just a squeak easily mistaken for door creak or car swerve.

Take from me this soliloquy. Cut it out like the tongue of Romeo.
Make me mute as a tree where I can be found like Nietzsche
absorbed in vibrant discourse with the origami birds of my fingers.
Some resignation will have taken over.
Dumb to my own inadequacies, the shackled limitations of my body,
my brain short-circuited, my heart functioning only as an organ;
my head, cocked permanently in befuddlement, no longer tormented.
My eyebrows knit but without the focused scenario of actual worry.
My emotions reallocate to a kind of way station, relieved of urgency.
I'll want but not know for what.
I'll quickly forget except for a mild sentient aftermath

of dull pulsation that could easily be mistaken for anything—
symptoms can be so heavenly ambiguous.

Take from me like a coat this circumstance,
this circuitous mode of living, claustrophobic as the arena of a placemat.
Excuse me from this table, the dimension of my future, the depth of a spoon.
Undress me then completely and carry me to my cradle of straw.
The closet will have shrunk then to a dark corner of my psyche,
the documentary photograph filed away in its archive.
I'll fear only at a distance, like flooding in the Midwest,
or rape camps in Bosnia.
The coffin, buried empty, tessellated with wildflowers
plucked from the untended cemetery, or sawed in half before an audience,
demonstrates the disappearing act as a ceremony of survival.

Take from me this child I cannot save, stillborn that rots
in the tomb inside me. Although my womb has shed its walls,
I'm like a snake who cannot progress from aging to death,
an internal myth of Tithonus.
Show me just once my dead child's face and I will accept my barrenness.
Show me just once the face of God and I will pardon him like Nixon.
I pay homage to each shrine of my future, to the cradle, to the falcon.
I pay homage by merely walking beneath the crest of the sky.
It's as if in the end, we are all, if only by default,
absolved as blameless, whether or not we die in prison,
whether or not we die of a terminal illness (another kind of prison).
We are all caught in a spatiality that reserves judgment;
caught but not released, the way children are to a playground
or POW s to their homeland.

I know, because I know what it's like to be there, to be dying
but not to die.
I know because I've acquiesced to the face of Hitler,
to the face of God, and watched myself as if through the eyes of God
engage in an act inconsequential and benign.

The Part of Me That's O

What assembles a locus for understanding cracks at the foundation,
a fountainhead of a troll's facade, against which all means of identification
flee, Haitians from their homeland, or become troll-like in appearance
as I regard my face distort accordingly, my pink hair, a shock of radioactivity,
my flattened nose desensitized to olfactory tethering, my red eyes like a rat's,
panicked and immoral. But inside the werewolf I am the same, though smaller,
diminishing inside the bell jar of this werewolf body.
I experience the tumult of my isolation like a kicking fetus
who accelerates its growth on a trajectory of delineation,
becomes more, not less, ambiguous in gender, its limbs more
a blur of purely molecular congruency than the aestheticized flesh,
than the Giorgione cameo that wavers in lakeside twilight,
profane by virtue of what it lacks in profanity,
a purity superimposed upon a purity like a testudo
forming a bulletproof sky which ultimately fails to protect,
as art fails, to provide shelter from the mammal in us:
from the carnivorous, the banal, the rupturous, the pitiful.
There will be no birthing, but a series of swallowings
until gaunt from longing I will have settled into a state of impoverishment
normalized finally by some property of physics that adapts
the disassociated to the hemisphere: like *E. coli* in water, I will live.
My erotic impulses curtailed so many times that in ringlets they will lie
like sheaved hair, as fertilizer fulfilling its wishes
by fulfilling the wishes of others
for which I will not receive pleasure
for which I will not be responsible
for which I will always be rendered impotent by this surveillant privilege.

SACKCLOTH-MOLD, tower-high

crows circle the stink
when my body dies

Vision slot
for the destarred

it be not heartwork worked
to death, collapsed under the intolerable
sickbed-tomorrow

at the end of the sorrow-fibril.

The cart pulled, famished mule
stick-scarred, water-fooled

The eyelash seam, at a slant
to the god-blazes.

I always stood up, crooked tree.
Never say you expected more.

In the mouthbay the place

I ran the machines,
dug farther into marrowlard

for rowing
Kaisertwitter.

Oil-milk to personless worlds.
When cruelty purifies,
it's time.

The.

No mind no country
deserved the plague-pit dedication

And the Going-with-
him across smokeblue,

but you, Beloved,
but you, Mean Ocean

blank
tableland, you.

The you in me, garment cindered
and from headstone breed.

Paul Celan, "SACKCLOTH-MOLD, tower-high,"
Threadsuns, trans. Pierre Joris
(Los Angeles: Sun and Moon Classics, 2000)

Woman, Resurrected

It floats like milk skin upon the inconsolable river,
pink, murky water of a mid-winter twilight,
the nickel-dull conformity of it.

It rises from fog grit, pulled forth as if by the mortmain
of what's beyond human thinking. Wind gusts ceremony
the recondite dimension out of which skullcap, hair part, neck nape,
fetal wet from river fluid, bob to surface
like some drowning victim retrieved in routine dragnet.

It rises slowly in jolts of ascension, an angel of humiliation,
feet arched, toes pointed in permanent pirouette
on the joyless horizon; the mayhem of its history exploited
in the freak show this recovery dispenses.

It emerges as if roll-called,
quarantined to the city's outskirts, faceless silhouette
framed by wormwood and ivy.
It emerges in response, like any spasm,
the way eyes of the freshly guillotined blink in disbelief
as they tumble into a straw-bedded wagon.
Out of pink water that crystallizes immediately
in the sub-zero temperatures, frost forming on brows and forearms,
it emerges reborn of ice, blown into existence by cold climate,
tallied side of beef suspended by meat hook,
or female inmate hog-tied
for repeated sodomy rapes never reported.

Ropetowed to full frontal, it rises, appears, arrives,
it does not triumph, surmount, elevate, or surge.
It returns merely, it returns resigned, listless, traumatized,
jerky succession, puppeteered by mare's tail cloud and lilac soot.
It follows dogmatically the imperative of some regained life
like consumer to capitalist fetish-object, exercising brand loyalty.
It follows somnambulistically, as if to the beat of tolling bell,
a procession of black horses and carriages,
the life that was, its life that was,

its embalmed face of achieved ascension, wax-museum-worthy.
Each step triggers like an anniversary those innumerable "what ifs"
that read like a palindrome their potential for enactment,
as if sequence had nothing to do with outcome.
The memories vivid, sensitized, influential,
embossed like brocade on the immediate future, respond quickly
with time-lapsed growth, almost frightened into awareness
by this moderate level of recall, its light touch sending a quiver,
a melancholy shudder, as if drapes disturbed by a nefarious breeze,
throughout the brain of reconstituted life.

Out of heat, bougainvillea, starvation,
out of mammal fornication where rooted the original fertilization
that determines gender, genetic formation, and sexual identity,
it emerges, compelled, it emerges, beckoned
as if by an atavistic master's crooked index finger,
dirty, unmanicured, curling landward
in sync with the enriching minutes of nightfall.
It emerges as if seduced, exorcised, or selected
(as if spared, as if not spared)
responding to a spiritual summons, the way Lazarus conceded
to the grief cries of loved ones.
How he lifted his epigenetically erected eyes obediently
to the prescience of a solitary cross,
a mirage that motivates only the most dedicated pilgrimages.
How he followed and flinched, smiled while driven by the antonomasia
of his place in the Bible as if doomed to a life of haunting,
enslaved to the invention of miracle like a wheel cog.

Out of pink water,
ivory anaglyph against the wildfire fuchsia,
extreme and panicked in an otherwise everyday eventide,
those out-of-the-way thoughts finally broken free from a confined mind,
endorphin induction compensating for cell damage.
Out of glass shards, stainless steel, tunneling blankness,
out of glutinous tedium and discarded passports,
driver's licenses and bus stop billboards advertising

an ostensibly healthy Hispanic gay man who's compliant to Zerit.
Out of newspaper headlines, boxes of rubber gloves, sharps containers,
and late-night phone calls spreading the news of another gone.
Out of dark suits and young faces at their memorial services,
in churches, in restaurants, in homes;
or in your home, alone because you're too sick to attend.
A friend updates you on the phone, describes the flowers, the elegy,
the diminished community that showed up.

Out of checks written to estate lawyers for living wills,
expediting your wishes for how you want death to come down.
Your death steadily approaches, a darkening sky that builds in momentum
like lake ice starting to break. Your death, a crack, black zigzag
amidst all the healthy whiteness, ekes its way toward you more rapidly,
a kind of divining rod for determining your damnation.
You will sink, you will freeze while trying to make the effort
to recite the loving things you've rehearsed in your head,
keeping in mind that your life belongs now to those who are watching;
as if simultaneously you're able to witness,
and by virtue of that vigilance,
exercise control over the evolution of your face
as it transpires into belatedness,
into afterward, the ambergris image of what's been known,
temporarily cohered in the tangibility of bedside handholding.
What you have left as a send-off gift
like a pendant always worn or a scented handkerchief,
or waving handkerchief spotted along the jetty
before sealed off permanently from view,
will be the concealment of your own grief and swelling regret.

Out of reversal, spinning wheel of tragedy and privilege,
which happens to stop for no apparent reason. The clicking plastic tag
lackadaisically allocates a fate, any fate, wherein the violent
violet horizon brings down, like a government, previous expectations.
They fall, a landslide of sepia mud,
stunted trees, shacks and partially dried laundry.
They fall with crescendo, pummeling avalanche, as if within the quiescence
of white ice, a buried body which lay for years
were suddenly seanced back to the living.

They fall, familial fallout, relationships severed and ensuing silence;
fall with imperceptible sound like pill to carpet;
fall, a silence, sudden, almost redolent, that fills up the pitch void
like an embryo latching onto a formerly barren matrix.

And what we mean by the beautiful turned monstrous
retaliates with the beauty of what remains, a post-disaster vigil
of lachrymal reflexes, candles, and extraneous flowers.
The body as vehicle of suffering survives regardless of its suffering,
first emblematized in the little torches ablaze beneath their destiny,
then as they're extinguished amidst a giant pampas of diligent misfortune.

Soaked clothes, dark as the bank water,
cling in rivulets to the exhumed limbs.
Missing eyes, like the shallow graves of SIDS victims,
rove in their absence with a phantom vision
that penetrates to the core those parasitical onlookers
fascinated by this postmodern resurrection.

From the example of suffering, they glean the necessary clichés
for courage and strength, the upside of tragedy so upbeat
that when they look into the faces of their children,
it's their cherubic expressions they'll focus on,
not the skull and crossbones of future time's possibilities.
So they smile a slightly forced smile to disguise the horror,
unable to tear themselves away from rubbernecking this car crash,
from the concave sockets of a body brought back from flatline
as if upgraded to titanium;
this wildcard second chance, a kind of Second Coming,
though not savior-worthy, more of a defunct hosanna,
blip of a female mortal, the inventory of which
is constantly downsized in China.

The future unveils itself as amorphous and foreign.
It lies wide open as once did her coffin, pontoon prepped for departing.
It's as if she could live any life from here on, anyone's life,
walking forward into eventual disappearance more final and total
than her annihilation could ever have meant.
Images of sunrises and sets, high noons, and soporific sunlessness
sprout like wildflower sprigs in the feral world of her memory nest.

Throughout this whole thing she's observed herself in the third person,
experienced the trauma then extracted it, placing it,
like an object, say a piece of sculpture, in the appropriate context
for viewing and comment. How else to negotiate with the physical panic?
She could smell their fear waft off the miniature atmosphere between them.
She could hear their inner battles, moral versus animal.
Most gave up to forces of the latter.

Those who die are transfixed within us,
caught in the web of lasting impression.
In a way, so too are those who survive, floating in the limbo
of what could have been that almost was.
But for them there's the opportunity, and also the pressure,
of reinvention, to soften the kilned clay
of how people have come to think of you, and moreover,
how you have come to think of yourself.
I should kneel to the earth, kiss its molten surface
in a thanksgiving ritual for the gratitude I am expected to feel.
This soil that refused to cover me at the same time it refused to save me.
This soil that regarded dumbly my faceless, irrational struggle.
This soil I regard dumbly myself
where lupine, like edelweiss, faultlessly grows.

Out of depravation into ambivalence,
out of misery into bravado, partisanship into evidence, crisis
into narrative: she enters, recruit for scientific demonstration,
the Frankensteinian specimen of newfangled experimentation.
She ascends, new moon in old sky, yet not a new moon,
adapts to the star-fragmented expanse,
sheds chilled, translucent light upon terrestrial offspring.
Her past rotations, small and senseless, retain themselves
within her hidden roundness, a wasted womb.

My old face, full of life, camcorder recorded, pulsates
like a transplanted organ beneath the sheened patina of this new face,
so new-moon-like, as it pleaches into the desolate char of beginnings,
the false transcendence of my overcoming AIDS,
which is the myth of survival.

Black Milk

in memory of "HIV, Mon Amour"

I.

Black trees, blue trees, white trees, bare trees—
Whatever was my life has been returned to me
in a made-of-trees coffin
killed in action like a veteran husband, its flag
a pitiful consolation,
its flag a smug presupposition,
for some greater cause more important
apart from what you know to be the *most* important to you:
his voice, his smile.

To me, the world now held away, irreversibly,
that once was just (now "just"?) suspended,
when I thought then there could be no greater torture.

Life's truest truth, it's that truth itself
unravels in ways that reveal less not more sense or comfort.

Consolationless is the tarmac wind, the kickback of jet fuel fume,
the bulkhead of the coffin wherein only regret to be alive
alights in contrast.

It burns like eyes burned out by cinders,
a hot poker waved amidst laughter.

It burns, a torch's temporary pathway
improvised within black trees, blue trees.

It burns like a novena unerring,
pure prayer within the black trees of longing.

It burns, the ultimate act of atonement,
the cremation of what I tried to save.

It burns in order to drown, ash in saline,
May fly rose petals of burial at sea.

II.

It burns in order to drown, ash in saline,
the May fly rose petals of burial at sea.

The regret burns like its converse property,
the hope I had (so fucking much of it) now retarded in me,
a tumor, inoperable, contained by chemo, a perverse kind of cancer
where the desire to live only prolongs the suffering—

I wish death upon this desire, I wish AIDS and cancer
upon this desire, let the desire suffer instead of me,
this pathetic willingness to live regardless of consequence,
regardless of indignation.

Who am I but the vessel, the holy vessel for this desire,
and for the natural spasms that confirm somatic reality:
vomiting, allergic reactions, orgasm, coughing;
involuntary humiliations, proof of living, of precious humanness.

In order to suffer one must divorce the pain,
divorce the vessel, until you become a slave to the vessel,
a whore to the harpy's needs, its spasms, its pathetic desires.

Its moanings must be tended, its shaking and sweating,
its fevers, its ailments, its medications—copious, expensive.
What are these drugs but a very refined life-support system,
science at its most powerful, most phallocentric?

We were not born for this, this stainless steel,
this sanitary lack of love, this medicine-vacuum.

III.

For this, this stainless steel, this sanitary lack of love,
this medicine-vacuum, we were not born.

Yet every twelve hours I take my drugs and refuse to capitulate
to the desire, acquiesce to that most base, pre-conscious motivation
that's common to humans and dogs, from scavengers
whose howling in the distance we detect as equidistant to the canine
within us, the jubilee of inconsequential behavior.

We enjoy acoustically the disowning.

But under the weight of one life-threatening moment,
concretized and extenuated by its repercussion,
what distinguishes us as civilized, as generations apart
from the medieval acts of our ancestors, collapses,
so fragile is the rope bridge of its construction,
reducing us all to dogs.

Let no more natural light befall, thus, like shiny hair
upon pillowcase, this crying face.

Let no more jealousies assemble in my heart like migrant workers.

Take me as a life can be taken in a car accident,
or at gunpoint then exterminated,
taken from the pack, a succulent carcass extracted
from their exhilarated jaws, for too well do I identify
with the hunger, the taste, the smell.

Take the needle, arrest these senses,
excise the egg-shaped moon from my field of vision
and silence the bark.

IV.

Take the needle, arrest these senses,
excise the egg-shaped moon from my field of vision.

Close off the whispering heart of my will.

Take from me shelter, from me food and water,
for food is rot to me and water brackish.

Silence the speak, the tongue and its elocution.
Numb the skin, the capacity for touch, the lips, the feet,
the sex, make them one and null, and null again memories of them.

Eliminate as in annihilate sad visuals before me,
cruel visuals, crystal-cut beauty crashed and splintered
as a windshield in the all-dead-but-one automobile accident.

Take from me or take me from as a mourning mother from her dead young.
Smaller grows the small carrion from the aerial view, the crying sirens,
the blue policemen and their radios' grim narrative of my future,
so far in the distance now you've finally listened.

You are who I need now, not doctor or officer, and no, let no
loved one near this burning house I've arsoned.

All I ask is to make the world what I experience it to be—
and show me my place within its godforsakenness
as you did seagull or jackal.

Every window, every memory, every dream,
represented by rank in this funereal cortege.

Destroy it now,
permitting just smoke to twist and waft.

V.

Destroy it now, this funereal cortege,
permitting just smoke to twist and waft.

Allow skeletal structures of museums and churches to remain after,
serving as scarecrows to any future's cursory good fortune.

What good could good fortune do me now?

No revision could be great enough, no benefit redemptive
to supplement this grief which extends as fields do beyond the Lager;
deep into the purple throat-cut scar of the horizon
without irregularity or illusion of narrowing
in their projection of irrevocability.

This grief mushrooming up, more life-altering
than any loss of a person: not my father or lover or girlfriend,
the distillation of their cremation dust still detected in the air.
Granted their photographed faces provide poor semaphores,
like lousy translation, for the sculptural distinction of their voices.
Yet I inhale the death-smoke like exhaust, adapting as eyes do
to darkness or appetite to liquid diet.

But with somatic losses, instead of adjustment,
an act of abjection, a salaam to genetics
happens and a submission of the soul performs outwardly
as an acceptance which can no longer refuse
like prisoner prison routine,
breaking down desire, giving up, giving in
to the venial totem of instinct & need.

VI.

Breaking down desire, giving up,
giving in to the venial totem of instinct & need.

Breaking down desire like gunfire overhead,
the hell-bent agenda of the shiftless sky and empty spills
the sunlight that tries to fulfill the deprivation.

Breaking down desire, until you become devoid of want,
sobbing on the ledge of your bathtub at 4:48 a.m.

The greatness of your regrets, the awesomeness of their magnitude
hover like a death you feel certain you're responsible for,
like the death of a child where that will always be the case.
Life events unfold with such a maniacal intensity, the moments
of choice short-lived as crib death. And the aftermath,
the braincrushing hours that force you at knifepoint
outside the perimeters of that crucial decision,
and your delusion of ever correcting it,
unveil a plagued destiny of staring into its open coffin.

There the event replays with a Gregorian density, a punishment
akin to rehabilitation techniques in *A Clockwork Orange*.

There the hierarchy of pleasure dismantles
and every screen memory that once triggered a modicum of happiness
collapses into a deletion that brings no final blankness.

What remains transforms into a savanna of locusts
for which you'll never forgive yourself.

VII.

What remains
transforms into a savanna of locusts
for which you'll never forgive yourself.

What remains
persists in unchangeable terror, as if a nightmare,
if only a nightmare—a death mask which adumbrates death
but brings no closure.

I wander alone, through the echo chambers
of its dull landscape, the bleak, undifferentiated daylight
refracted off the terrible silence.

I am utterly lost unto myself
in the absence of a god, of belief in or hope for anything.
The unmitigated pain like radiation contamination
reaches every cell, every fiber in aorist distention,
branches frozen in lake ice.

I am more alone than I've ever been in my life;
more alone than on the cusp of death,
tubes of hospital fluorescence buzzing, yes, buzzards
over my head, or at home in bed my skeleton shaking
with hallucinating fever like the death rattle itself,
my chattering teeth, the sad attempt
to exorcise it from my marrow.

I was less alone then
for death is not the extreme of aloneness people fear,
not even the death of an atheist.

There is the ocean for us god-ravaged souls,
terse, teal waves belly-cold and winter-mean.

There is the dirt, dry and punishing,
whose clouds kicked up upon car wheels passing
mimic our own mortal dust. So, so aptly.

VIII.

Clouds kicked up upon car wheels passing .
mimic our own mortal dust. So, so aptly.

Behold the sky, deaf, mute and blind,
idiot sky, autistic sky, the *I know nothing,*
I'm not responsible for anything air of it: blue white,
dark blue and starry sometimes, a moon when it wants or not.
It gives no more than a handful of seeing-is-believing things
such as flora, pollen, blood, the wonder of blooming,
the wonder of decay. I was not alone when I was dying
with these reminders, these companions, reflections
of my future transparency.

But left now to life, the midday sun of it,
the full flour-sack bulk weight of it, burdensome in length,
its relentless "pleasures" tallied up like pence in a piggy bank,
I'm pressured to squeal about, lucky, lucky me, runt pig me.
Each day a rebirth in the statistical glare of AIDS,
a day of gratitude for my survival rolls over into regret
I'm ashamed to admit, into jealousy for the dead released from this,
the medical discard pile, totaled car sent to the scrap metal yard,
wasteland of having done all they can do.
The stench of their best efforts makes me gag.

This is evil poetry.
Resurrect John Doe who died of KS in his lungs
and bestow upon him what's obviously been wasted on me.
Runt pig me.

IX.

Resurrect John Doe who died of KS in his lungs
and bestow upon him what's obviously been wasted on me.
Runt pig me. Ungrateful, frivolous me.

What life I have is not enough, a vandalized Rembrandt ruined
by razor cuts when others have lost utterly all beauty,
lost as in buried, flung body into self-dug grave
or cattle stock submerged in mudslide. Graveyards now are
the memories of seeing, the irreplaceable intimacy of looking
into someone's eyes, even a stranger's eyes—
the power of it, pure Machiavellian control, pure vulnerability.
You could watch it form before you as breath does in cold climate.

For me this should be nothing, just cross-eyed crazy
like looking underwater, patches of blur floating in a frenetic,
rapid-motion galaxy; a stocking over my head, just a mask,
the isolation I've lived with all my life increased a bit
but a bit too much this time. The snowy landscape's still there,
just a little skewed, but enough not to recognize it
and thus lost as in buried like the death of a close friend.

O to hear her voice again. She of all people
would understand how I long for sight unmarked,
without filmy transpositions of black dots and cobwebs,
the snowy landscape resurrected in perfect handheld-camera clarity.

X.

Resurrect the snowy landscape in perfect handheld-camera clarity,
mass-produce my prayers for it.
Take the mimeographed pages and tie them to branches
exactly as prayerpoems flagfly on mountain sides in Burma,
or by rope drag me through the village.

Culled from the warfare, I have been spared but I am not relieved.
I loathe the mechanism of life I fought so hard for.
What was my motivation, my conviction?
The optimism propelling the conviction escapes me.

I bite the hand that held me away, apart, up and out of
the perished millions, the unfinanced, the persecuted—
break skin and suck the way vampires subsist in their counter-life.
Shorn for this ingratitude, spit on my head,
for as if I'd slept with a Nazi is this expectation for an unscarred life,
a morning when opening eyes reveal the world I used to see clearly,
my eyes as once they lay like ampoules filled with a roving, fearful,
penetrating source wherein, just by looking, I'd save myself.

Now no longer can I distinguish white body from whitecapped wave.
What are these tears? Alien saline, black as the blood
Lady Macbeth hallucinated on her hand. Black tears,
where do you come from? You trickle down, bloody trail from the bullet
I pray to be put in my brain.

XI.

You trickle down, bloody trail
from the bullet I pray to be put in my brain.

Black tears, you are my prayers, the evidence of their anguish.
Only the worthless are tortured like this
with prayers clear and black, with prayers for resurrection
or final death, enunciated in hot whispers or self-pitying sobs,
in delirious silence I consciously contain, for I cannot recognize
what is whole among all that's disfigured both interior & ex.

I pray for ultimates, for extreme circumstances,
not for patience or strength or any of that human enhancing stuff.
Pellet my flesh then with black tears from the sky,
the tears of gods for this embittered poetry.
May each letter catch like a chicken bone in my throat.

Doom me to sew the AIDS quilt from scratch, to re-engrave the names
on the memorial wall in San Francisco with my Bic fine point,
alone in the fog and wind. Rape me there with rain,
the black tears of my shame while chiseling in the dark,
for no atonement, I assure you, will come.

Show me the blind man, the madman, show me
the names on the aforementioned quilt and wall,
EEGs grafting the grief reflexes of their beloveds.

I will not say I'm fortunate, I will not say I'm lucky,
traitor to the living, traitor to the dead.

XII.

I will not say I'm fortunate, I will not say I'm lucky
not to be a part of some goddamned quilt,
not to have my name engraved on a wall,
not to be pitied anymore.

All of popular culture and biblical literature
tells us that life's redemption is life's beauty,
that these moments are worth it, worth the prophesying of either
the lucky or the deluded for one glimpse of the snow-laden dogwood.

But what justification could there be for that optimism,
at this point, at this point,
when suffering is caused by the very beauty
that's supposed to be its redemptive property?
I can honestly say there was more hope in the expectation of death,
for even if death be slow, the humiliation exasperated,
there's an end that provides, as if nourishment for living,
relief from this.

Traitor to the living, traitor to the dead,
I regret that I cared so much to live. I regret.
I hate myself now for surviving, willing to sacrifice anything.
No, I don't feel that determination within us we purport and enunciate
with mannered, aesthetically acceptable level of grandiosity,
that sense of moral and ethically admirable desire for life
regardless of circumstances or vulgar litany of precursive events.

There are two truths no one will ever admit to:
it can always get worse and there are things worse than death.

XIII.

There are two truths no one will ever admit to:
it can always get worse
and there are things worse than death.

What remains, not above and beyond,
but within and as definition of,
remains like chemical residue, stubborn, resistant,
no quaint keepsake left behind to calm the flutter
of separation anxiety. What remains prevails,
like the enigma of evil, as an intangible, brutalized
counter-beauty or anti-beauty, persistent, worsening, and incurable.

What remains preys upon the weakness for longing
and remembrance, provokes nonstop at precise intervals
like sleep-deprivation torture, your vulnerability toward regret
which is, which will always be, the rejection of its catharsis.
And time arrests in the insanity of exhaustion.

Propped up on one elbow, blinking from half-sleep,
you regard from your bed how long, how wide darkness casts itself
across your past, lengthening still, shadows bleeding out
from a sun's departure. Ferociously they swallow up
what comes to mind in defense against your self- recriminations
as you float then sink overwhelmed by the watching of a water level
rising to final closure above you like heaven sealed off
to your redemption.

Fish fight over the delicacy of your eyes.

XIV.

Fish fight over the delicacy of your eyes.

And those leaves, those terraced dimensions of green grass, bush, and tree
that once moved almost muscularly, as if isolating the movement
of a particular body part, thigh or back, in the midst of athletic endeavor—
the synchronized interworking of bone, muscle, tendon
that signifies spirit and a kind of holistic integrity
in its undulating texture—

it's what we admire in world champions, this brush with immortality,
the freedom of superseding physical limits with an energy
usually reserved for children. It's why we look to nature,
the inviolable mountain range and butterfly-like recycling of bud
to withering, to lead us by its history and pantology,
as well as its papistic submission to the unknown,
as omnipresent mothership for our fledgling nature-made selves.

But how still those leaves lie now, pressed against
the gray cement cell wall of the overcast sky as if they too have lost,
and lost badly, to others, to themselves, and eventually to the gods,
their strength expended in the effort of seeing through to its vespers,
to homesick sleep, this protracted day,
which forces even desert flowers to relinquishment.

XV.

This protracted day, which forces even desert flowers
to relinquishment, how do I fight you?

I've tried hiding, gray swallow immersed
in a cavity of twigs, dry leaf and bramble
from your crow-culled stalking light,
but always the shriek of discovery breaks
like the will of Moloch in the styptic air.

I have tried becoming like you, painting my face
with primary colors, chanting until entranced
by the ritualistic drumming of my self-imposed mindset,
until the neological narrative of your mode of preservation
formulates inside me like some necromantic transfusion,
a werewolf transformation worthy of you.

But naturally I fail in fine-tuning my genesis.

It was then that I tried to love you,
to give myself to you, bathing in your acrid hourlessness,
urging you to make use of my naked body.
But no amount of moaning from a calla-lily-white torso
that shifted with sidereal delicacy beneath you, that writhed
there in continuous play the way patulous shade
dapples across summer grasses, could rescue me

from your red dirt, your arid field, the barren life
you point to silently in your ecumenical expanse
as your gift of freedom, a freedom without liberation,

from how by you I am permanently marked.

XVI.

A freedom without liberation,
from how by you I am permanently marked,
is what is left of me, that which can never change or heal,
that which subsists as the truth of my survival—
antithetical to the mythology of truth, of our desired perception
of truth as something bright, something clarifying, the ends to the means
of prognostic testing which should unveil appropriate treatment.

But for truth that lies on the cold floor of my soul,
its telling aspect, the reminder of how cold my soul has become,
there's no response precisely because there's no expression
to be lured, extracted, or demanded.
There's no expression save for its rocking,
an obsessive attempt to console and contain,
that unsteadies my walk every now and then,
or the two or three tears I reconcile myself to in the morning; so loud
and radical are those sobs that pierce the lemondrop sunlight,
I'm taken aback anew by what refuses me to refuse
like a ghost limb's reflex.

Its destiny dislimns reckless dreaming
when caught in the briar patch of retrospection,
when prone to forgive, to fall victim to pop tropes,
i.e. , rebirth, letting go.

It truncates relief from the responsibility toward your history
as if such loyalty ever mattered to man.

XVII.

The responsibility toward your history, as if such loyalty
ever mattered to man, is something to accept like food stamps.

It is something to agree to, like love,
or what passes for love from physically abusive parents.

It is something to assimilate
like a certain level of toxicity, weighing you down
as if tied to you, ankle and wrist, cadaver tethered to deep-sea
eternity. And though such loyalty has never mattered to man,
one should for some reason, if only a reason in theory,
proceed as if it will. Proceed taking comfort in how music
used to compel you, the recall so complete it's hypnotic,
your twisting body transported to a trance of rhythmic beating.

Proceed losing yourself, as surely you will, to momentary forgetfulness
of your history. Like wind gusts upon which dust rides,
you too may, say driving on a wonderfully winding country road
with the radio off, be lifted up by forest air,
by the good the blue sheath above should only bring.

It's something to submit to like a test of faith,
Old Testament tribulation and trial. It's something to suffer through,
to survive still that which your history has done to you;
to discover and discover further
what's been done that you've yet to fully understand.

XVIII.

Discover and discover further
what's been done that you've yet to fully understand.

But I've just to think of it, and what's been done keeps doing,
does more, and will do again. It's that simple.
In a glance, my profile turns toward that which waits,
like a snake coiled in its basket for charming, to outlive me.
It waits prostrate with tail thumping, bestial, invidious, black tongue
lashing out in serpentine curls at the vermiculated soil of my future.
Its grunts, loud-long and echoing, devised to torture with PTS flashbacks
of that vortex, mammoth, carnivorous, giddy, the death hole
of my impending diminishment.

How it whined, a dog chained in the snow.
How it overrode, an insulin overdose.
How it pressed its sweaty cheek against my face,
relishing its weight, relishing its thrust, like a pedophile.

How it made me beg for it, and I did, O I prayed for it
only to wake in the woods, in the desert, in a motel alone on the highway.
How it held me in place with undertow force, told me not to scream,
shrugged off with a smirk expertise, intervention, self-love.

How it preys upon me still, *in petto*, feeding as crows do
off roadkill on what's left of me in its stultifying afterglow.

My protests rise up, amaranthine wails from the starving.

XIX.

My protests rise up, amaranthine wails from the starving.

My eyes close, silenced
music boxes, to disdainful darkness,
for what feckless freedom could be sucked
like breast milk from stark abandonment?

Where do I lay my head that's not thorny and sharp?
I've moaned for rescue, a white wolf to errant stars
whose papilionaceous configurations just watched
and listened and decided to do nothing.

The trees that swayed sympathetically
concern themselves only with themselves.
And the ocean to whom I surrendered gladly,
to its eternal nothing and hence my own,
consoling me like a maternal heartbeat, only verifies
the death knell of its tidal pulsing.

You would have to know such deterioration,
that detritus which is to the soul
what the skeleton is to the body.
It stands alone at the end of your life
as if archived by your merely living.

Pared down to a singular longing,
it pumps independent of blood and oxygen.
What gathered as a predicative desire for beginning
calls for termination. Let the alpha and omega
take hold, noose of relief and redemption.

But the promise for sanctuary beyond godlessness
retracts its promise.

Churlish forces I once read as emotive
revert to indifferent tumult and torpor,
alien as an artifice of vinyl.

XX.

Churlish forces I once read as emotive
revert to indifferent tumult and torpor,
alien as an artifice of vinyl.

As if by headlights I'm blinded, by a brilliant void
churning in untouchable eminence, a serf lord
represented in the unforgiving radiance of the sun
that surveys with rapacious enjoyment.
I've trouble breathing in its thick, verdigris air.

What should be a post-whatever,
call it recovery or rematriculation, conquest or celebration,
reveals no distinction from the previous.
I'm as alone in life as I was in death
and I didn't think that would happen;
as alone in the icy containment of civilization
with its calendars, complaints, and sensation headlines.
What's the difference, surviving in order to live or solely
to defy that which is committed to kill you? I've forgotten.

I've forgotten the teachings of all those 4 a.m. pleadings,
hurled out into smoky, laissez-faire oblivion.
Where did they go, all those wrenched reconciliations,
determinations for acceptance as I gulped down, then kept down,
gratuitous pain? Where did it end up,
that which I listened to in the end, the voice
that soothed *sotto voce* from beyond, above, within,
within me: rabbi, father, animal instinct?

I can't hear anything now.

XXI.

I can't hear anything now
except the clock, that foreign face
I stared down from the start.
Where did it go, what the clock became?
Its heavy hours and aching minutes, and that second hand,
how brutally it swept like a bayonet
through the fabric of my days and nights.
I was afraid of it, the insanity-producing ticking
like water torture, the tick, the drip, inane and ruthless,
a quintessential symbol of how mechanically heartless
it had all become, as if ruination ran on a schedule.
Whole nights I would wait for phone calls from the doctor
who delivered mostly bad news like automated weather;
or that fax to come through revealing game-point blood results,
some specialized tests taking twice as long, their clicks,
styptic, staccato, the clicks, the ticks, incessant, surreal,
the clicks, the drips, like Luftwaffe RED code.
And me trying to decipher from just the tops, those digits
that determined how much time I had to live.
Where did all the patience go?
It's as if patience died without me,
stayed on course while I, ejected from the passenger seat,
just beheld from my parachute the spectacle of its endgame fires.
What part of me sacrificed itself for me?
A kind of natural selection of the personality occurred.

XXII.

A kind of natural selection of the personality occurred.
Qualities innate, principles, beliefs,
those variables in the inexhaustible nature versus nurture debate.

What died instead that could have been me, like a foxhole buddy,
expired without my noticing as if asleep in a crossfire riot.
What of me, of my heart and mind and soul and flesh, has remained
in the after, shivering in pajamas, barefoot on the snow,
while I just watched it, like a house, burn to the ground.

That excoriated terrain still smoking into the daybreak
of an Everyman's morning, today, yesterday, and tomorrow
demarcates in gradations according to the sun's rotations
this so-called survival, which I call The Continuation.

What should have been transitory has become permanent,
ossified. Stupidly, I thought I could bring it all with me.
I am but the representation of those morals and values,
their emblems and monuments; for something else I am living.

This that's left of me awaits me, less like a new recruit,
too green for my liking, I'm too tired to befriend,
and more of something else, say, a seasoned vet,
the one who bonded inhumanly with the land
in a garret of bushes, eating worms and drinking his urine
whom I've come to meet as my maker.

XXIII.

I've come to meet as my maker
that which threatened to be the end result,
that which stood insurmountable beneath the pink rays of dawn
as if materialized not by daylight but by its advent of breaking,
by cracking instant, glaring rip in gossamer blackness,
cool and quiet, dainty twinkle scattered hither.
They melt, lovely elements of night, weak, irrelevant,
into obscurity upon the fiery pressure, one tongue-lick
of aggressive warmth for whom breaking is the food, shelter, the love;
the breaking, a soul-standard up to which I'd be measured.

Little did I know. All this suffering proceeded as my measuring,
my momentous heartbeat, the switch of his crop against his boot,
setting the pace like a metronome. Hoodwinked by its beautiful days,
I naively thought this my overcoming.
Now that I've touched the rock, there'll never be
the outpouring I craved, that primitive utterance of relief,
great heave of agony culminating in private exhalation.

No tender victory endured to hold as mine within me will be mine;
no sacred body experience to sanctify the finished body in final communion.
Perhaps you're there beyond the future, held out
like an engraved invitation, a promise for sanctuary. I can wait.
I can always wait.

XXIV.

I can wait, I can always wait.

I can wait for speaking, for the god-mute that's life
to regard with ineffectuality my intermittent repose and torment,
exposed in the hissing surprises of my sleep.

I can wait under the clean blackboard of a December night,
then in the lithe pine of a suicidal morning.

Through it, I can wait, within my namesake body,
small huddle of a sea urchin with its pleasure-seeking tentacles.

I can wait distracted by the strong spiders of my fingers
as they finesse their way across sheetscapes and keyboards.
When they stop moving, the day of the poison, of manna,
of cryogenic suspension, I can wait for I wouldn't have been wrong
about how peaceful the ascension.

I can wait while clouds waft and tender themselves
across a tilled insignificance. Someday
I'll be a part of its modus operandi,
of colorfree flotsam, of the moiré of sliding doors,
the muscular shadows of the dead moving in slow,
disc-throwing motion behind them.

I can wait for the lamb, the fig, for the rains,
for the parchment-filtered light from my desklamp to exploit
the nakedness of what's left unwritten.
It melts, snow and ice, under the heated fan of luminescence.

At the end of a rubber-riveted carpet,
I can wait to retrieve its fluvial conception.

XXV.

At the end of a rubber-riveted carpet,
I can wait to retrieve its fluvial conception,
the nectar sucked, the injected junk
of earliest thoughts and loves, little shocks
that served from the start as motives or instincts.
Holding on to the projections, I'll grab the gauzy curtain
of what may still happen until it tears like tears
running down the cheeks of orphans.

Only memories mark a day's difference
when I split them apart like a chicken breast
in the morning and convince myself to continue
along this wacky tangent, the dismembered evidence
of my loss of control—where legs move from prostrate
to upright, feet into slippers, torso pushed ahead
for possibility's sake, because it's not for me anymore—
what else could launch me, dinghy from dock,
out into peaked teal and the crying gulls of my orphaned dreams?
Tears of disappointment bead up, seaspray against my face.

Cruel the rechallenge to make something out of the question,
this plague-rebus of discarded images, not book-pressed
corsages of yellow belatedness, but enormities of pain
collapsed into places imperceptible as shrapnel.
That I'll be able to locate their origins
like a dream's driving wish, I trick myself into believing,
in order to get up again tomorrow.

XXVI.

Like a dream's driving wish
I trick myself into believing, in order to get up
again tomorrow, so too fools the dream held in life
that entices me forward with perennial carrot-stick image.

I alternately hate then cling to it,
hate because it won't let me go;
cling for more time with the people/things I love.

It tugs, jerky, imprecise through the white rapids
of disease crisis, each resolution ultimately temporary
'til it shatters within weeks with involute ingenuity.

I'm as far removed from the healthy body
as the pedestrian onlooker is from perfume advertising:
my gaze at the exotic, olfactory promise of sensory
fulfillment, just as brief and jaded.

Only the uncompassionate stars who blink and bob
like heads of Supreme Court justices ostensibly deliberating
their denial of your plea for clemency
perceive this infinity of torture, which is much stronger
than any argument for pleasure.

The great imbalance indefinitely offsets itself
by our burning need to rationalize existence,
distracted for decades are we by art or author
redefining the meaning of life—

why it's worth it this morning to try after failure,
to work in the world when skies deny a farmer water
and vaccines to infants in developing countries.

XXVII.

When skies deny a farmer water
and vaccines to infants in developing countries,
there is no reason better than this, than mine,
minute in comparison to those popular motives of country, family,
religion, pontificated by politicians and newscasters.

Reasons like mine live alone, reclusive, paranoid,
replaying favorite albums each evening hour,
night's snowy falling allowed to reclaim the room
with its granulated opacity.

It's these "Strangers in the Night" stages of darkness
with which I identify, their communion and confiding
similar in propinquity to those depictions of death
I viewed in Rothko 's final series at his Whitney retrospective.

The fifth protocol had just failed
and I was mostly bald from the madcap yet widely practiced attempt
to add chemo to the mix, so desperate was the drive
to make something work, but nothing did.

Nothing did, and that's what confronted me, what comforted me
in his paintings, that largesse of dark within dark,
present tense fiercely withheld, fist-tight as money, amidst future death,
too palpable in its precipice, its warble of mourning.

They made me cry abruptly in public, for someone understood
my shorn-head humiliation, this fundamental defeat
at mere living.

XXVIII.

Someone understood my shorn-head humiliation,
this fundamental defeat at mere living.

But that someone's only a configuration
of my need to communicate, the sometimes recognition
of a refracted ideal absorbed in stroke, syntax, or gesture,
of painting, poem, or film, just a hungry projection
no matter how enlivening the sensation, a touching
that never belonged to this world.

What belongs is this vacuum-sealed isolation,
watertight as an ocean buoy that contains the keen pain
of physical malady. Its silence turns on you,
police attack-dogs. It eats through your coat, then negligée.
Even when the teeth puncture your breast and hot breath
blows through you, how this longing burrows deeper within,

as if even beyond death it will continue to live,
unhappy ghost, phenomenon of unidentified noise
heard after midnight.

After all, it's after midnight that you grow
and connect with the unique contortions of its frigid brooding,
so like, so like you and all you are, more of the nothingness,
the white noise of snarl, a trilling aria
that forecloses finally this futility, a simpleton's
reduced perception of the future,

the effort to reclaim what you were born for
suspended outside the periphery of sated Amazons.

XXIX.

The effort to reclaim what you were born for
suspends itself outside the periphery of sated Amazons.

How we all need to think that what happens
matters regardless of outcome, though it doesn't.
Our struggles great and small do go unrecognized
for the most part, the impossible disappointment shared
by you only with yourself inside the walls of a flesh hutch
ultimately ephemeral.

Still, we lift up our faces, mutter stuff
regarding strength, courage, forgiveness, slightly
self-conscious of the lonely movement, the regressive desperation
forfeited in return for this ridiculous proposition—
already you know you'll suffer a predetermined vacancy,
your sad plea lost along with its precursors to eternity
within a chalky cloud maze.

You picture their heads frozen to death, uncovered
by fresh sun in the morning like Jack Nicholson's in *The Shining*.
What's left over, that exsiccative aftermath
which makes up a distal trajectory
so far from what you originally had in mind,
remains unfalteringly before you, like the unanswerable glare
of blank paper, that authority figure you could never master.

Yet under its squinting disapproval you learned.
Of something you've made and done and loved.
Despite this hateful lack, you overcome.

XXX.

Despite this hateful lack, you overcome,
but by default. You do not succeed, but sit up.

You wink at your stylish reflection in the window
with full knowledge of its plain-faced reality.

You do not give in, but you can't fight back, entirely.
You're better off today at great cost
but just breaking even with the norm.
You have no five-year plan, you have no children.

You're still, seventeen years later, thoroughly dependent
as a sucking, squirming infant on the uncanny brain synapses
of a socially problematic genius who can barely speak English
but from gristle and saliva was divined for medical research.

You imagine their lab coats clustered like white mice,
speaking in algorithms, hovered with goggles and gloves
over test tube and Petri dish. It's drug-experienced blood
like mine that their laser-like perceptions aim at
for the good of man. I revere them like swamis,
follow in karma their ideas, treatment du jour after trend,
obey rule and specification, trained dog for hotdog reward,
the way pilgrimage devotion holds the promise of spiritual salvation.

Such piety's referred to as "compliance" in this community.

Regardless, protocols have failed. What will humanize me
from faceless mammal? Catholicism is kinder.

XXXI.

What will humanize me from faceless mammal?

What will find me crouched awake late at night,
unable to beat it down, this cold suspicion,
this fundamental neglect?

My monotone cries deflect like traffic noise
off the semi-gloss sheen of white walls shined blind
by my bedside lamp, a flashlight waving for help on the highway.

And all that stares back is made of dead pavement,
its two lanes a diptych of necrotic sky.

Who will save me from the brushfire burning,
enveloped as I am by unnoticed instant,
unable to be traced like nitrogen?

Who will hear when only an echo
and the chain of free associations in its reverberation
intimidates with a glamorous chaos, 0 complexities of silence,
the refracted paths of regret and resilience, their many mutations?
I grow dizzy at the gateway.

We think what comfort could be lies in faith, in the soul-myth
as point of connection, as child of god.
But faith is reflexive: it outfoxes us, manipulates the mind,
preys on its fears in exchange for fraudulent reassurances.

What then after faith for the lost? Just flesh,
unreliable in its warmth, fickle in its tendernesses,
as fragile and sickly as you? Yet closeness
is what makes anything matter, ineffable or otherwise.

It's why we try.

XXXII.

Closeness is what makes anything matter,
ineffable or otherwise.

It's why we try, stretch taut
unto breaking, bridge-like into the beyond,
and though no one's there on the other side, we still search,
blinking, into the palmate dark, so pervasive the demand
for our loved one to materialize. Its impulse cuts
through the common sense of corpse palsy and blood drought.
Surely, if we miss them enough, they'll gravitate to the pull
like cloud swell to rain dance or responsive subject to hypnotist's spell.
Why else keep moving through the tar reek of midday
where life's average elements conspire with a persecutory objective,
and it's not neurosis taking over (sadly, it's not neurosis),
if not to be rejoined, by them found?

Only love as overwhelming can keep us earthbound,
bring us back from the netherworld at night to their breast,
provide with hairstroke and hush more reasons to stay than leave.

We can wish for and work toward that,
what's unforced, real, worthwhile,
squandered amongst the sugary accoutrements of an external world
spared from suffering.

What am I inside without?
Like a play within a play, our soliloquies are swallowed up
in the sarcophagus of their loneliness,
tongues of epileptics withheld from intervention.

XXXIII.

Like tongues of epileptics withheld from intervention,
interminably I'm untouched by what's available,
dependent upon the extraordinary, the miracle—
and kept there to languish in exile, hung from a branch
along ghost-town streets. I barely catch a glimpse of the winter sky,
gray mastaba from which I inhale a stone-cold breath.

How quiet the cruel recourses of the body—
the way it all flatlines after a while, health & illness,
life & death, happiness & depression—the routine of movement
is all that's left. Life becomes the homogenization
of morning, afternoon, evening, midnight; of youth,
prime, and aging; your concerns, fears, excitement, the same
just in different translation: the pills, the shots, the schedule,
the side effects, waiting rooms, doctors, the substitution
of food as medicine, sleep as medicine, everything turns into medicine
that maybe works then doesn't. Nothing's voluntary anymore,
not a bagel nor the hour of retirement.
There's no reason for it like parenthood—O yes, survival,
this postmodern AMA version of hunting and gathering.
Everything's forced.

The mind's mythical extension,
my soul folds back into its black bellows like an accordion,
then wheezes forth to play.

XXXIV.

My soul folds back into its black bellows
like an accordion, then wheezes forth to play.

My eyes fixate the way the eyes of the blind do
on an invisible entity just above the head,
somewhere in the distance yet close at hand,
a dimension we cannot reach although we know nothing's there.

No heaven from pain awaits us
but wait we will anyway, dogs behind iron gates,
pawing the ground and barking at clouds
in anticipation. We will go hungry from our dreams,
curled up on the street in the cold, rocking this cage
of a body that won't break or shake apart
despite its abandoned interior. Where do I belong?

Illness both stunts and time-lapses growth,
a hybrid of child and senior I've become,
my prime wrested asunder as if drawn and quartered.
Who will look at me with full recognition of what's been lost?
All gods are subpar in such circumstances.
My sobs evacuate in the sadistic silence.

You don't need children to fight, or peace of mind
in not having children to decide to stop,
if it be the purest argument for euthanasia:
not bitterness, or anger, or even resignation,
but acknowledgment of the segregation between you and life.

There's no lesson, moral, or resolution when I lean
into the concave space of crushed morrows.

XXXV.

When I lean into the concave space of crushed morrows,
there will be no crossing over
the line to take me back this time like the last,
caught up as prey en route to hiding by
the swooping grasp of an eagle's claw while I bit
at the knuckle and kicked in mid-air.

The undertow of discovery and experiment was too strong to tackle,
of moral expectation to keep trying for others.

This time the DNR will be executed
and I'll step comfortably into my silhouette.
This time I won't be seduced by second chances,
that impressive gravity reversal of natural progression
that wind-tunneled and time-warped
my return from graveside to sickbed,
coaxed me with soft words uttering lore of the future
like flute-playing off the ledge.

This time I won't succumb
to what's known as the Lazarus Effect.

Either you end it or you take it further,
but that doesn't mean it gets better.
It means only that you wait longer,
conscious of the containment of your brain
in your head, a fetus in formaldehyde.

Familiar landscapes, loved ones, & everyday objects
become Rorschach-like.

You wince from the glare of interpreted loss.

The black moths mar your perception as if bloodstained cloth.

Your body, perpetually end-stage,
arches in fallow triumph.

The Legend

Death be not proud,
you stand alone, just a man, all shoulders and brows
beneath the cloud-webbed moon, a wound wrapped in gauze,
suspended like some mummified specimen exhumed
or head of a burn victim whose one working eye
watches your every move. The leash of his aching gaze
overextends on the verge of snapping,
the way my body breaks down in degrees of disease progression,
crumbles as if created from sand and dirt, that essential substance
which eventually lies flat as a grave plot in front of you.
But credit not my demise to your sage-spotted hands,
your brainy expertise, mostly myth and thrill of unproved hypothesis.

though some have called thee mighty and dreadful,
I have the strange privilege to know better.
Once, twice, three times we've met like old enemies and exchanged
the frigid certainty that someday ahead we'll meet
again in a surreal rendezvous. We sense out the other with sniff
and cocked ear across a room, vacant save for the vicissitudes
of the solar route and the sad breathing we share, shallow
like staccato strings in the inconsequential street or bar
where subsequently we screw. Like any desperate two
we're turned on by the equity of mutual loss,
that low level we've let ourselves dive into.
For now smoke and beer, bad country juke, and graffitied wood
paradoxically make us feel special, wanted with a speedball
concentration, the pure stuff cut with baby formula.
But whatever feels good, good enough,
spurs us to spill what was once real passion,
its kaleidoscope assimilation feigning the muscular spasm
of waves, the twisting of leaf-like limbs, wind-blown and sweaty
with rain, almost as if . . . in the basement of our shut minds,
we each strain to perceive *that face* again, the one we loved.
Gleaming, our green cat eyes cast a verdigris glow to their nose
and cheekbones, the beloved who redeemed your life as equally beloved.
Its piecemeal desecration brings us here.
The pain of want and being wanted by what's left over

results in unsatisfying climax only.
Not loved are we by each other, nor liked,
not and never,
for thou are not so.

For those whom thou think'st thou dost overthrow
—the sick, the elderly, the disabled; the infant, the innocent,
the inconceivable tragedies we digest like mincemeat via HBO;
the POWs and the imperceptibly lonely, the vital tennis players,
the diva stage actresses, the abhorred CEOs—
die not, not yet, not soon, do not give in

poor Death, as helpless as we
are you without us
standing alone, just a man, a man sick, a man lonely
waiting for two hours on that worn sofa
in the doctor's waiting room

nor yet—not yet, not soon—
canst thou—I do not, will not—
kill me—give in to your love for killing.

From rest and sleep, which but thy pictures be,
much pleasure; how intense the soothing, the release
of those dreams I barely see before me in a blur of melancholy
like bluebirds nonsensical on a sunless February afternoon.
Hallucinations of freedom made concrete by morphine, fly,
happy bats of pitch and 4 a.m. darkness, into my neck, my all-pupil eyes,
and bygone breasts of womanliness, a pile of kindling
sticks upon this secluded raft of bedding and I.V. lines
intricate as a narghile from which my body inhales false life.

How acute the wicked drip to which I listen
and with which I rock my agony away
into a lake-lapping lack of cognition.
Far gone am I from my donkey flesh, pulled by rope bridle
and frothy bit, from bloody belly nicks, fur and ribs,

incurred by those mandatory spur kicks,
the tyrannical manifestations of healthy impetus.

Let such night, such
paradiso asystole fill me up with a pill-potion
bitter and final. Fill me up with your death ecstasy, greater
than secular accoutrements typically cherished:
drink, food, or lovemaking in marriage.

then from thee much more must flow,
like milk cartons and empty Styrofoam cups
in the overwhelmed gutter when it rains, sharp and polluted,
tears of departure. We imagine in response to our fits
of injustice, gods weeping with regret and shame
for the configurations of fate they've force-fed us.
But do they too rub their foreheads
with feelings of powerlessness, experience parasympathetically
like us these untimely circumstances
as if tied to a universal clock, mercilessly inanimate?
That little hand, its sweeping seconds, the curt demonstration
of those secrets, those reasons why
we were meant to be born blind but acutely sensitive
to how faint the din, eerily repetitive, of pennies
on the modern equivalent of beggar's nickel, a homeless person's
cardboard cup that reads "It's a Pleasure to Serve You."
It's the same sound of life overflowing with milk and emptiness.

After efforts to communicate, to rationalize, barter,
talk sense into twilight, its stubborn menu of aggregated darkness,
we kneel defeated by our limits, a muddy knell within; that threshold
of self-control, just a stick-drawn line in the dirt.
There we pay homage, finally negotiating with terrorists,
to reason beyond our control—
by resigning ourselves to the befuddlement,
the dizzy, invisible taste of it,
the idiotic sublimation of you, Death.

and soonest our best men with thee do go, like firefighters,
like airplane pilots, like a flight attendant who smiles routinely

with her slit throat bleeding as she offers more coffee
and requests politely for seats to return to their upright positions.
Her face, offset by the ghastly pallor of resurrection
as if a flashlight were held under her chin, spirals chimerically.
Her garish features beam, a full moon foreboding stark incidence.

How the stories coursed like MRI dye through the brain:
of charred skeletons huddled together in fear and community
on the Concourse floor below the towers as backdraft fires
torrefied Commuter Cafe, Perfumeria Milano, and Sbarro Pizza.
What they saw coming.

Wafts of burning flesh seep still in genie-like puffs.
Voices and facial features suddenly formulate then disappear
as if drowning anew into what's left: that which hangs unrippled,
impartial as an object, coffee cup to be fondled or not, a thick, viscous
light we must push against headfirst, stooped in plow posture.

We push against the phone messages, beknownst and unbeknownst
last testaments from men and women who jumped through desk-chair
shattered glass during breakfast meetings at Windows on the World.
We push against their pictures on T-shirts, on picketing posters,
the yearbook details: loved animals, would have helped others,
hardworking waiter, father of three, fiancé, expectant mother.
We even push against the newscasters who finally broke down,
allowing reality to catch up with the viewer.

Flyers pasted to the armory, St. Vincent's, NYU/Mount Sinai—
souls trapped in intimate snapshots press themselves against
their protective plastic covering with exhalant force,
suspended indefinitely from burial thus, like unclaimed bodies
refrigerated in the morgue, or those few on view in a public wake,
greats like Lenin and de Gaulle,

rest of their bones and soul's delivery.
Our best men, at least twenty I knew of personally, and our best women
and children, gay or straight, died from AIDS, more people
than soldiers in the Vietnam and Korean wars combined
(it behooves me to restate, and will again so no memory fades)

from the barbarism, the "evildoing" of an impotent government.
So brainwashed by the media are we today, turkey-stuffed
with reassurances of current drugs and pipeline hopefuls,
and Andrew Sullivan with his End of AIDS proclamations,
that no attention's paid to the seriousness of drug resistance
and its rapid development as well as the unlikelihood
of developing more new drugs.

Was I supposed to supply a metaphor, beautify the language,
make pretty the fact that the USA's increasing HIV population
consists primarily of inner-city teenage girls?
What linguistic twirls would you prefer about their woes,
how peer pressure drives them to skip their meds,
or how much harder it is for them to comprehend geometry proofs
when combating those nasty Norvir side effects?

No Yankee Stadium tribute saluted those citizens.
Patriotism turned its patrician cheek away,
ignored their heroism. No appearance of the mayor,
nor did Mariah Carey perform.
And George W., who threw the first ball
in defiant tribute, honoring the American Everyman
before a backdrop of televised tears and frantic flag-waving,
where was he when his dad said nothing about the plague?
Did his father urge the Old Gipper to say it, to warn the country
of the disease that's now dramatically reducing world population?
He could not say it. He would not say the word "AIDS."
If he had, half my friends might be alive.

Did they argue? I want to know! Did they fight bitterly,
Reagan and Bush, son and father?
Were there words, risks of estrangement?
Did chests swell and sting with principled emotions?
No, I will not forgive them.
They should be forced to build the children's coffins
in Botswana, Bangkok, Ukraine, and Buenos Aires,
the number of which has now redoubled.

Thou'art slave to fate, from no higher power do you come
or independent source, no cracks in the heavens

through which caitiff eyes peep to keep track of our actions,
spy on our mishaps, betrayals, or just lazy, vindictive thoughts,
evidence gathered for subsequent judgment,
gaunt-jawed and gable-happy as if another kind of God.
How many prayers you must intercept as they proliferate
from contorted mouths, fissile as fallen leaves,
in their gravity-defying journey up.
You devour with closed-lipped smile, like counter-fan mail,
descriptions of how potent and manly the swipe
of your Chinese tiger claw. Your reputation stands
as someone always hungry, wildly indiscriminate like natural disaster
in what you choose for momentary satisfaction. You gloat
at the inference of screen-star persuasion in your capacity to seduce
the suicide-prone into velvety lappets of false peace.
O the garlic necklaces and rabbit's feet, the bevy of ritualistic superstitions,
fantastic contraptions to stave off
the tools of interrogation you wield over their crying.
With vampire fangs and Father Time's beard, you fulfill
all the lofty requirements for our concept of evil
as you ride the Death Card's black horse
through kicked ember and straw-roof collapse
of bubonic-stricken village burning against mimetic sunset.

If only they knew as I do, watched you feed upon *chance, kings
and desperate men*, like wild ponies off a paucity
of midwinter grass. Educed as in an x-ray,
you're like my shadow, an oxygen tent
where from interlunar nothingness I breathe in and out,
and dost with poison, Percocet, morphine, *war*, Vietnam, Somalia
and sickness cancer, AIDS, heart disease *dwell*,
a fraternal twin from whose memory I wake with nightsweats,
dream remnants in which fractured symbols and visions
appear as prescient of a union soon to follow.

Parasite to that which thrives, and crushable as I am ill
I depend on these drugs for life, but you depend on them as well.
Hidden in my frontal lobes, the lymph nodes of my groin,
you wait poised for covert operation, reinforcements received
from a bloodstream which shares in your end-goal.

But when I imagine the aftermath of their imminent failing
you have no blackened teeth or Goliath-like stature,
all I see is a compassionate face—
and though *poppy'or charms can make us sleep as well*
and better than thy stroke; I will choose your friendship
when the drugs stop working. You will never seize me.
I refuse to say you beat me.
No fight will be ours in Zaire like Ali and Foreman.

why swell'st thou then?
as if punishment, as if message?
I've seen through your bravado,
your doves produced from interior sleeve machinations,
your impressive history compounded from simple darknesses.

One short sleep past, we wake eternally—
mortised in the *petit mort* of postcoital consumption
or storybook comfort of parent and child.
I used to wonder in whose disguise you would come . . .
As female friend who died of breast cancer?
Will you arrive single-breasted, crippling tumor
ventricose in your arm for which hospice care
denied palliative treatment?
Or will you step tentatively toward me
in the form of my father, bent over the steering wheel
in cardiac arrest where the ambulance
finally found him, his breathing so shallow?
Will you hold me then, Daddy, the way you used to?
Although this time it will be with I.V. catheters
stuck in your hands from the efforts of paramedics
and doctors to revive you; the way I viewed you
refrigerated in the funeral garage
and apologized to inanimacy for whatever reason.

There is no message in you, death,
you have nothing to say
when you reach with largo stride from exiled forest,
strong-limbed and hushed as the lave of pine
beneath divested branches

and lead me further away from where,
within the hermetically sealed consciousness
of medical vigilance, I've been already removed,
the way lepers were sequestered outside city walls.

I place my hand with olfactory familiarity upon your shoulder,
as the blind do when they follow each other in shrouded exodus.

Resubmerged into underwater concrescence of cellular beginning
I'll return to a riveted essence that's love absolute
despite bodily dissolution and without worship
of winged endings.

and death like my father *shall be no more, death* like me,
my facial index, in its final measuring, gone gray
as your tin repoussé reflection, excoriated amid an ocean
cold as chrome, or dispassionate continent
where within parched clay and thistle-pyre *thou shalt die.*

John Donne, "Holy Sonnets #10,"
The Norton Anthology of Poetry
(New York: Norton, 1975)

Birth of a Masochist

This host that burns within me, out of which I was born to burn
like psalms openfaced upon the feverish Christian Scientist's forehead,
like a speculum that investigates the presence of the host itself,
a communion wafer which refuses to dissolve inside the atheist's mouth
until I outlast the body like an IUD, copper coil discovered in a sifting pan,
an artifact of mistakes never made, a pastiche of the defunct love-child.

This host that burns within me, out of which I was born to burn
admits me to the charred aftermath of an arson's massacre wherein I confess
I am the arsonist, my orange tongue dismembered from my skull deranged
with absence, with the absence of fire as substitution for the home,
until a lack of substitution becomes the substitutive home
and deprivation the equivalent of the first bed: the womb.

This host that burns within me, out of which I was born to burn
writhes and wrangles like my mating parents, an allegorical ménage
of vice and virtue, a successful sadomasochistic relationship,
successful in that it's lasted beyond the atrophied phallus, the
cavernous cunt that after birthing several litters lies lethiferous
in its mindset, wrung out by a history of having drowned the kittens,
the crime sheet, an egg-crate mattress pad undulating under the pubic hair.

This host that burns within me, out of which I was born to burn
out of polar opposites like the evolution of two continents
plants the cotton seed of my crooked future to set its path
like a serial killer, the rodent fetus destined for abortion
until the monarchy of the clouds as representative of inexplicable phenomena
shifted in configuration during a session of lovemaking torture
and focused in on my mother's uterus not unlike a fascist officer
who targets the neighboring villages before usurpation of the capital.
How oft I've felt this force zero in on the bleeding knees of my capitulation.

This host that burns within me, out of which I was born to burn
a freak of nature, spawned godless and born of shit where back into shit
I continue to be redelivered into the world like a prayer poem tied to a twig
a sponger for the negative feng shui of the bedroom where I was conceived
goldfish floating on the surface of a fishtank, a thoroughly modern Ophelia

rafting naked and dead and wreathed with flora unidentified down the river—
I wake and crescent in the hydrodynamics of restitution and refusal,
of humiliation and relief, the seasonless swimmer who gladly risks
her drowning in the familial definition of familial: beloved lacerations.

This host that burns within me, out of which I was born to burn
until my ribcage foregrounds itself like the modern wing at the Met
until my skeletal structure stands a kind of primavera wasteland
until out of ash I transmit by example the eternal placidity of Lake Como
until out of the evolution of two continents a chasm wells up, a slit artery,
with restitution providing an oceanic mechanism like a tape of the sea
for prenatal cognition like primal scream therapy or Munch's *The Scream*
where relief begets relief in the silence of identification.

Broken Consciousness

The askance ocean darkens, anachronistically, and I admire its solidarity,
its whitecapped disparity like the clouds that frequent the sky,
offsetting the tethered soil, the belovedness of what appears a handswept field.
I operate within a similar lexicon as desolate in inscription,
identifying with disparity *per se*, i.e., sky, field, or ocean.
What I wish could hold me in a way I've only imagined
and experienced in the ubiquity of constancy offsetting fragmentation,
witnessed ad infinitum in the demonstration of a glass dropped and its shattering.
My mother, armless and decapitated, flies stationarily
at the top of a tiered flight, away from me, my continent sense of externality,
winged and victorious, perpetuates her ability to give
belatedly, a product of consequence, contrived
as truth or whitecaps, my disparity.
What arrives D.O.A., a newt delivered by Mercury, nebulous as a sentiment,
parsimonious as a net that retains nil, I lunge forward anyway
and in such an empty gesture mark at least a gesture
the way a soliloquy must always locate itself in some vernacular.
Similarly, my longing replenishes itself within the canon of my longing,
though not solipsistically, for longing by its nature makes up a disparity
between evidence and expectation that provides for my starving
a kind of feeding, a food forever deferred like virtual reality.
The closest I've ever come to closeness is waiting
strung out as if suspended amidst the air into which her corpse has been flung
thus into marble and therefore into nothing.
Her would-be loving embrace fetters, her alabaster lips
chiseled in perfect partition almost smile, and I reciprocate
with social reflex as an infant first mirrors the mother's face,
before cognition culturally fans out into recognizance,
before response moves beyond the automatic like a Roman calendar
into genuine remorse, into what love connotes
before it gnaws away at the stomach.

The Window

I was born, at the age of fourteen, in a small room. The room was extremely narrow and dark, its wood-paneled walls of fake mahogany had a way of closing in just in being themselves.

There was no furniture in the room, just a narrow cot, poorly sprung and too old to be of use since it sagged considerably in the middle. I remember that the blanket on it was green, a warm forest green, perhaps a shade lighter, though, than a forest. It was nubby and warm and soft and added color to the room and with that color a kind of kindness that altered in degree according to the intensity of light that was shed upon it through the window—the extraordinary window.

The window, the only window in the room, was enormous and expanded across almost the entire length of the west wall. The window made the room a room, as they say, a room that it wouldn't be cruel to put a person in if you emphasized the attribute of the window, that is. It was a bay window, shallow in depth with no window seat, that curved out and carved a space outside the room, that indicated, though it was shallow, the depth of its view, the depth of the world outside the room.

Of course, it was the view from the window that made the window exceptional, although, I suppose, in retrospect the view was not exceptional but ordinary yet beautiful like the window itself, if you know what I mean, that the beauty of the window depended upon its view and the beauty of the view depended upon the window. The view, as I best remember it, was always of early autumn. There was a mountain range, leveled and distant, with a jagged horizon of trees, lush and profuse in their foliage, orange and red and green. The grass was just beginning to yellow, and the sky, of which there was so much, was clear and practically cloudless. In its clarity the sky felt friendly and even wise. You could say I looked up to the sky and not just literally. I knew that if I concentrated on the window I could live in the room until it was time to leave it, survive in the room if I concentrated on the window and its view.

So I came to be good friends with the window. I would sit on the cot facing the window and talk to the window and look to it for counsel and give counsel in return, which naturally was never necessary but I was ready and willing all the same to be as good a friend to the window as the window was to me. The window was always there for me to confess to, to cry in front of, to express my confusions, my despair, my exasperation at having to live in the room one day longer, which sometimes I didn't think I could do; I would lose hope that there would ever be anything beyond the room, and in the moments of silence when I had nothing else to say and just lapsed into staring, though not blankly, at the window, I could hear the window and I would listen and the window would say:

"Be like a window, live like a window, have perspective like a window, try to accept like a window, hope like a window, write like a window, love unconditionally even the smallest thing like a window, breathe deeply like a window, sleep peacefully like a window, endure like a window, show compassion like a window, remain vulnerable like a window, be ambitious like a window, respectful like a window, able to face the world like a window, be honest like a window, prove nothing like a window, share everything like a window, show promise like a window, live humbly like a window, be pure in intention like a window, courageous like a window, adoring like a window, be merciful like a window."

Lamentation for My Right Eye

for Stanley Chung, M.D., & Adrienne Rich

I wake and feel the fell of dark, not day.
Long night, with your velvet pansies,
a gored sun's dying bray,
you blind me, you tighten the fold,
fist-like knot rubbing bald into my brain.
I grasp, as if gulping air, chilly walls
of a room I can't recall. No paintings,
no light switches to provide a clue.
I bite into my knuckles for proof, feign comfort
from dreaded spiral deepening further,
pitted crater beyond ember clay dismembered
where no bedrock waits as anchor
or core or center.

What hours, what hourlessness, amorphous stain of fluids
unnatural, spilling out of cinder ray its anorexic light.
Skeletal shapes, caustic, resentful, linger within larger
shadows like the latent viral strains we all carry—
poised to seize and devour.
             O what black hours we have spent,
in effort to decipher the familiar from tunneling hole,
haul up in buckets what wood warp's evaporated.
Our pupils dilate from the delirium of starving until
the hours collapse as they transition into oblivion,
where noise suddenly ignites in the pitch,
pinched and reprimanding.
All that's left, that's to be done is to listen. Listen! to the lisp,
a Celtic rasp, foretelling events, mere suggestions of which
flay, whip-like tongues against your bare skin, ribcage
protruding out of protective hunch. The grainy minutes
of pain accumulate and compress into the obliteration of time,
until the strap that slaps with hot breath its grimy coax
convinces you as unworthy of the window's burst:
lilac, yeoman, and infants. *This night!* Wound tight
like dunk ropes that bind me, ankles and wrists,
into a bone for Mercy—not much meat left.

what sights, you, heart, saw; of hiss and spur, the razor wire
of its tedium. And within as if held to the breast,
ways you went! If only feeding itself could break loose
this loneliness, a dwarfed hope, daunting and corpsecold,
that was there from first memory on,
wide-awake and suckling.

What images, you, eyes, loved, plucked out in order to forget,
not by red pokers but by daylight's slow erasure, the world
swallowed up by a centrifugal bleeding that stems from
membrane tears of your interior drive finally rupturing.
Greedily it eats its way to the edge,
this macular degeneration of the soul
where desires drain like verjuice into the earthen night,
worm-swollen and star-stung.

What sounds, you, ears, are forced to absorb, louder
with each resonance, the repetitions of hell.
They sink like gravel into impending mind-rot,
the mud of dementia, the way liquid soap swirls
into a dish-filled sink, gravel-blind with grease:
today's gaunt-cheeked identity juxtaposed upon what
once was, like a double exposure or dust cloud of flies
swarming above gutted fur.

And more must, in yet longer light's delay.——
like dug graves and their bespeckled mounds of dirt
that lie inert, coupled as if long married
beneath dawn's communion veil.

      With witness I speak this. But where I say
Hours I mean years, mean life.
Longest night of my life, you have become my life,
while everything else has become life's abstraction, including
me, its amputee, torso floating void of what's human
as if transfused by embalming liquid
or spotlit as exemplary likeness of anatomy fragment.
Like the precious remains of a dog tag and two limbs,
arm & leg, of another casualty sent home as if whole

in a casket scaled to grown man or woman——
tantamount to what wolves walk away from,
their bellies warm and full of flesh—
I no longer live but remit like archival evidence.

And my lament, for roses, pregnancy, and wing-clapping
migration *Is cries countless*, as extreme in tenor
as these slaughterhouse poems, macaw screams
that infiltrate the jungle, that humid density of my future——
days drive ahead, indifferent to each other, industrious
in their gluttony as the steel stomachs of gulls;
or a recording of chain-gang ballads I heard once, each song
a requiem for the suffering expressed on the previous track,
the many ways of suffering indistinguishable and unnamed,
rooted in their throats' laboring through
thick hours, dusk dunes; their vocal cords necromantic
venues for death's croon and incomprehensibility.

      cries like dead letters sent, the blurry words perceived
through saline-filled eyeballs and hair-pull——
like raindrops on lakewater, they amount to nothing——
To dearest him that lives alas! away.
surface pings and circumferential rings round out while
below mindless depth sleeps, steady chest heave, undisturbed.

      I am gall, I am heartburn.
I almost never cry anymore. The sadness,
full-term, has sunk with silent thud
like a blue baby to the ocean's floor. No momentum is left
either way, no choice. My dry-heave cries no longer emit
tears *God's most deep decree* so that of pity spit
Bitter would have me taste: of pity spit, *my taste was me;*
licked clean like an animal, isolated and chastened.

Bones built in me, flesh filled, blood brimmed the curse.
I drag your heavy coat like a bearskin
through rooms and streets I cannot see.
The heat of the sun always scares me at first.

Selfyeast of spirit a dull dough sours. I open
my mouth, palms, heart, but only an emptiness, hollow
as institution hallways after hours, follows, the meandering
paths and stale ammonia smell known by rote.
Show me the door out. *I see The lost are like this,*
condemned to an exodus that reaches no homeland.
We wander in perpetual flee.
We mourn within our collective unconscious
for the nourishment of stopping—*and their scourge to be*

As I am mine, defaced bust broken irreparably—
the former likenesses of Mahler or Schubert,
mounted, like the decapitated heads of traitors
on Old London Bridge, along public park promenades,
deliquesce into more graffitied rubble—their marble eyes,
webbed over as if with cataracts, dimensionless
in their stare from the beyond
the way the dead stop and look back at us before they pass
over with a glance both foreboding and wistful.
We investigate the horizon for a long time after.

As I am mine, my black lips petrified in kilned cry,
my agony silenced as if never having existed;
I push it forward, unkillable determiner,
the sound that will outlive its mother,
birthed calf of a dumb tomorrow, organs intact.

As I am mine: slug-gray as a tumor, an entry beast
that besieges the morn. I howl, an epidemic of baleful moans,
but the leaves, unstirred, adore the sky and refuse
to give off either shade or dew to the beauty-starved,

who point to their mouths to convey hunger,
who point to your hand for food
their sweating selves, emaciated and confused.
They await like turtleheads retracted, sun-allergic,
beneath the moth-masked moon, God's voice-piece,
taciturn and cruel—
the tragedy of promise tangled at their feet
like the hair of the drowned—

As I am mine,
moon mimic, moon-negative,
bloodshot eyes blinking postmortem
when the hood sack reveals what's freshly hung
from the gallows: a souvenir of butchered conquest,
of my landfill-doomed devotion
but worse.

Gerard Manley Hopkins, "Poem #44,"
Poems and Prose, ed. WH. Gardner
(New York: Penguin Books, 1975)

Odes to Delayed Gratification

a.) furious retraction of a prayer

for you, lost pine, Atlantic air, I told the island exactly where, I spoke
but no response rescued me there on the rock, path-end, an hour's walk into
lookout excess of nature rich like aristocracy of wig, cake, harp, silk-clad
servant, orgy of excess, green and blue, immovable clarity, for bits, just a
morsel of natural bounty—but cold mother like my own are you, narcissistic
wood and salt, no pleading ever does for her now you too, monstrous health,

health to spare, minerals, rainwater, your cycles calculated machinery, a
callous factory refuses, then forgives no one, and I stupid, ransacked of
hope. Only our opposable thumbs distinguish us lonely dogs from apes,
we believe from one bone tenfold returns, indication only of how deep, core-
through disappointment stares into dirt juicy with groundswell's wet grass,
your brown eyes angry with rejection since my beginning rooted inside.

Aloof, Amazon-alive, indifferent to my patched eye, my I.V, my cane, this
survival despite you. You did not care—you do not care, from your bigoted
blue skies, your milk-and-honey sunsets, I learned not to expect. I learned
the hard way as if handcuffed, from the stark cabin out back where blues
originated—I learned anyway to keep sucking leaves out of revenge, while
acquiescing to the rotund belly, frigid womb of my burial ground, holy ocean

whose icy whitecaps like arrowheads impale my aqueous body, another soulless
transparency. I learned to look forward to it like a lookout view, maintain
hold of its vision, to balance desire and abandoned desire, expect nothing,
accept everything, expect nothing but from myself the will to fight
this fundamental feud against disappearance. I spit into my shadow, just a
stick figure to you, onto your mother tits distended with immortal milk.

Overrated your reputation, regal mountain range, I never experienced the
awe, too self-absorbed with reflection in still lake, clear sky I thought.
And some of us as if punished, which is most of us, suspended interminably
from gentle touch, the manna you hoard. Their open mouths but sores, blue
hollows of disease and war, yet diminished faces pray for elliptic bloom
from monuments of impoverishment that remain recalcitrant to foolish praises.

I say I'm not afraid for what you can still do to me you've already done—
my sickness born from chilly interior by you reclaimed as if inherited, eaten
amidst knife-precise waves—but that which is mine, buried like an infant's
coffin deeper than disappointment, than its reverberating pain, remains lost
to your hungry horizon, withheld like breast milk, comparable breast milk of
my love, well spent, spent all, by path-end reached to which I look forward.

b.) death rapprochement

returning to me early spring, my late winter, the infinitude of a colossus
withers, hopeful trajectory reduced to a breve, miniature pleading
without lachrymal accompaniment, this pre-sleep acceptance of dark blankness
and its hard-won bereavement, a fundamental breakdown at core of mine being
small in contrast to everything, to snow on daffodils or my praise of them

sick tree girded to the ground we discover in downtime evening stroll
barely decipher between wires and branches elaborate effort at forced
blossom, now bare fortitude—identity with the lush and wan of sad might
returning to me too, like you, tree, despite operose drive, despite coo-like
prayer-like dreams otherwise, the signification of try and love, I try hard

which poem which sentence it doesn't matter as long as I type a letter,
lifelong shapes, old friends, become an assemblage of want, of reconstituted
desire, until to anabatic heights I'm brought to climax deeper than some
adolescent shudder plight, this tiny soul moving inside like fetal stir
echoes larger than any, than all—How close to threshold of pain reduced it

comes but never null this cruel pulse, what feeling good was once, first thing
last thought, my mourning. I ask forgiveness for my survivor ambivalence, though
the fear hush of imminence, of returning to me early, I say, I believe, I fear
not the belt-strap bite of sky pictures and conch-shell conjuring of ocean sigh
focus into uniform white, compassionate surrender suspended above just flesh

I recognize in the lilac branches where my death should land and take me
quickly, long last, in ordinary gasp, but where breaks my chance for a natural
end amidst this? So many medications girding me like my sick tree to public
soil, to cultural life, and the domination of heart's need, bending forward
like bedridden reach, its wish-upon-a-star wish to be more than that, ignored

law of medicine like law of ethics imposed upon us to organize unfairness,
the division of church and state keeps clear which way we see it—yet how to
designate wire from wood in edulcorated concoction that keeps me here, forced
to blossom, failing to blossom, the flower-hope science bears shared no longer
for I, bare fortitude where birds alight petal-like, refuse to say it's life

c.) wilderness

what can, why does, who hears, must I, I must, but I do not want
not so silent cry, stolen cry, ignored cry, pierce flesh, busy passersby
mercury tears at thermometer's tip, snap the glass, scrape with broken
fingernails more than just atmosphere this once, only once I ask

of an 800 prayerline, of secret feedback mysteries, those brain crevices
untapped, curvaceous, fertile beliefs like frosted-over bulbs come March
what color, tulip or hyacinth, I'm trying to imagine, imagine more than dirt
rise over, rise over this bent head, flogged forward, but no more than dirt

rises like rising kite, a cruel spirit I try to imagine some crescent sky,
this feathery dome but you turn away, chiseled cheek, embittered sundown,
and I can't, I do not want anymore the illusory anymore yet I ask anyway
it's no longer a choice, my imagination, a bygone impulse, I hate its path

yet I ask anyway, hint, whisper, plead with penciled grimace, short breaths,
steeple eyebrows, black church against mauve night, mauve hawk, I ask from
what, from why, why does the belltower fail me? See how it relishes its
failing? How stick-still the belltower rope hangs in ineffectual evening?

These cries, absorbed too quickly by clouds, heard in transit then uttered
not, these ignored cries, these questions flat-out breaking, snapped glass,
separate tears of mercury self-contained, roll away, further outside my aching
the edible, the tangible I must, must I?—Again imagine? The only respite

from dirt, from interchangeable fields and streets, from loathsome journey
I hate its path, tormenting cul-de-sac, what's effectual is the only knowing
I know nothing for what effects, fervent conviction of prayer, passerby with
carousel of worry, diehard tulip's ironic bloom, rolls outside my aching

d.) death hiatus

strict slap held-out hand—quicken retraction or else slap harder
truncated want not desire, not longing, pea-sized peacetime emotives
truncated want, abort, abate, behave, obey until self-sterilizing, yes

dark hallway darker, my hallway, my darkness, darker yet make blacker black
by adding tinge, cigarette ash, demarcate, trace the no longer in nothing
like break in bone breaking originate what internal brokenness now speaks

alone, alone, wind voice bifurcated between graves and grasses spoken
soft as dirt submerged in massive memory collapse, memory fire, memory fugue
truncated listenings caught off-guard from where I've been thrown far-flung

what was what was what only the moon, blowing cold blue, understood not now
but once where I stood underneath a darkness, my darkness, a subversive night
in itself, unto itself now no longer understood as I strain in night proper

for the trace of no longer, the tinge, like a needle prick prick me I ask
of nothing, brutal nothing all that suffering where did it go? Into brutality
with its camouflage of sweet-smelling air—no longer, what was, prick me

all that suffering would be better than this cold moon, this perverse way
station between graves and grasses as history expands despite memory fire
expands without me, without voice or memory fugue to subvert sweet air brutal

e.) nightsweats

from the Easter blue of reissued spring previous where withal perishes
within this cherry-blossom interstice, a mad fusion without differentiation

dilated minute myopic its inspection of body stretched upon medieval rack
tendon tear and futile scream in face of immanence matchpoint at every moment

what all this fighting is for crashes like a hard drive dives into purgatory
of fallen information, loose-leaf memoir burns in accord with spoken instant

I watch the fey fanfare as Dirk Bogarde did blond Tadzio in *Death in Venice.*
It's the fatigue, makeup melting in sun streak, not lost youth or eroticism

I identify with, ancient desires devoured as if amidst applauding coliseum
recessional hymn subsists in silent gray of few cells overwhelmed by symptoms

once in everything phantasmagorical hope swallowed up in process of evolution
my airtight universe opened long ago then closed with cold-blooded precision.

f.) inexplicable drive

why wake from inert blankness where ending sooner entwines us? Betwixt I lie

analysand of revised motives, cloud slave, abject, hungry 'til nil appetite

from shatter exhumes broken still broken but crazy pull speaks over drum

reasonless of movement meaning yet spine tall before sun beat forced swallow

or dropcloth waste to stagger drown. Stripped chance, sole impediment, I

burn through bleak instant, bursting reflex, no specious curiosity this reborn

Time on Fire

in memory of Robert Farber

Again I drive my pencil point as if to make unlined paper bleed,
drawing out of its naïve and lily-like dimensions
the history of its pulp, the history of its leaves.
By virtue of this reconstruction, both minute and grandiose,
I seek out as an end to its means some kind of absolution.

Like a torched village, small and undistinguished,
from whose burning boundaries spirals of smoke urge upward
like the chanting of hungry mouths, of mourning mothers,
in order to warn of plague; the urge to witness
urges upward the way vertebrae of the moribund arch
in their final stages of rigor mortis.
The stench of incinerated hair and melted-down personal effects
infiltrates the air, intermixed with spark and ash,
until the chant and the wind become inseparable, imperceptible.
It whistles in our ears like screaming in the distance.
We listen, cringing, helpless until oblivious,
until simply seasonal weather outside our windows instead we hear.
Out of instinct to survive,
the brutalities of war, disease, and deprivation
mutate into weaker renditions of themselves,
shapes we can recognize then put aside:
a photography exhibition that catalogues the plague into "event,"
or a memoir of the plague, ten years ago its publication date.
There have already been too many of these memory prods,
efforts to manufacture the unimaginable,
to protest against the communal mitigation of nightmare—
and all losing money due to the gruesome thematic and macabre overtone.
Later, they're dumbed-down to melodramas on "Television for Women."

Although my life mimics, even mocks itself
in the rapid progression of its illness,
the way society mocks the plague in the rapid progression of its forgetfulness,
again I drive my pencil point, like the countless needles
with which I've been forced to puncture my skin,
allowing "access," in medspeak, to my veins and hence my interior world.

In order to appropriate conscious thought from unconscious tableaux,
the letters falter like some demented love-letter composed
by a mutilated ego. My negotiation with my past,
invisibly inscribed upon its remnants, those frail moments
which hope to foster some concept of future, operates like a mode
of surveillance that denotes my life into a prototype of itself:
my body demystified in the autopsy light
of its anticipated corpse, factual skull void of gray matter
extracted from facial flesh as if exhumed
or resurrected by the rubber hand of a transplant surgeon,
denatured, sepia heart inserted into another's
for the good of all, not the individual, before assigned
to the homey boneyard that will be the signified of me after.

I touch the paper delicately, tentatively, as I do my naked body
in the mirror, the joy of initial regard and study,
its deft innocence, a baby that I believe can be reborn,
conceived in open-legged, organic underbrush of coupling,
its wet head popping out covered in blessed blood benign.
What I touch that's innocent is tangible faith formatted in pills,
syringes, and I.V. medications. And then the potential to believe
in medical theories and histories,
when quantum-leap discoveries arrest cultural massacre.

But then again, why I touch, driving the pencil point
almost to breaking, is an attempt to erect via words
(as the very compulsion to write reveals merely the desire
to affirm identity by signing one's name over and over)
the effort to accept that such discoveries may not occur in my lifetime.
I already buried the baby last winter,
its miniature coffin set in a grave shallow as I insisted,
for I needed the assurance that if finally mad, willfully crazy,
I could unearth the stillborn and embrace it
with a desperateness redeemed as love—until its soft head burst
like soapstone against my useless breasts, into dust
of her or him, in whose scattering I foresee what eventually will be me.
I lick my dusty palms with its would-be nativity
and my greediness to die, dust more refined than sand
or the declined cremation of my child.

I want my child differentiated from the wild, devouring
distortion of land and populace, its infirmity set apart
from even a tender though violent diminishment;
from the outbreak of fire, the lit hours unleashed to scorch the sky,
its phantasmagoric flames taunted and fed with roof shingles
and dining stools, with picture frames and books
brought forward to the combustion in wheelbarrows—
while those who organize the disaster, their malicious features aglow
as if tinctured in saffron, stare on with satisfaction.
Branches blaze above their huge heads like death crowns.

I touch with the trust, palm upon psalm, that the cumulative effect
of all my writing will concretize as well as convey
the smoldering circumstance, the uphill futility of what takes place
primarily by what won't last; the happening flagged by absence,
the occurrence landmarked by disappearance, starkness, and terror,
those elements of slaughter, of mass graves outnumbered
by singular ceremonies. The bowed heads of loved ones, baleful flowers
lean obliquely toward the nothing with which their relationship continues.
I touch with the intention that something good will spread
like a medicine that actually works, forming a lifetime written
ostensibly to be read, yet substantiating, if only to myself,
if only to the archive of missing text, that I've lived.
By driving my pencil point relentlessly further into blankness,
into the void, nondescript and moody, that will replace me,
I try to touch my lifetime proper
reaching, like bedrock or weighted-down diver, the ocean's floor.

But what I touch also ignites, flame that eats alive my life,
polluted reservoir that freakishly ignites with only one lit match tossed.
And though I scream out at the forceps I encounter
when I drown in the jaundiced reflection of approaching fire, its march
almost military in precision, paradoxically, I'm stilled
by the pitch of my voice, its distance, its defilement.
I'm humbled by the recognition of it as that screaming we learn to ignore.
And though shaken by the increasing warmth I understand to be my ruin
I always feel love for the defunct in me,
regardless of the deteriorating green,
the world of disease within the world of life.

Like the incarcerated who regard freedom through the grid
of its limitation, I proceed, I crave anyway,
I spit out at it and give no information than otherwise instructed,
risking disfigurement before betrayal.

Out of what is short, then, allow shortness to be demonstrated,
in halting breath, in early fatigue,
in an immune system of someone young identical to that of someone elderly.

Like the War on Poverty, poverty will always lose against the Fortune 500.
Twist tears of acid out of the sky, beneath which,
like torn flesh, umbrellas disintegrate.
One glance upward
and my scarred eyes shut to pleasure,
by what should have been a summer shower, an iridescent downpour,
tears that would be, in another circumstance, permission granted
to relieve, easily relieve, the overburdened mind.
The taste is no longer salty but of bitter clinical methods, the medicine
an immaculate poison which emits from pore and orifice, an intervention
mandated with a kind of virility, invasive as a livid alien
made of heat only, my essential nature marred, my innards reordered.

Compound the victory bonfire, encourage the russet horizon to burnish darker,
hotter, red as a Doberman's tongue and as reliable in destructive motives.
Just as happy moments in life shape us, so do its horrors.
Survival is simply the witnessing of beauty metamorphosed into the ugly,
along with the ability to bear it, bear up under it;
the weight of one's head, the weightless echo-chamber of loneliness
in what you've seen, in what you know.

Ochre

so pale a beach she
   faces his back
and he sleeps
    oh he morning
       to smooth her hair

the smoothest of hair
    bed linen she so

when he is the loveliest of boats
    his turned shoulder on pleats
       sand falling
this wood bend

her damp knees closer
    the cloth sun is weather
      and she high land

us

in your arms
it was incredibly often
enough to be
in your arms
careful as we had to be at times
about the I.V. catheter
in my hand,
or my wrist
or my forearm
which we placed, consciously,
like a Gamboni vase,
the center of attention,
placed, frail identity
as if our someday-newborn
on your chest—
to be secluded, washed over
in your arms
often enough, it was
in that stillness, the only stillness
amidst the fears which wildly collided
and the complexities
of the illness, all the work
we had yet to do, had just done,
the hope, ridiculous amounts of it
we had to pump
from nothing, really,
short-lived consensus
possibility & experiment
to access
from our pinched and tiny minds
just the idea of hope
make it from scratch, air and water
like manufactured snow
a colossal fatigue
the severe concentration
of that, the repetition of that
lifted for a moment

just above your arms
inevitable, pressuring
it weighed down
but remained above
like a cathedral ceiling,
strangely sheltering
while I held tightly
while there I could
in your arms
only there, the only stillness
remember the will,
allow the pull, tow against inevitable ebb—
you don't need reasons to live
one reason, blinking in the fog,
organically sweet in muddy dark
incredibly often enough
it is, it was
in your arms

Drug Holiday

The flesh is sad, alas, and I've read all the books.

Far away I detect my body breaking down
In a series of seemingly inconsequential snaps,
Indiscernible as the rustle of leaves & twigs
Underfoot someone approaching.

I touch my face, oval instrument, incrementally devoid
Of features, first nose then eyes, a Brancusi bust.
I behold from a distance with an objectivity that's evidence
Of a disintegrating self, as my head rolls slowly over and above
Its finished life—shadows departing on a wall of bookcases filled,
Volumes read and reread, just gray against white, calligraphy and parchment.
That's what the air I've breathed has always consisted of.

To flee, to run away! I sense the birds are drunk

Let me go, let me leave!
Like an unleashed dog on safeguarded grasses
Render me entirely to my own devices, to my miniature capacity
For effectualizing. I'll focus on the trees,
Regard their opening like tulips unto the royalty of sunlight,
While my ambition abounds despite reality's grimness.
Free me! I refuse to be helpless anymore!
No more drugs, no more doctors, no more needles—
Stop your prayers mid-sentence.
Like birds overhead who veer in almost drunken flight,
I sway too inside, above and beyond this useless fight.

Intoxicated by the unknown of surf-spray sky!

Into water I disappear, this seascape sunset, its white waves pinprick
My arms with foam, a painless acupuncture of rain.
I'm possessed by that which no one ever has the courage to say—
Because they're afraid. Must we choose life under any circumstance?
No! And I'm happy, happy to dissipate into a bird-like vaccuum.

Nothing, not even the ancient gardens reconfigured in my eyes

What your love once manufactured in me was a reason to stay.
It took the amorphous problem of a diseased heart and remade it,
Unable to be broken down the way the rest of me is breaking.
Now it too melts, a glacial slope at midday, my killer cells
Declining against the impossibility of their reconstitution.
My body falls sway to the depreciation of its marrow,
Caves into bone-hollow and the dispossessed resonance of plaguy echo—
Collapsing eventually upon your chest, my idyllic grave site,
With somber whimsy like strewn paperwhites.

Can restrain this heart when it bridge-jumps into the sea

Forgive me. There are choices.
The future of longing, the "want" of what I already have—
Trees, magazines, appetizers, tidbits of life that decorate and crowd—
Provides a poor argument against the ferocious focus of disease progression
As it moves closer to the closing umbrella of time.

We can demand out of what we had, only what we had,
Its invisible pulse, that which beats behind all else.
But what presents itself to us now defiantly eclipses our contrary desire
And like a skylark, nothingness swoops large enough
To dominate the forlorn, inopportune horizon.

O nights! Not even the stark clarity if my lamp

O nights, not even the comfort of the silent company of my desk
Can convince me otherwise. What was once greater than a passing and pause
For retrospection spites me instead, a tool for longstanding torture.
Mysterious words and sentences turn into duplicitous systems,
Mere semantics for survival, not the ingenuous expression
Of my incapacity to express the delicate depiction of living alone and sick.

And the wounding arousal for more, just a disparate reverie,
These pillow-muilled screams at dawn butcher what waking used to mean.

On blank paper protected by its whiteness

I moan for that for which I no longer have an image,
My cry, blank and empty as unused paper.
It mesmerizes my exhausted eyes with the potential for peace.

Hence, the most meaningful portrayal would be to say nothing.
After all, there's nothing to say that I haven't already said,
And worse, failed in the attempt to articulate;
Those words that could never matter enough
To mean what they meant.

Now the refusal to speak best mimics the bleakness of snowfall
On sidewalks. Its cold brick and hazy glory of impermanence
Encapsulates uncannily the history of my impotence.

Nor the young woman who nurses her baby.

She once gave me hope I would feed my own.
Adoring tendencies that spun and wound like some solenoidal apparatus
Pulling me toward an infant's face, its translucent beginning
Of pre-socialized consciousness glowing like raw marble,
Stung me next into a sonant isolation,
The behest of another woman's child.
The Madonnas keep me closed down in palsied instinct,
Not too hungry, not too envious——
All that innocence swirling into a hallucinogenic happiness.

It's the choicelessness that cramps up,
spasms that come after a D & C procedure, or belly-kicks
Of a ghost pregnancy from the stillborn you named anyway.
It's the box, the ropes, and the metal tin of this mental compression,
My limbs mortised to a spatial destiny of progressive deformation
And no way, then, to crawl out of it.

I'm leaving! Steamer with swaying masts,

I'm finished, fixated on liberation from this sand-sack of a body,
Spiteful, inert, unresponsive to love but not to pain——
These useless limbs that flap and jerk like debris in the wind;
This torso embowered on the precipice of rigor mortis,
A diver set to launch into the bliss vapors of incineration.

I beget relief from the rocky depths, from my someday metamorphosis
Into ash and pebble, tooth and nail, never too soon, not a bad substitute.

What is the will to live finally but masochistic,
If living with a sickness rarely provides release from suffering?
And what's deemed worthwhile, "those little things"
Become instead the dissilient products of an engineered concentration,
The discipline of needing only, reacting to, then withholding;
Desiring just that which cultural consensus weighs in on with correct emphasis.

Lift up your anchor for some otherworldly place!

I wade through the refuse.
There's no self-hatred involved if I've already been disowned.

I'm allowed to cut loose the dead weight of this body-harness,
Defective parachute pack, in order to achieve ascension.
Like luggage jettisoned into a flogging sea, I will to be free
Of the topsy-turvy, of the hand-wringing, of the identical seasons;
The internal push and pervasive failure, the salute to stoicism & bereavement.

I will be unkind to it. I will avenge it.
It has pursued me all my life, throwing pellets and vocalizing insults.
I will to overpower it and make it my slave, make it beg as I've begged of it,
And made myself vulnerable to needle and tube, to x-ray and scope,
To the medications, twenty-three pills a day.
Yet despite this massive loyalty
Of subject to superior, patriot to cause, child to parent,
My body refused me, refused me like a stray, like refugees aboard
The *SS St. Louis*, who, when denied admission to U.S. harbors,
were forced to sail back to Hamburg in 1939.

O what you have made me do!
You deserve to dwindle in a hospice, in a nursing home
To be left to your helplessness, diseased and dissenting
From the efforts of others—friend, husband, doctor.
I leave motivated by the knowledge that from my neglect
You will first go blind.

You rise in the morning where morning no longer exists.
When the heat hits your arms and face, its sting is black instead of yellow.
Your panicked outcry, shot without aim into a dark crypt,
Lands muffled by water lap and its curvature of sand.

And you will wait as I have waited.
And you will want as I have wanted.
And you will pray where there's no one, when
Nothing but dune grass and suffocating wilderness surrounds you.

A boredom, now grief-stricken by cruel hopes,

My future as amputated from me
As any dream, a single cloud out of reach,
The repetition of goodbye, the awful au revoir.
I'm tired of the long-waving arm.

Hope-work is like grief-work.

Allow me to be hopeless. Take the burden from me,
This dead child I can't resign myself to bury.
Hope on my behalf, the way trees do in their regenerative cycle,
Or tulips upon which we project temporal happiness.
I try to be like tulips, content with the ephemeral,
Eager to brush against what's real,
For implicit in its silky, tactile petal, a lasting although minimal.

I tell myself it's enough,
Stupefied from my worsening situation,
A kind of dementia that passes for coping.
I listen to the plans of others, their comings and goings, wants and makings.
I listen and smile. I've learned to give over everything
So I can join in, even on the periphery;
To join in on the purely speculative effort of the newest protocol
As I try again to take the medication.
I join in, at the very least, by not committing suicide.

Why indulge in such an aggressive, painful act if death be there anyway
Within arms' reach, like my likeness, like tomorrow, its closeness

An intimacy almost sexual in the depth, penetration,
And devouring length of cohabitation?

I lean forward and wave my arms around in unresponsive air,
Clasping at its concept. Speak to me.
But impending death it remains, index finger pressed to its lips,
While I cock my head at the vaguest intonation
And watch from outside myself, myself struggle within the bondage
Of earthbound purgatory with no promise of departure.

Still believes in the supreme farewell of handkerchief waving!

If I look into my husband's face, up close, let his features
Become my visual field, I can forget, or rather justify, this shrunken world
And give up, give in to his encouragement,
Let it sustain me like a trampoline. A little scenario we never tire
Of rehearsing, the repetition of reassurances and proclamations of love.
"I feel it coming," I say about my death.
I whisper this to him in his arms as if afraid someone might hear
Though we're alone: just walls, ceiling, and space heater whirring
In the corner while a single window reveals the monastic landscape of winter.
"You've felt that before," he reminds me quietly, equally alert
To the discretion of our discussion.
I protest, "But the drugs won't work," which has happened before.
In fact they've never worked, not for more than a few months.
"They may this time," he reassures. I believe him. We dupe ourselves,
Just to be together some more, take another snowy drive,
Or other ways we find distraction.
I want to forget, make use of moments like this to forget
The bare, coffin-like subterranean station
From where, as if buried alive, I stare up at charming, pointless flowerheads;
Like receipts or ticket stubs, mementos of lived life,
Evidence that I succeeded in forgetting this inconvenience, this great
Interruption—succeeded in admiring and subsequently triumphing
Over my jealous disdain of all things prosaic and pretty.

And, maybe, those masts inviting storms are the ones

Maybe this earth wherein we automatically presume rebirth
Proves most meritorious as solely that which disguises dirt—
Just dirt, whose dimension of power reaches no further than underground water,
The murky stream soon to immure me in the catacomb of its drybed stasis
And provide, at last, like a goblet of wine
The equivalent for quenching this shapeless desire
In the form of cold certainty drunk, dank and numbing:
My right to refuse treatment at last acknowledged.

Among those which the wind bends over wrecked ships

I reserve the decision to stop, to draw the line—
Not to give up but to point out what can never be, despite;

To catch with one splayed hand, then close into a tight fist,
The falling leaf, birch, oak, maple,
Thrown into high relief by virtue of its increasing deficit—
A kind of performance art for what my body now signifies.

A series of exhaustive actions, the compartmentalization of functioning,
Each gesture singled out and forced forward, my brain synapses slowed
To a chain of events like frames of a film in their editing process.
Living has nothing to do with instinct anymore.

Lost without masts, without masts, or lush islands . . .

I reserve the right to choose nothing instead of almost-nothing—
Not to give up but to point out what can never be, despite;

To catch, steal, devour the smallest evidence of good health—
Hold tight in my fist the private hope, the private love,
The private experience of loss.
Please know how hard I fought, how badly I wanted it.

But, O my heart, listen to the sailors sing!

How badly I want it still,
The freedom, the thrill, the passion, the complexity.

All this suffering for nothing?
We need to make up something to rationalize it as worthwhile.

But the body does not.
The last sound heard will be my stomach growling.

Stephane Mallarme,"Brise Marine,"
Oeuvres Completes, ed. Henri Mondor and G. Jean-Aubry
(Paris: Editions Gallimard, 1945)
Translated by Tory Dent

Early Poems

Dilated Hours

The house cannot be seen from the road.

Only a trail of incongruous leaves
                    that track inveterately
with amorphous feet, up the asphalt driveway;
only a vague tierra of light, sanious
        that betrays the otherwise salutary sky
fleshes out the home's necrosis.

So blows the prodigious breeze . . .
       voice-over for a subliminal scream.

                 ****

So only insects, birds and house pets
                  herded by the pitch
    salivate for the anabranch
sewage pipe for the spontaneity of smiles,
                 and drink

    the pabulum of pretend, the apophasis of humans
                   and acquire

     by consumption a comprehension of their death
for where
    there are a thousand faces (more or less),
              only one mouth opens.

For where
    there floats a promise,

                    there follows its perforation
and tiny hands faint from yearning
beneath smaller flowers.

                    ****

Blame a belief in blank paper,
                    or the need for a mother,
                              or the deceitful obscurity of clouds.

Ambient.
Avaunt.
Amen.

                    ****

Watch the unwanted walk now univalent,
a pacifist who finds solace in desertion.

          By passing the vertical, implacability of longing
                                        landmark to absence
                    like intarsia or convoluted petals
                    denial became embedded within its denial

and from the salt content of tears
                    was invented a vaccination
cleansing from the yellowing teeth
                              little golden morsels of spit,

                    ****

Now the limp is barely evident.
The glassy stare of the epileptic,

                              alert and halcyon.

With perfection achieved in their ability for abstraction
            they've even found people

                            (good people!)

who can love them,
in the finalizing light of their failure.

Before physicians they can fake equivalence,
        that's how well they've come

                        to brave the aberrations.

****

O no word's a freak accident they've discovered,
            nor a gesture,

                        a slip of the tongue.

Not the arms of a giantess outstretched in the distance,
        the serpentine driveway writhing before her
                    the front door forever opens a tunnel to China
while the windows consume slowly their own curtains,

                                    suicidal

            as illustrated by the chimney;

and the effervescent eyes of the father,
                    diffusing, dissolving

 at the head of the table
where his head hangs, empty.

What screams he swallows when he climbs the staircase
        and thinks of his child perpetually thrown,

                        as if stuffed, a toy animal.

271

How the spiral stairs closed in like an accordion
and the child's eyes

                               now buttressing their past,
               never quite close again.

Save for watershed of self-pitying tears
                    that overflow into the garden
          where no more conversation is allowed,
      the heartfelt having been absorbed, long ago, by the clouds
where, lo,
              a lame vernacular, as ghost writer, slinks about.

                   ****

If only you could divert your attention
or explain what you think might have happened,

              the stories, stretched over the years like a canopy
              that splits apart in the middle from the tension.

So only a few remain in your favor (and what a bad hand of cards
                    in comparison, for that matter).

Their solidity fragile as a house of cards, or matches
                       a flicker upon the fire screen
           or a tiny chapel in the midst of a mansion
               that's undergone mid-century restoration;
a tourist attraction,
         where you, the atheist, stroll upon piousness
               a floating island
within prison walls
        of the supposed perfection
              of childhood.

****

Does the beauty of stained glass,

its spiritualness

penetrate the atheist

if only in retrospect?

Yes,

if the atheist believes in actual glass.

There's evidence enough

in the aorist architecture of your daily life:

just looking up

at the virgin mother

perched upon her marble pasture

with that infamous infant

positioned in her arms

already riveting his wisdom to the world,

can make ya wonder

Do her kisses smell of Scotch and Norell?

The way God's wife who once held you close (the closest ever)

breathed that smell

and your name whispered

became your first love letter

festering its many versions between your childish legs.

Wise to the sensation

but ignorant to the adumbration

of retrograde responses

trigger later

by your lover

when two, past and future, become one.

****

The heart has no seasons,
no cycle to follow like the fern

                       that we follow

in our fight against the centripetal

                    force of the heart.

****

Yet even if we surrender
and walked its radius, blindfolded,

              as if a ship's plank

    our desire for a center, a mirage in the desert

                would only move further from our grasp,

for that is its nature:
to live off of lack.

****

The heart that has four chambers,
        four vaults that unlock with an olfactory key;
                mummy chamber of a mastaba
    where the diastole of a mummy's soul still beats:
The heart that has four chambers,
        four vaults that unlock with an olfactory key;
                mummy chamber of a mastaba
    where the diastole of a mummy's soul still beats:
The heart that has four chambers,
        four vaults that unlock with an olfactory key;
                mummy chamber of a mastaba
    where the diastole of a mummy's soul still beats:
The heart that has four chambers,

four vaults that unlock with an olfactory key;
              mummy chamber of a mastaba
where the diastole of a mummy's soul still beats:
The heart that has four chambers . . . .

****

Autumn branch against winter bank
         dead leaves dangle like prayer poems
or abandoned fortunes tied to twigs—
      only the bad fortunes, that is.

****

Is there such a word as an apology,
    a word with grace and elasticity,
              with such audacity
      as to swaddle the sore of your experiences,
        like newborns
and deliver them back with enough benevolence
that you love your mistakes,
           for you're healed because of them?

Inside a minute stone carved into a heart
    isolated within the context of your bedside table

                 (alarm clock, lamp, and novel),
     a smaller heart beats, the heart of a fetus
    curled up upon a crêche of literate pages,
         its barely formed body barely lit
by the clock, the size of a ladies' wrist-watch,
    pulsating like a bedside lamp inside its breast.

And the apology,

a minute stone carved into a wrist-watch,

delicate as a ladies',

guards an even smaller flower inside,

a blue rose made of blue crayon

that colors over the pastel flesh to be of this infant.

Many apologies bloom in a bed of roses beyond these hedges,

like a real rose laid upon a real grave.

And though tiny hands faint from yearning beneath even smaller flowers,

streaks of rose rise against the disparaging air.

You thrust your hand deeper into the pocket,

of the earth and it's expressionless like the face of a buddhist monk——

that which encompasses all expression.

Your arms then root with the trees in apology,

your feet fold obediently in the grave of your regret,

just a little bit larger than you.

Your truancy unfolds, continuous, plush, and velvet

a theatre curtain flung down from above.

Hot and musty, it forces further,

and further down your head,

the curse of the curtain eternally flung.

Accordingly you drag its gold satin fringe along the curb,

and listen all the while to the life you might have led

as if actually taking place somewhere

like Muzak piped into a shopping mall

or xylophone played without xylophonist in the attic.

****

Forgive me
   for my weakness, the amnesia of my strength.
I fall into a pit of quicksand,
     indulge in the gritty sinkingness.
  And shut my eyes, petulantly, to the neighboring vines,
my limbs pillowed in atrophy, a luxury,
    a dog who allow himself to be put down.

   I beg with my brows to be held until I die
  but no sooner has the needle been routinely removed
     than do the two nurses (identical)
   turn about-face as if synchronized

  leaving me to a convex blur,
    the shrinking world of my vision
     where I wade through my impending death
      that weighs me down with its imminence.

Forgive me
   for my fears that pummel the earth
 with candywrapers, beer cans, newspapers, inkless pens;
    empty milk cartons thrown delinquently into the river Pishon.
  I watch indifferently with involuntary tears
      thickened into blood
  that run askew in rivet upon the churlish land.

Leaves may be all around me waving,
  though lie they will eventually upon the merciless earth.

And though the fallow sun
             singles out in pyrite the solitary jet or day glow sunfish
                         it abandons as well the coffee cup
                         it abandons the black baby carriage
it abandons as well the brainwashed child that once the black carriage fit.

Now when I look back at it,
                              with my chicken-wire resistance to love,
             the holes hallow and widen inside me
                         and consequently inside us.

My field of vision, a field frozen over
             a skating pond I've already slipped under
narrows to a spectrum, a flashlight's circumference
                              stationary as a butterfly of pain
my gaze,
             that strains through layers of cake and ice
             the fallacious sun kindly illuminates.

                         ****

Spotlit, so to speak,
             by the shell-shaped shadow of a cloud

                                        the unwanted
                         incubates in her circles of isolation
face-down and flexed
             as in a penitential burial,
             the grave of a Cro-Magnon girl.

See the debris of sympathetic magic!
Tiny teeth broken from the eating of seashells,
the stick scrawl on a stone of a shell,

a half-shell, actually
drawn in memorial to the beaten.

Shriveled orchids tossed in for forgiveness,
their animistic heads, voodoo dolls,

                    parasitic.

 The early rope of sterns
binds her soul to her circumstance—
call it karma or the inability to forget.

                The memory is a monarchy
                that belatedly begets.

                ****

In the middle of the night,

                the night falls ill,

        where her eyes spring open, oyster shells

                        from the twist of an oyster knife.

        She hides in the trench of her bed,
listening into a conch shell
            to the dull, oceanic yelling beyond
                    the closed door while within her closed breast
whole orchids of apology
                    bud and yawn in fast motion
        their petals press plaintively
                        against her ribs and larynx,

pushing out her heart trapped in tin, a Jack-in-the-box
pushing out her heart veined with blood, a birthing head
pushing out her heart fostered by mossy twigs, an egg in a nest
pushing out her heart cartridged in lead, buckshot
pushing out her heart, a drawer in a chest of drawers, overwhelmed with seashells:

>Green Stars, Violets Snails, Lightening Whelks,
>Warty Cones, Flesh Pea, Solid Bubbles, Silver Clams,
>Graceful Pyrams, Eared Ark, Horse Mussels, Junonia,
>Loveable Nut Shells, Black Worms, Boring Turrets,
>Fragile Spoons, Flexed Sea-hearts, Paper Scallops,
>Jewel Boxes, Bleeding Teeth, Glassy Teardrops,
>Lion's Paw, Angel Wings, Dogwinkles, Tulips,
>Wretched Aspella, Sunrise Tellin, Cylinder Sundials,
>Pearly Lyonsia, Zebra Periwinkles, Nobles Lora,
>Carrot Cones, Cock Stromb, Queen Stromb, King Helmet,
>Immaculate Moons, Glory of the Atlantic, Baby Bonnets,
>Goldin Oliver, Prickley Cockle, Deer Cowry, Ivory Horn
>Emerson's Cerith, Magpie, Hairy Triton, Beautiful Caecum,
>Bridle Rimula, Caribbean Coral, Coffee Bean Snails,
>Ram's Horn, Disks, Sand Pandora, Perverse Whelks,
>Writhing Shells, Snowflake Marginella, Flame Augur
>Rosy Keyhole limpets, Fat Doves, Lamps, Fancy Lucine,
>Incongruous Arks, and Purple Venus.

Stolen shells

cracked and causing internal bleeding,
spill over from my chest;

the drawer of desire (all purpose)

that ejects at the onset of bereavement.

Break away, pouch of wampum, from the hip of the brave

                              and scatter your contents along the riverbank,
        brandishly,
                        promiscuously,
                                        to procreate in your own image
        the countless volutes strewn already
                                empty homes shaped the same
                                as the empty home of the birth canal

where just like snails we've egressed into the world.

        And so our home comes with us;
                                        it is, as they say, where the heart is—
                        (the way the monk instinctively deems sacred
                        any patch of grass upon which he pauses).

On our backs we carry the heart's house
                                and all the horror within it.
                                                                All of it.

                                ****

The half shell cupped in the half shell of her palm . . .
                        which came first
The privileged form of her palm or the privileged form of what that held?

        In whose or what's image was the transistor made?

        The digital watch?
        The snowmobile?

Scalloped edges wallpaper the room
                        anatomize the pool of her prepubescent body
                into the pink shells of her breasts and knees,

into the pink shell of her freshwater flesh.

Which came first,
                    the shell or the image it fits?
          An open fan, an open magazine, the oval toenails of her mother,
                the meat of the clam, the mussel, the oyster,
            the intestines, the tiny brain , the bubbled lungs
                    panoramically projected
from the souvenir shell
                                                of the souvenir heart
            laid upon the altar of the threshold,
              the cold wood of her parents' bedroom.

One tear of forgiveness
                    like a drop of holy water,
        cleanses the spirit.

                    ****

I'm sorry   for the way our driveway darkens at the end
I'm sorry   for the deficit of smiles
I'm sorry   for the single television station of our lives
I'm sorry   for the implications in my walk (there are
                                                    so many)

I'm sorry   for the shrinking box, our home
I'm sorry   for the dirty counter top
I'm sorry   for my failures that label each part of my body
I'm sorry   for what makes you want to hit me
I'm sorry   for milk spilt
I'm sorry   for my voice thrown in every room
I'm sorry   for my ubiquitous quietude
I'm sorry   for the rain you so identify with
I'm sorry   for the abysmal kitchen sink

I'm sorry   "I'm sorry" isn't enough, as you've said

I'm sorry   for the china dish I'm unable to make of my hands;

                        for the medicinal water I can't obtain from the springs

                        for the tendering cure as I won't watch you drink.

                        ****

Baleful are the petals played upon the floor of the grave.

        Their dried edges, sharp as crude metal and as sharp

                                        like spearheads.

        In the burying of the casket, the casket pries open

and the skeleton of a girl puppeteer's on the lawn,

                        mimes for us

        the life lived in fear of the hand (great or small),

her bones glinting their betrayal.

        No I can speak and so can my friends!

                                Shells deflagrate

around the memorial stone . . . a headstone actually and actually

                        a celebration.

                        ****

With no parole

or option for good behavior

                        just the off-chance that the mood might improve,

                        the will of a rain dance to manipulate the weather;

the unwanted lies afraid

                        looking into the night

as a tarn might spend its day in awe of the mountain,
or jailbird, the ceiling of his cell.

Particles of dust shuffle in the air.
The moonlight, a searchlight, scans the monolithic trees.
There's the high-pitched buzz of infinity.

If betrayal were a sound what would you hear?

        The depth charge of self-hate?

            A woman sobbing inside the tumbleweed of her hair.
            Or your oleander "Au revoir" that so oppugns me, Dear?
            Or the decadence of bombs
                    against the Herculean sky
                        now deodands on High.

Perhaps it's sorta brief, more of a noise really:
        the squeak of a turned heel,
      or a pale chink, very sweet
        as a teaspoon makes with its teacup.
                          So sounds
the shell thrown back at her door,
    a cross and bible, painted white.
                  It lands, *point-device*

where Christ's head would slump.

        The refrain of sorrow / stop
        The sorrow of refrain / end-stop

                the shell, a stone

thrown strategically into the lake

where estimated the most rings will appear,

     relentlessly rippling outward as does the agony on your face.

     The stone: my hope for you and me

     The stone: my belief in the stone as a rock

     The stone: my need for a word that means "stone"

     The stone: my love for the shell

that flung through the air, its meaning is won

         like the flight of an arrow,

from the loss, the loosing of where it came from.

Suddenly forgiveness spans the distance of betrayal.

Suddenly blood runs down the linen lining of the orchids

     that encircle her, that surge through her,

      that buoy her up from her hell—

since the shell is only the shell of the word "shell,"

   the little animal inside,

     a chameleon of signification,

since the shell is only the shell of the word "shell,"

   the little animal inside,

     a chameleon of signification,

since the shell is only the shell of the word "shell,"

   the little animal inside,

     a chameleon of signification,

since the shell is only the shell of the word "shell,"

   the little animal inside,

     a chameleon of signification,

since the shell is only the shell of the word "shell" . . .

It builds its helical house in the motion of a circle.

****

The word

                a chip of kryptonite

    aglow in the cave of its context,

           illuminates the lips in the act of speaking,

           illuminates the eyes in the act of reading.

Beheld by meaning, its magnetic force

        that renders impotent with a blaze

              of what should be warming,

the body gags

      in a gown of mail,

        and cold gold locks about the wrists and ankles.

Could classic demolition unleash the limbs,

             left spineless

     disrobe a Michelangellan statue of the body

     reveal a Frankenstein, the construct of omnipotence

     demystify the way a map does human anatomy

     de-pure by laying bare and vulnerable

          the bare flesh of the body:

The truth like legs slowly opening?

The truth like penetration,

             or permanence?

       ****

Once upon a time

    in the blood stream of corpuscles and brain cells,

red and white ladybugs
our name germinated,
first fossil of a private vocabulary
that grows inside us like a family tree.

No wonder
when atop a kitchen table, the empty dish of the word is placed
round as a breast or childbearing tummy
or bowl-headed beginning of our birth,

we peer over into it for manna—

Milk that spurts from the tit
into the pomegranate-red mouth of the infant.

We think we move instinctively toward language
the way a plant leans toward light.

We hold on for dear life, make the word flesh
pull from the air
or out of a hat

from a generic term, the specific rabbit.

We draw a fleur-de-lis in blue
and appellate underneath "fleur-de-lis"
believing it's forever.

And from the monstrance of love
we immortalize the dying one,
personalize the word
and manifest it as our mother.

****

But in my love for you My Love,

        the traces flow from few to few, and to no 'other.'

      ****

When poisonous snow spills freakishly onto the poppies

      and onto the magenta field you faint, gliding,

               a handkerchief:

        feel it inside your body.

When the voluminous hand of the monster inside the monster's chest

      swings, a boom out of control,

        hot and branding onto you face:

          feel it inside your body.

      It stays there, doesn't it?

White scar on white skin:

      a flag of surrender against the winter sky.

To mark,

        though arbitrarily, the certainty of a spot,

        the way a plaque of an unknown soldier does.

But there is no memory that stands for the rest,

                no poem exigent enough

                nor relic, holy;

    no essential metaphor or metonymical event.

A multitude of crucifixes are produced daily.

****

Rebuild from scratch, from a foundation of pain, the body again.
     Like Coventry, from the rubble of a bombing,

inscribe without anguish
     in the high relief of your prostrate limbs.

Inscribe in pencil on white space
                       the body of the text;
         drawn and quartered, word by word.
                     Resurrection only occurs while writing.

If not from the inscription the message evokes
                     a holy ghost,
     than from the inscribing itself—
           like the indecipherable hand
or signature of hope.

            The fear, the fear, Nosferatu,
      the one that persists in the open hand of the child
until the hand closes into a fist so tight
               it turns white and red,
     resists ever opening again,
             never ever,
closed like a mouth, like a mind, like a book.

****

Dear Reader,

        why are you looking at me like that?

        I didn't find you, you found me;

'found' in the sense the stunned gaze

                of an infant

         finally focuses on the mother's face,

     into the nothingness of her pupils,

             black spots that determine depth in the ocean.

Underwater,

       the opus warps to distortion:

            underwater, your abridged desire, her ruination.

             ****

Whole, you find yourself in front of the mirror,
albeit a fragmented whole, like a stained glass window.

You read into the text of the body refracted,

            what you see &
            what you see as missing;

like the fascist sun that insidiously pervades
or the insecure star that emulates meekness—

        a wallflower in the contour of nights,
         (just a speck against greatness) . . .

or a rock that marks the crossroad

        from which paths stem, many,
         countless and useless,

again, none leading to you again.

****

Wave goodbye to the body
      as it floats to the surface in a lake of melancholy and giggles.
           O hydromancy of personality! Your little eyes, your little mouth,
                        all alone in life.

Wave goodbye to the body
      with scales and webbed toes and longing roped,
           umbilical cord of ambergris,
                    around its throat;
                      looking backwards, homewards,

veins bulging in the effort to look ahead—
                  the non-descript hair, matted.
      Is there no comb?

Wave goodbye to the body
      how it peers warily into its soul.
           The wildcard of desire, the wildcat and the wildflower
                  separated from the rest

as the bed is from the struggle to get out of bed,
a bed of wildflowers,
               dark purple, almost black.

****

What's missing surrounds your silhouette,
          a white aura or nun's habit

or a zillion tiny fish swimming in a zillion directions;
piranha or goldfish, filaments of orange, red, and yellow;
a Japanese screen that adds contour
to the evening.

Each, a soul having lived or yet to,
their destinies circulate, a whirlpool of the unfinished.

You crave their so called 'existence' don't you?

O to bond (again?) with that motion.

****

The jettisoned coffin seesaws over,
buoys up for a moment on the churlish sea.

The white covering cloth slips down, gown of a seduced woman.
The coffin is your mother's, and then your own,

sinking with suction
a great ship or junked television,
sinking into the blurry garden beneath.

It waits, a delayed torpedo, to ultimately implode.

****

Tears pellet the ocean, a hailstorm, or bits of granite thrown.
Tears to harden from sorrow, or so it feels.
If I cry hard enough you will be willed back. You will.

****

What you remember suits you perfectly,
                            comfortably, like a suit.

You choose to remember solely the coffin
                            with exquisite detail—
                    the conscious mind, an exquisite suit!

What's inside? Buried like treasure, is it only the mystery of
What's inside? Buried like treasure, is it only the mystery of
What's inside? Buried like treasure, is it only the mystery of
What's inside? Buried like treasure, is it only the mystery of
What's inside? ...

****

"Why are you looking at me like that?" she says
as I stare into the face of my mother, thirty years later
                    all gnarly and contorted and neglected, like an orchard.

Into the hollows, the helical vacuums of her pupils
Into the eye of the staircase, a tornado, into the vertigo of its spiral;

        and watch my desire domino with the child
                    perpetually thrown headlong
                                        as if stuffed
a toy animal.

            She falls phantasmagorically,
ricochets off the steps,
            a pinball eternally propelled by outside circumstance,
                    each step a metaphor for the next:

The Step, the insecure star

The Step, the text, the wildcard, the missing step

The Step, the many steps of love transferred, metaphor to metaphor

The Step, the opus, the fascist sun, the ocean

The Step, the steps off infinitum

The Step, the shell, the stone, the fish, the sign of the fish

The Step, the face of my mother lost forever in my mother's face

The Step, her omnipotent breast

The Step, "Why are you looking at me like that?"

The Step, the television, the treasure chest, the pelleting tears,

The Step, the effervescent eyes of my father, diffusing, dissolving,

The Step, my father at the head of the table where his head hangs, empty

The Step, the child's eyes as if buttressing their past

that never quite close again

The Step, the pupil. the orchard, the body

The Step, the staircase

that closes in like an accordion

or lid of a coffin, airtight.

****

The white plastic diary inscribed in gold "My Diary"
    shuts of its own accord, the miniature gold-plated key

    swallowed up by the infinity of inscribed pages.

Moribund, the prom rose pressed inside,

finally transcends recognition:

    a skull.

Its soul, smoked out from the pressure, looms up,
>> a waft of smoke from a fire defunct
> or genie rubbed vigorously out of its bottle.

> Lead me, barefooted Gandhi, though the desert,
> though the pencil be too faint to go on.
I lumber dutifully behind within the idiocy of my flesh,
>> a number clipped to my ear
>>> fattened cow about to be slaughtered;
>> a Jew on route to the showers.

In stocks the villagers guffaw and throw eggs and pebbles.
> My towering dunce cap sits askew.

>> I let you test, test, test me
>> tube of blood in a lab
>> that I am.

Lead me across the boiling hot grass, the streets
> beds of red stars, sharp bottle caps.

> Before the guillotine I cannot see,
> before the firing squad I am shot by my own countrymen.

>> There is only action.

And so I listen.

>> They told me the news on the telephone
>> in a telephone booth without windows.

The small walls, stork-white, of claustrophobic definition
closed in, staircase, lid of a coffin, accordion,
cover of a white plastic diary inscribed in gold "My Diary"
closed in, the small walls, stork-white
shut of their own accord.

There is only action.

And so I listen.

They said, "We want you to lead a normal life,"
as they dangle my perdition, the possibility of not, before my face.

I stare into it,
in all its eschatological glory:

A lake, pronounced 'lough,' if you wish.

Elusive depth.
I strain to detect the bottom
and decide on an end.

Wherein, everything that could unfold has unfolded
fall has fallen, and lies cracked and broken

at the illusory bottom,
which focuses after all as simply another horizon:
platitudes of malm and silt.

Wherein, bicycle wheel, heirloom, or mitten
amuses me with causary origin:

blank windows.

****

If only to pinpoint the pain that permeates so radiantly,

                                my perennial radiation,

       and in its discovery, the ablution of extremity,

                and in its ablution, eloignement,

(though only seemingly)
       at last.

****

But sparse the sky remains matt to the finish.
Totem poles, creak the pines.

Wedged between the spaces, the splintered self-narration
       of my history, my precursory history pervades
Wedged between the spaces, the splintered self-narration
       of my history, my precursory history pervades
Wedged between the spaces, the splintered self-narration
       of my history, my precursory history pervades
Wedged between the spaces, the splintered self-narration
       of my history, my precursory history pervades . . .

****

No wheel, glove, or broach

                       preens specific enough to seize upon
      to catch within the upside-down cup,
           a poisonous insect caged by your perception.
Of many wings was made the wasp.

      Take this page, for instance, as a sign of some source,
      operative only from that to which it already pertains (itself).

This page, not the place where memorabilia stores up

for eyes to dart and long for,
as if shoebox transformed into my beloved's face,

But this page
I stare into

in all its eschatological glory:

"We were driving in the country. The sky was overcast, and the hilly landscape, a distinct kelly green. We came upon, almost involuntarily, as if the car drove us there of its own volition, a small provincial town, dark and cobble-stoned. A mob gathered in its center, jeering and shouting. We drove straight into the middle to see what all the ruckus was about. A couple was being arrested. An armed wagon was parked nearby with its rear doors swung open. The woman was having her hands cuffed behind her back. She was barefoot and wore only a hospital gown and underpants. The gown opened in the back and flapped in the wind, exposing her fleshy, overweight body. She was both voluptuous and muscular, her skin, a blotchy pink from the cold air. All of her hair had been viciously bobbed, obviously cut off by the mob. Parts of her scalp were bald and some of the bald spots were bleeding. And where her eyes, nose and mouth were there were only little stitches. The mob had carved out her face as punishment; they had defaced her. Her cheeks ballooned in and out furiously like a blowfish as she tried to breath. She stood there puffing, her legs astride to steady herself against the angry crowd , her face stitched up like a ragdoll's. She stood against the mob and the overcast sky; she stood against her husband who still had his mustached face, wore a suit and appeared almost dapper, definitely less dangerous next to her. She must have done something really horrible I imagined, more horrible than her though both were on their way to their execution."

****

Raised on a Grecian pedestal, the bust of the defaced woman

swerves west toward her perdition. Godforsaken?

As snow predicated whiteness,
> the hybrid body predicates the soul.

> > A body of snow whirrs into oblivion,
> > > > a stark quintessence
> > > above gnat or angle.

where
not sky
not space
not ponies
not secretaries
not feminine
not zonal
not cuneiform writing
not fuchsia
not shoulders
not a toastmaster
not forestry
not antique
not tousled
not Gladiolas
not aerosol
not a coliseum
not allegorical
not a youdles
not Tampa, Florida
not new
not shocking
not carbonated

not graceful

not angora

not a compact disc of Stravinsky

not lovers

not turquoise

not paradoxical

not a fiddle

not obscure

not mountainous

not clay pigeons

not fashionable

not vanilla

not digital

not incense

not intelligible

not March

not a Zebra

not a saloon

not penetrable

not impenetrable

not a cupola

not a vampire

not destiny

not a wedding

not necromantic

not honey

not worm-eaten

not precious

not absent

not a rock band

not homogeneous

not a grotto

not form

not Homeric

not gentle

not a yellow hammer

not tangible

not a Lady Slipper

not a toilet

not comparable

not a sports car

not heteromorphic

not a dinosaur

not salty

not a tunic

not fickle

not a dinghy

not Aphrodite

not wintergreen

not bewitching

not an apricot

not athanasia

not an afterlife

not a dinner jacket

not diluted

not a fawn

not Zion

not a lake

not nothing

(This is intentional):

                    this vacant prairies of the open promise,
The fluid shredding of flowers until, unmarred, a silence field.

                    As testimony to blossoms, no petals.
                    As proof, the spoken promise, "Petals."

                         ****

Mouth to mouth
Match my face, defaced, within its acrimonious promise of, "face."
Word-of-mouth to word-of-mouth.

                         Palm into print it will fit
                         or prom rose pressed into the indented page.

Place my shredded face against its features,
          its absurd petals against their absence, the field.

The place, its promise congealed;
                    misery, retribution, and apophatic prose.

The place, the grey room, larger than last I looked,
          delineated by pain into walls and dead-end corners.
          The definitude of pain with its many graduations,
                                        like a rainbow
               distinguishes ceiling from floor.

The room, a necropolis, larger and smaller; both.

Large as the squadron of stars, my own countrymen,
                         that fire all at once.

Large as my desire to go to bed with you again.
Large as my fear concealed in hour-tight compartments
            that expands, fed on fear, to explosion—
                exploding in and on in itself, over and over

until just helium, just fear, everywhere,
            above and beneath, translucent bubbles filled with terror
                expanding to explosion, over and over . . .

Large as the infinite inscription of pages, fawning open, loose-leaf.
            The promise of the page, blank or filled (still blank windows)
                tossed from a cargo jet and scattered across a nation,
                        across the impartial ocean.

        You watch the event from the television in your bedroom:
            the promise of chaos and lack of inscription.

                    ****

Small as a lake, pronounced "lough,' if you wish.
                                    I look it in the eyes.
        Its trick depth shallows and shrinks

            to the size of the face upon my wrist-watch.

Now at the bottom, the mythical hour,
                        defaced and stainless steel.

Small as the walls, stork-white, that close in
            lid of a coffin that shuts of its own accord,
                            airtight.

And so I listen
　　　to the promise
small as the miniature space of spoken word, "Mother."

＊＊＊＊＊＊＊＊＊＊＊

The Blue Ridge Mountains at dusk are made of flannel,
　　　　　　　　　though blue, they are a ghostly blue.

In an iron strong-box buried at the bottom
　　　an odd crystal formation spackled with zinc and copper
　　　rises to the surface, the tip of an iceberg
　　　　　　　that exposes itself in a receding ocean.

It fills up the interior of the mountain like guts.

'Til the beam of a microscope, my narration
　　　　　melts the alps of snow into salt,
　　　　　　　　　　　　pool into pool

My past reconstructed by its recollection,
　　　　　　　　made of the same substance
As the blue flannel childhood I fabricate
　　　　　　　　　into my death bed;
　　　　sand-cast shells, identically made.

They drift to the perimeter of the ocean's spectrum,
inconsequential as today
or the chattering teeth aglow in my dreams--
　　　chatter, chatter, chatter, chatter, chatter, chatter, chatter, chatter

Poinsettia leaves make quite a fright wig:
the infinite inscription of pages.

Each petal sequesters the myth of I

turned sepia in the course of its revisions
and matches so well the sepia floor
where from my lips the pages bleed into the parquet
to the dirt beneath,

a coming or going home of sorts:

The skull brought forth in the skeleton's hand
The heart torn out and dripping like a chalice that overflows
The prom rose produced in the form of a grey room,

the grey room, a shady vale
the vale, the necropolis of the analytic sofa
where lost like maggots

my past miscasts itself, procreates to fecundity
from fecundity to feces:
my mouth, my history, the famous patchwork quilt.

Dismantle the staircase as if fifty-two playing cards.
Fling them up, pell-mell, and in midair, regard;
they usurp themselves.

And the shell that prototypes the promise of "shell,"
And the skull that prototypes the promise of "face,"
And the voluminous hand of the monster inside the monster's chest

that fits the voluminous glove of pain,
that fumbles the comb for my matted hair
that forces me to sleep on a horse-hair mattress--

Baleful are the promises that splay themselves upon the floor of the grave:
playing cards, petals, poinsettia leaves, loose-leaf pages.

Baleful are the pages, this page, for instance. This page.

It tricks depth, shallows and shrinks
to the size of the face upon my wrist watch.
Now at the bottom, the mystical hour . . . .

The Specific Ocean

Finally,
            on the seventh day,
                        all twenty-six letters are tossed into a sea.

Tears,
            glistening like breath mints,
                                    tumble onto the catalogue
                        undulating the oblong outdoor sculpture
                        (represented here as an actual size)

Through and through
                        the horizontal blinds
                                                white brick drops back
            while the branches of the trees
                                    impale a height—
                                                held yet higher,
                        farther than a kiss blown to the father...

            A distance covered by amaranth,
            dotted by the sins of women and men:
            blue nudes who swoon before another Homo sapiens.

As if flesh tinted pennies sprang eternal from public spicates,
chipilin like the fountains in the gardens of Tivoli.
Tiny fingers begin counting
the jettisoned blessings that circumscribe their feet,
                                                awash in looking up.

Gazes ricochet off the alto-stratus,

an alulate feudal system

that remains impervious to upturned faces.

Alas, their thoughts have been lip-read in transit

and returned, consequently, to their rightful owners,

still spinning in place on their menology calendars;

dates circled in the tail chase.

A novena filled with helium hits the cathedral's ceiling.

Gargoyles wink at one another in the rain,

fledged by the raindrops.

The angel of mercy shrugs her wings.

But stand you will before the sublimated flame.

A self-initiated candle tips to ignite another name.

O unknowns, dozing in an ozone

far fetched as eternal rest:

I picture   you now   stretched out   as if sunning

or floating   on your backs   draped   in tucks

and folds   camisoles   sheer curtains   billowing

at floor   length   windows   blithe smiles   affixed

in yawns   Aryan eyes   slightly closed   the dazed look

up lighting   lo   cambric   tones

sound-proofs the heavens from those kept below

Where leaves, posthumously, skim the streets.
The wind lifts one up like a Christian from his knees.
On the river the sun surfaces, exit-red, for oxygen.
Gulls swerve near to my feet buried in saffron.

B is for blue, whatever shall be, world without end,
before me at my wrists, my ankles, feeding off of each.
Who sent for the doctor of a thousand leeches?
His little locked box in the crook of his arm.
His grin diminishes the room to an angle
to which my height proves the hypotenuse.

I offer myself up as if silver-plated,
the arch of my back, *l'arc de triomphe*.
Ordered to count backwards I'm anesthetized by numbers,
tamed like the virgin anointed for slaughter,
or a stone thrown into a pond, kerplunk.

The talisman placed (foil heart!) on my chest
auscultates an audio-video installation,
and somewhere amongst the syllables,
snapped twigs beneath my feet,
I happen upon my face
peering into the water at the penumbral rings.

Quietly as I watch me I am watched as quietly.
I wander about this auricular forest
and the elocution of its leaves,
where the sun seeps down as it does upon the Vatican,
the cardinal's song just as I expected.
Honed notes sew together the hem of a mantelletta
as it drags past the Pietà, up the scarlet stairs.

My hair rises in hope.
The sky's a magna carta blue,
though the diaphanous moon's plutonian.
A palomino's hide turns to wood.

Splayed by the grass is the gloryless flower.
A scream bursts from the severed vein.
So sweetheart rose goes the river
as the house I grew up in floats yet further.
Held hostage like a house I watch it float
creaking under the weight of my woe.

Broken dreams hover like the shadow of a branch.
How, I wonder, do I begin again?
What leads me ahead
once lead me from above
the way the Japanese were led by their Mikado.
Barefoot, I slept at the foot of the mountain.
A breeze could cross a continent then.

I lick my lips dry from the distance,
the hiatus between what's spoken and what's heard.
All that time that I thought I had listened
the history of music slipped through my hands,
exposed conversations spoiled like film.
And these words as I speak them
though voiced in your direction
barely graze your ears, ammunition misaimed,
their cadence disintegrating
down the caliber of my throat

It's pouring rain. Back at the motel, I walk into a dark room that becomes a theater. From the corner an answering machine is playing back a message.

"Hi Tory, it's David. I'm stranded out here in Indefinitetude. The plane leaves tomorrow. Lets meet at the airport in the afternoon . . . who's that singing in the background? A baroque soprano. How funereally beautiful! Be good."

We're travelling together like snowflakes. It's at the end of our trip and I have yet to type a story of his or mine, I can't remember which. I'm already behind schedule when you show up at the window and enter by it. You caress my face as the rain grows louder. Black letters type of their own volition the story on white paper. A car passes on the road. Wet leaves whirl upward, almost touching the trees.

The next day I meet David in a coffee shop at the tiny airport. The hour's rough. It's still pouring rain. A bald woman, handsome as an apology, is seated across from him in the red leather booth. Each holds their cup of coffee by its saucer. David spots me and waves. I walk over.

"Tory, this is Mme. Revoir, the famous teratologist. She's studying to become an architect. We were just discussing her career change." Then turning to Mme. Revoir he adds, "I've always wanted to write a book on the teratology of the phobic personality in twentieth century architecture."

She nods vigorously, searching madly in her pockets for cigarettes. Meanwhile, I produce a brand new pack of Rothmans which makes her smile (although I sense that she smokes non-filters). We hit it off. Lighting up, she inhales through her nostrils with a gasp and tells me a story about Corbusier and herself when they ran out of cigarettes on New Year's Eve.

"We thought it our fated resolution to quit!" she beams. I notice then that she wears the same style eyeglasses as Philip Johnson. Conversation stops when the plane lands. I watch a bird overhead leading many.

Suddenly distracted, David flags the waiter. It's time to take the plane. It leaves at seven-thirty, the same time as the local movie starts at the only movie theater in town, which is located at the tiny airport. Thirty-seven raindrops fall at once.

Just as we start to leave I remember that I forgot the story and must re-
turn to the motel. David jumps over a puddle and boards the plane. Mme. Revoir
climbs into the cockpit. I watch the plane take off. Things are touch-and-go for a
few minutes. Then blinking lights evaporate into navy.

Pitched against the road I start back to the motel. My hair's completely
soaked. The way is long like folklore. I cross two bridges before coming to a gas
station. I ask the attendant when the next plane leaves.

"Not 'til seven-thirty, same time as the movie starts," he says with a big
grin. All of his thirty-seven teeth are missing. I wonder what movie is playing
but decide not to ask him. I thank the attendant who winks spasmodically from
the rain. It's pouring.

Certain as a signature
are my last words to you, pre-recorded in my brain.
If I touch the tape it will self-destruct.
So I trace the Braille footprint on my heart.
Singed, it stings.

Think of the people you've loved but never reached.
Humans can teach monkeys to act but not to speak.

Like a document I played into your hands,
making love for my motherland.
Under your command I killed a bird
whose wings once spread beneath my lungs,
to stitch the ardent vest you wear today.
That's my imagination pinned to your lapel
calling to me like an exotic flower.

Under your command
I shaved my head and stood naked upon the wagon.
Spit scorched my breasts

as I walked through the crowd,
the scent of my village still moist on my lips.
A rock in my hand, I held onto my innocence.

Commitment ditched like a stiff into a Cadillac.
Murder committed in a country without laws.

I wrote you letters
but they were censored.
The guards, the guards, were they your parents?
Common as a comma in a sentence
were those occasions of hesitation,
the insults and then the devotions
thrown at each other with such velocity
that we bypassed our targets,
our promises piercing the stratosphere
so that they outlive us,
not in time as we know it
but in a time lovers feel they've tapped into,
the hollow behind a secret panel.

"Forever!" said Franklin of death and taxes.
Forever was said of the expulsion from Eden.
Now I understand what we meant by 'forever'
when up the spiral staircase we climbed together,
history leading us by the nose.

I suck from a blue vial
the sweet drought of forgetfulness
and still I know your body by heart:
the length of your legs and arms
the width of your hips and shoulder blades
your profile you showed me as you would a postcard,

your chin and forehead refined as a Pharaoh's
silhouetted against the sun—
a chrysanthemum,
deflecting desire with gold.

I see you in red for reconciliation.
White fences yield backward in pink,
small ships twinkle like earrings afloat
as I approach you, my red dress reeling,
a servant girl from the sixteen hundreds.
I pour evening into your cup.

I see you in red with no relation to pink,
a matador's cloak dropped before his bull.
A clock wrapped in a note yells against the air
and a thousand reckonings unstrap their belts.
Flaming ran the arrow, finally driven into sand.

After losing everything
destroying one more thing
is not just a macabre celebration
but a respectable tribute to loss.
Our story finished, ended and edited,
proofread by the light of a raised torch
is torn to bits and pieces by a banshee
flung up like confetti
to scatter like wedding rice on a lime green lawn,
like snow falling on a cemetery.
What's left adds up to no more than a ransom note
that wouldn't stand up as evidence in court.
The rest has been sent back from whence it came,
from a globe of brokenness
where moments gain value in their disappearance.

So go, and take with you your comrades
our last looks that litter the Luxembourg gardens,
the rubber mats of Tenth Avenue buses,
not to mention the Lido beach in January
where in July the tourists bathe nude on our legend.

The Learjet recedes like a prehistoric reptile.
From its bulging eye you wave goodbye.

If it is not your return I wait for
then it is for the ghost of your return,
for surely someone will fill the form of this phantom
just as your name became a sign to my love.
Who is it then that I've loved all along?
Who was the first?
Was it even a person?

I simply long for what was familiar,
the way a dog might dig up the grave of his master.
                              walked to the river—
                              boats pass by without a word,
                              day in and day out.

Edelweiss	Baby's breath	Narcissus	Gardenia
Austria	America	France	Malaysia
Ocean	Lake	River	Sea
Indian	Como	Thames	Bering
Moon	Sun	Star	Flame
Phoebe	Samson	Stella	Aiden
Albert	Helen	Dolores	Duane
Noble	Light	Sorrows	Poet

The creases in your palm
match the cracks in your wall,
        matched yet mismatched,
                like fingerprints.
And as you beg the sky to break—
      for surely there is above it
           even a greater sky—
homeless is the wind
     that breaks down at your feet,
         newspapers lap against your knees
your forehead bumping up against the horizon,
          a rainbow roped
   imminently around your neck.

Memories do grow on trees.
    Their promiscuity sets fire to your cheeks,
         since only hours prodigally spent
         can sift the real from the rest

   and in that attempt
subsequently add to the orgy of events
      yet another inscription
           in yet another hand
   upon the illuminated palimpsest
        dipped again in red.

Abandoned by your century,
      by the ordnances of your sex,
   mistakes surround you like a barbed wire fence.
        Bluebirds veer in the opposite direction
where the snow covered mountain
turns its back toward the moon,
      so pure, so aloof

absolving as a communion wafer—

Just as one side remains concealed from you,

we too

are forever held away from one another
like the fourth side of a cube

clandestine and unruled
(as a rule).

It is, perhaps, your closest friends

that have of you

merely a first impression . . .

I am off-center I am on the brink I begin to speak of me as we I walk beside myself
(literally!) in the streets this is the time the frozen hour when a memory of myself
embodies a vision that looms up beneath street lamps an aspen premonition and I
feel close to her as I would to a stranger that strikes the resemblance of someone
I loved "Remember!" she says "Remember or Resemble!" and sure enough the ob-
jects around me flaunt their autonomy like objects of transit a plane or train that
stationed symbolizes change or some form of justice no strings attached save for
those which you explicitly asked as if for a window seat in the smoking section
one must take their chances after specifications and nestled there on stained tweed
or turquoise plastic footsteps have passed the remorseful have departed as you fall
asleep to the theme of footsteps bare feet on the beach slippers shuffling in the
kitchen a sneaker floating in the river a pale pink sneaker floating in the gutter of
the street where no larger than your thumb though becoming larger is a little girl
walking someone has blindfolded the child pulling on her pigtails as reins to herd
her uphill where snowflakes tattoo the street behind her shoelaces trail while the
snow comes down much harder like the anthesis of snow covering the street com-
pletely a car drives by making tracks and snow covers the tracks slowly but surely
I wade through the drifts yelling out to her as I go until I hear muffled footsteps it's
the remorseful departing I think and just as I reach them I'm so close to them wait!
wait! I trip on my shoelaces trailing behind me in the snow that's no longer wet but

dry and smooth like the folded cotton the blindfold rolled out in the street thick as a mattress and I'm so tempted to lie down on it I'm so tired I want to fall asleep on the giant blindfold that's tattooed with tiny footprints as small as the pawprints of a kitten where a child has stepped where up ahead she's sleeping on stained tweed or turquoise plastic in the window seat of the train that's leaving

The way a believer needs no proof from the real
(what we want is Mary Poppins not Julie Andrews),
so do children who listen to their parents fight
night after night
find a melody, eventually, in the white sound
of their shouting,
a melody that plays in the place of a song
first heard in the unhinging of tears, now nigh.

The way ashes upon stones in an ash tray
seem meant for each other,
so do your parents in white & pin-striped gray,
wait for what's to come that has yet to be spoon-fed
to the happy couple's apparently happy future,
bred from eating out of the other's hand
a wedding cake that glows in the dark.
Boxed in by silver at a tender age,
their quitch-bliss preserves itself in a two-dimensional portrait;
the double exposure of icon upon ideal.

A down wind shudders over Idaho
An astrologer shuffles her deck of Tarot

Pretty pink dust falls from above
Populations stick out their tongues to taste some

There is so much

talk

of eternal night

but

it is eternal

day

I fear deflecting

light

dove-gray so

now

there's no night just

lasting

day lasting light

years

and the moon

once

a famous trouble-maker

becomes

a fable found like

stars

in storybooks

save

rare book

libraries

our knowledge of

constellations

Latin's equivalent

planetariums

having become non-

existence

What was the original sin?
Comparison?

Opposing forces, you are co-operating
and you don't even know it.

Example:

   Outside the movie theater on 57th street where Godard's latest film "Hail
Mary" is playing, hoards of Catholics, outraged at the director's blasphemy, pro-
test behind police barricades by furiously counting the beads on their rosaries and
chanting "Hail Mary, Hail Mary" as if hired for a promotional rally.

Our little earth spins in a spurious universe.
It rotates in remembrance of a galaxy that was genuine,
or at least justifiable.

Still, we scan the skies as if panning for gold,
our foreheads stitched in temporal confusion
as the listless distance returns our look
with that indigo of an infant's eye
or of the very old—forever open
and one step removed, albeit a baby step
they know more than we do; we to whom
perception congeals as a kind of feathery pool
we toe and squint into, its vapor
used as a facial for the future,
hope's anadiplosis ever raining on our roofs.

But beyond the august sky,
the rococo choreography of clouds
there floats the alleged heaven
that entertains millions in a manner
to which they are accustomed.

For at the prestigious Trinity Asylum
only the hypostatic are accepted.
The public (as we know)
can go to hell.

Emerging from this myth
is a mist pink-thighed and buxom,
auspicious in her paleness
autogenetic in her birth.
Dawn enters disguised as the present
and produces from her purse
a seething haze
seemingly innocuous and pearly
as she hurls it with demonic strength
into an unsuspecting world
where soldiers still are sleeping
defenseless despite their nuclear weapons
against this dead weight
that deliquesces into endless day,
diminishing dimension.

                                     The sea grass is frantic

                  trees quiver

                        as if Parkinson victims

              their leaves flap convulsively

                            almost epileptic

          the willow cramps over in a bout

                      of self-recrimination

      my spine curves like an appetite

                    in sympathetic reaction

           the sun stares on mum-faced

             as a Freudian analyst

                        vanishing like an oriflamme

     o'er the horizon the moon melts down

                                        and petals close in on flowers
        birds nest on stone
                                    oceans evaporate within minutes
                                        minutes within seconds
    rivers flood the forests
                                    mammals become amphibian
        piano keys   pouring black and white
            forget their notes
                                                into the city
    clouds   bounce
            curled up   along the street
                                            sticking
            to whatever's trivial
    menstrual blood
                flows in the gutter
                                where stringless violins
                                        set sail
        people half-dressed make love
    on the sidewalk
                                    to the beat of a child's
                tapping toe
                    and the earth whirls
    to the drumroll of children
                                                numbers run wild
                    throughout the sky
            flying in one ear   and out the other
    pencils   tennis balls
                tools   pens
            knives   syringes   juggler's pins
                    teeth   china cups
            and all missing things
    sink upward
                into the antiquated air

                                                            a snowfall
            of rosebuds and tulip leaves
                                                    spills
upon the bones
                    that build upon
                                            building rubble
      books burst   open   in an effort   to erase themselves

                  women turn into windows
                    windows into boys
                      boys into tables
                    tables into baskets
                    baskets into noise
                      noise into music
                    music into shells
                    shells into beaches
                    beaches into beds
                      beds into bathtubs
                  bathtubs into chairs
                    chairs into churches
                  churches into clouds
                    clouds into diamonds
              diamonds into mountains
                mountains into horses
                    horses into houses
                  houses into blankets
                  blankets into ceilings
                    ceilings into nets
                      nets into apples
                    apples into telephones
              telephones into mouths
                  mouths into envelopes
              envelopes into cells

                    cells into atoms
                  atoms into acid
                    acid into rain
                    rain into acid
                    acid into acid
                    acid into acid
                    acid into acid

I see them assemble on the onyx ocean
Their arms wired to the stars
A crowd reflected, signed and dated
Categorized by their Ages
Steps onto an extended wave

The bell buoy tolls like a call to supper
Their sighs swarm together
As if the voices of the famished
Single file they follow each other
Up the spotlit aisle like acolytes

The moon regards them as the angel Azrael
would separate the soul from the flesh
There is no smell or taste only motion
As people once ossified jump from their bodies
And dive one by one into a spotless sky
That opens like a mouth taking on a smile
Humans arch and wince in remission
Before swimming into the inhalation of light
Not blinding but sallow and dense as a cinder's
Where the late gods reappear
Like a panel of physicians
Each holds in their hand a copy of their legends
On each of their robes
Where their names are written

A constellation is embroidered in tribute
To their positions

I watch the procession
From a state of suspended animation
For I am the one held away from the past
The once who swelters in antecedent sleep
Dreamless and speechless
Though of speakable dreams
I am the one that was never born
Circling interpretations traces my birth
I am the I in I am that never lived
Yet when you knew darkness you knew me
I touched your lips, your pellicular lids
I taught you to teeth on foreign tongues
I held you tighter than your mother to be
Breathing into your lungs a warbling silence
Breathing into your eyes the reflex of trees
Breathing into your ears a melic idea
Breathing into your brain blind expectancy
Breathing into your heart the violence of memory
Twenty-six letters tossed into the sea

The Horizon

Pentecostal, the churlish bushes bend all at once toward the ocean.
Ominously, the ocean arches, in response to its audience,
like the nerve-racked needle on an applause meter.

Godforsaken rain begins to fall on the godforsaken dew.

What but a contrast of colors that clash actually controls?
Few are the flagrant pebbles tossed playfully, sticks to a dog.
My response to this like ocean to bush or reader to poem,
I'll pull like toffee the meaning within limits
to satisfy my greedy, bone-dry soul.

I'll wait at the door of nightfall on all fours
I'll wait for the mantelletta to drop,
its unstoppable weight, brave garb, of Virgin Mary blue.
I'll wait for my baby-doll nightgown to flutter up, petals on a buttercup
irked slightly by the breeze of your breath and your steps to meet me.
Deeper my nails dig into the dirt and glow belatedly in the dark
as the moon positions itself in mercenary surveillance
and pours its hot fluorescence on my obsequious neck, hell-bent.

Collared and chained to a stake from the start
I'm leased to a circumference
which by now I've run a rut steep as a medieval moat.
From time to time I'll stop, react, blink in homage to the horizon,
admire how aptly it mimics the radius of my leash.
O in just the idea of a bridge there's implicit the hope of my leaving.
As man's best friend I've come to understand man, a little.
Nothing drives the backbone, you see, quite like oppression,
the oppressive, boneless erection, my baleful stake, heroically driven.
And the rape of the collar in which I acclimate hourly, but never fully,

poor adapter, ousted forever for my unorthodox behavior.
Sound familiar? The horizon knows, although never irregular itself.
It broke our toes while we were sleeping with its immaculate foot-long ruler.

Against the sun's exactitude, how could we compete with such uniform precision.
We counter as cowards, ineffectually human.
How to mimic the horizon becomes the dog-day old dilemma.
How to keep another species more vulnerable, more human, more
obsequious by force as we were forced to feel in the beginning.
How to rule unilaterally with the ruler's edge like the horizon.
How to own the superiority of two legs
as opposed to the all-fours submission of dogs or women.

Well, we can keep our dog yards filled with women
circling like skirts or Ferris wheels for our amusement.
We can pressure them to have breast implants so we can have bigger penises,
('cause if there were such a thing as penis implants
we guys would want one the size of the Chrysler Building).
We can avoid the lone-dog look in their eyes,
take them, then say "You're welcome!"
We can snuff out the fear inside us like a Marlboro
forget the tremor the horizon offers as a reminder
of what minuscule space we puny mortals take up in its precious time.

Smaller than dog biscuits or corn-pone or river-rivets
and vast as the population of women who've died in childbirth
we can stonewall with balls of Hawkeye our specific existence
so that its specificity shrinks in proportion to the size of a BB
shot to no avail, gritty and worthless, into the evasive distance.

Blue Ruin

Welts rise up on the youth of paper
Where lead drags a tiny trail across its torso
As if threshing a path home
Trenchant and narrow

Ostensibly, I'm lead through the diminutive forest
To no definitive gate at the end
As I'm steered in a circle, a slow pirouette
The circumference disheveled with shards of sky
Of exfoliated night,
Returned oblations that graze the dirt
Psalms, bits of bread, the pubic hair of virgins,
And stars felled as if by sleight of hand
With itsy, glistening cloud chips
Tile the homely earth like mosaics
Splinters of moon protrude between twigs

The hierarchy of height dismantled
A subject fetishized to such an extent
Erosion began from the inside, desultorily,
Like metastasized cancer, like civil war
Where the blood of children brands the streets
The way blackness like blood makes viscous the rivers
The university of night overthrown by its students
Scattered at the shoes of a scholar (a pair?)
Loose-leaf papers loosened from a notebook
Thrown with love at the threshold of the professor
Eyeglasses, a bottled note, swept out to sea
A book tossed on the beach and left there, indefinitely
Lost as a passage read from a book
A passage as long as the length of a book

Its pages fading away like praise
Though the loss of content be equal to the loss of leaves
The way denotative and connotative are caught in a ceiling,
Generic as a lexicon that, unbound, bursts
Gluing together the late sky, piecemeal, leaf by leaf
For looking up there's nothing higher than trees,
Nothing higher than branches faradized from belief
For looking up there nothing higher than trees,
Gluing together the late sky, piecemeal, leaf by leaf
Generic as a lexicon that, unbound, bursts
The way denotative and connotative are caught in a ceiling,
Though the loss of content be equal to the loss of leaves
Its pages fading away like praise
A passage as long as the length of a book
Lost as a passage read from the book,
A book tossed on the beach and left there, indefinitely
Eyeglasses, a bottled note, swept out to sea
Thrown with love at the threshold of the professor
Loose-leaf papers loosened from a notebook
Scattered at the shoes of a scholar (a pair?)
The university of night overthrown by its students

The way blackness like blood makes viscous the rivers
Where the blood of children brands the streets
Like metastasized cancer, like civil war
Erosion began from the inside, desultorily,
A subject fetishized to such an extent
The hierarchy of height dismantled

Splinters of moon protrude between twigs
Tile the homely earth like mosaics
With itsy, glistening cloud chips
And stars felled as if by sleight of hand

Psalms, bits of bread, the pubic hair of virgins
Returned oblations that graze the dirt
Of exfoliated night,
The circumference disheveled with shards of sky
As I'm steered in a circle, a slow pirouette
To no definitive gate at the end
Ostensibly, I'm lead through the diminutive forest

Trenchant and narrow
As if threshing a path home
Where lead drags a tiny trail across its torso
Welts rise up on the youth of paper

Faux Poem

Lavender atmosphere downpours in powder-puff gusts
into the FAUX forest and FAUX life within—
an impressive amethyst mess—.

What's the real thing?

The same autonomical ambience that ransacks the trees,
as documented in meteorology textbooks,
reveals itself a closet violet like smog,
the forest where it filtrates fairy-like, as if animated
defines the height of FAUX.
How do we know what is genuine?

Is the phone call more FAUX than the kiss?
The handshake than the contract or vice versa?
The message left on the answering machine which is indisputably Memorex
FAUX in the feeling your vocal cords incur in me?

And isn't the FAUX sometimes much more preferable than the real,
the fluffy compliment than the parched terrain of an honest response;
and though the truth in its petrified state, like logs from the FAUX forest,
penetrates like a beam of wood, an arrow plucked from Cupid's back-pack,
shot to a bull's-eye from his harp-shaped bow,
catalyzing the inert brain to communicativeness,
the foolhardy body to the sensible act,
the lascivious heart held under glass to break glass in its zeal . . .

So FAUX can produce effects of the real,
for symbiotic are they like the companion poems
of "L'Allegro" and "Il Penseroso."
They're not even as far apart as our dreams are from our waking,
but as dreams are from our sleeping
or thought from conscious thinking.

Utterly FAUX is the world around me, both culturally
and organically, that I must in fact be FAUX too:
FAUX in my thoughts, in my dreams, in my being,
in my destiny wish-fulfilled by the great FAUX gods of Zeus and Apollo ,
the FAUXISM of gods punctuating and climaxing within the movement of history

like the FAUX phallus of my fantasies that enters me slowly, then thrustingly,
our flesh-colored bodies like FAUXISM and reality,
lapping against each other, as sea water against Grecian rock,
until water oozes from stone and becomes the inseparable
"L'Allegro" and "Il Penseroso" companion poems.

What authenticates an action, a sentiment, an intention?
Is not the FAUXIST dimensions that rally reality,
give it its zip that partitions it from the rest of life,
renders it larger than itself for its own amusement,
the way the gaze originated in the mirror?

Do the feelings I have around you which make me so happy
count as countless because of our limitations,
that bliss I've come to know in its raw state
dissipating in actuality into what could be labeled (ah me) as FAUX happiness?

Well, I don't care if it's FAUX, I'll take it!

For I don't love you less because I look at you through holes in a fence,
much the way a prisoner inspects the outside world,
or the outside world inspects the prisoner.

My love is not FAUX, not illusory in its greenery,
even when compared to the botanical counterparts
that stroll along in married couples,
their tidy contracted commitments projected obnoxiously onto the world
(me in particular), as if voiced from a bull-horn,
understood to have been approved by pop psychologists everywhere.
What love is not perceived through a fence, I wonder?

Yes, I have the right to be nostalgic
for a love that has yet to be and may never come or quiver
within the ice sculpture garden of my future . . . .
and fake a friendship just to be closer to you
with that implacable loyalty felt soulfully for a friend,
capitulate without resentment to what you need,
without jealousy, without disappointment,
the way with stray eyes we sometimes feel that we can see through skin,
peer from the mezzanine into the red theater of the heart,
adore the stage for what we imagine could happen,

as virginity is esteemed, really, for its whoring potential.
And even those who have been selfish and stupid
soften to benevolence when confronted with the innocent,
because don't I, too, live underneath my problems like a fetus,
so fragile and emblematic of beginning and ending,
the overpass subtly constructed in the figure eight of infinity.

Aren't fences, too, like fetuses beautiful in their defenses,
like the cliché of the angry, beautiful woman,
who becomes more beautiful with her venom,
the fences, natural borderlines of hedges,
erected to manicure the landscape of our future together
by defining our futures apart, each icy and green
and indecipherable from the long distance with which we speculate them:
O stormy, stinging uncertainty of outcome,
the mandatory race between the hare and the turtle
that has yet to be disclosed from the gold sealed envelope,
which species we play in our hackneyed revival.

But when I become so afraid on the freeway,
perhaps it's not genuine courage that generates in me,
though I happen to notice that my legs move anyway,
purely out of habit, I guess,
the way one is able to drive miraculously well when they are drunk
simply because they're so well practiced
at drinking or driving or in combining them both.

But if my emotion be FAUX, so to speak, my shoes are made of Italian leather
and regardless of the questionable authenticity of feeling,
my steps, if I were walking along on sand,
would leave footprints dogs could sniff,
which seems to be all that matters,

since my legs do their job (and not a bad job, frankly)
of moving forward.

The Flower Room

Within the white, white building where within the white, white
rooms, pale in contrast like a pale pink tulip
there exists the flower room within the body
of the hospital, complex and organized as a sestina
as profuse and varied as a wedding bouquet
that resides in the flower room amongst all other flowers like handwriting

within a text or a page without text or handwriting.
Both promising and promiseless as the overcast sky, white, white
are the walls altered only at times by a single bouquet
three days old, pale in contrast as a pale pink tulip
yet useful as something to focus on as if a sestina
they organize and recognize the arrangement with a body

of sensory appreciation, the ability to smell the only body
that they can recognize as themselves like a sample of their handwriting
reminiscent of their old life as the sophomoric sestina
abstracting into the obscurity of these white, white
walls, pale in contrast as a pale pink tulip
yet sustains itself against the demanding white like a bouquet

that understands its needs to be analogized, like a bouquet
of fresh flowers there is hope for the diseased body
perhaps pale in contrast as a pale pink tulip
yet helpful and comforting as the handwriting
of a friend jotted down hurriedly but with love on the white, white
card, and effort as forced and as intentional as this sestina

yet as ingenuous and natural as the first sestina
that was ever written or perhaps the first bouquet
ever picked and given to the outstretched white, white
hand of perhaps the first evolutionized body.

Sunday in Thailand

Hold fast to dreams

springtime's river bank branch
            that saves you from downstream death
its wet bark embraced as if in love
and like love
            the irony of pale petals budding pressed
against your forehead
            while twigs and snapped wood cut you
deep as wolf bite,
      as glass shards and jagged slate arrowheads of previous promises broken.
                Their scars branch out in a pattern across
your forearms, purple like blown veins, of tributaries that
feed into the larger disappointment, its repetition detected by a telesthesia
that rolls inside you like distant thunder: the dread, the familiarity,
the grim two-dimensionality which from now on you'll be forced to speak to.
Its horror pushes you forward.

It forces the
            focus on those gold filaments of late autumn leaves
like fleur-de-lis, you say to yourself, convincing yourself—
something appropriated from nothing, exactly what a dream is—
and a hopeful impulse catches in your throat.
You stare out your window with renewed curiosity and marvel, not
at what you see, but at this almost cryptic capacity for renewal.

Autumn leaves, blooming yellow and olive as the compatriot bruises
on your various body parts, organic tatoos of life gone wrong,
so too do they (leaves) emboss the air with an exigency,
scar that listless vacuum of exhalation with visual cues
of existent beauty and beauty implicit
in the possibility of existence's capacity
for relief, for overcoming grief, for waking,
glad goodness gleaned from ordinary daylight.

Hold fast, hold tight to that skeletal hand
that leads light-footed from a few paces ahead; its the lost origin
of your dream, now a blurry head,

checkerboarded by media censorship you recognize but cannot identify.
It's your dream reborn, resurrected from its levitated burial,
the stick tray on stilts where incinerated flesh smoked and hurled
with tunneling spirals into grayer skies—you stood transfixed,
you moaned a goodbye prayer, you hit yourself out of frustration
and loneliness—you breathe deeply the smoke until it makes you cough
for therein, in the Siamese twins of your lungs, the dream begins again
pieced together, piecemeal, a cracked china doll not a child of madness.

When dreams die splayed against the darkness, the cold mattress and white walls
when your cries, drowned out by bus breaks and car alarms, or just stillness,
as if held underwater until asphyxiated—that bloodless quiet
where your anguish whirls across field, fence, field, like vermin life,
yet not a wheat shaft shutters
under full moon fortune, a spiteful plentitude. Its bounty multiplies
by virtue of your depravation, or so it seems—feeds, as it were,
off the corn grain of your sorrow—sucks to lip-licked satisfaction
the nutrients of your marrow
its hungry jaws working away at the core of you
but only the dream—at the core of you—
fights back, bulwarks the deluge, stone garrison of glossy images
that cannot be gotten rid of.
Out in that wilderness, winded and anemic,
covered in dust-dew, amidst a cold-billowed cloud dawn
from which you rise up and out of, bringing back to life
by giving birth
from that gut nest where the dream seed first secured itself,
where godless need turned itself into a swan and penetrated like Zeus
and another dream, concretized with each contraction
dares to dream for you despite evidence otherwise,
to come back, to sit up, to thrust the dream head to crown between your legs,
to outlive some sickness, someday.

To exercise the muscle, squeeze the rubber ball, resist
a temptation to give into the fatigue that thwarts the work of dreams
like sparrows crashing into a plate-glass window—behold, with frightening
perception, the spectrum of dreams, hunt down their pictures
reflected in puddles punctuated by raindrops on rooftops—
the momentary rush you fend off in their coming true—

for a second you allow it, sugar cube of pure hallucinogenic
which coddles you inside its bubble-future, the innate womb of hope
whose innate fragility you stubbornly refuse.
And you must refuse it, for it's the only protection you've got
from merging into rainwater as if of only water, more than 80%, you are made.
Just water and gristle, and a teeth-lined jaw discovered,
the whimsy, the chaos, the cruelty, the ineffectuality,
the jagged edge of daybreak coming back to eat what' s left of you,
its wholesome redundancy which you could never break out of.

Hold fast to dream-offspring, the deaf-mute
and Down's syndrome dreams, precious as perfect originals:

Hold fast to dreams, the desire they signify,

        Any dream is strong in itself
as a cry of protest, as a poem of controversy, as an action of integrity
as the dare to love and effort to receive love from the same person.

though its contemplation teases you, its frustration burns through you
drives you to sob alone at night, to scream out at the ceiling, its
eschatological summation that's the only alternative;
it is its desire that continues to believe in you
the iconoclastic dream, the ridiculous dream, the minor dream
dreams begotten of failed dream, missing dreams found, forgotten dreams
half-remembered, even if just as objects
like cherished souvenirs between the expired pages of your journal.

For if dreams die,
so what becomes of them becomes hard to acknowledge
like what's hard to look at, an act of cruelty or suffering,
acute and sordid you're forced to witness—its image, its sound, every detail
none of which could be called gratuitous
not the gum wrappers or news pages crumbled near the rape victim's head.
There was nothing you could do to help her.

Was that true of you with yourself?
Did you let yourself lie there unattended, not scream loud enough?
Did you freeze at the moment, refuse to speak, turn away
down the staircase you climb down, only down
where you pace just to make something happen
for nothing will happen if you let go of dreams

Life is a broken-winged bird you watch with only one eye

reverberating in the frontal lobe
painful to think of though it persists in your mind

Their truncated sentences lie on the sidewalk when you pass

that cannot fly.

The fast dreams that save you from the body
save you from your mind
from your despondent heart
it battles like chemo the loneliness in your blood,
the loneliness that eats
you alive from your gut, the hole that as a child was the world
that as an adult becomes just what life is
everything you do is an offering to your dream
you feed it like a husband, like a father, like a king
obey your dream and one day it will free you
sacrific for your dream and though it may never materialize,
always it will hold you like the mother you should have had,
hold you like a lover, like no experience other, to be tried in life
will never have; You've had
the dream of love
the dream of strength
Frozen with snow
the dream of justice,
the dream of a cure.

For when dreams go
Life is a barren field.

Wait for your dream outside its gates, plant flowers for your dream,
pay homage, show respect.

Hold fast to dreams
like a screaming child—   like a screaming child—

The Courage to Surrender

I wish that we could lie down together, clothed
on a bed that extends endlessly outward like wall to wall carpet
and just hold each other for a long, long time
undisturbed as a house snowed-in.

Like snow I wish I could relinquish myself,
not exactly abandon which implies betrayal,
or with the sense of surrender that underscores defeat—
albeit I've toiled, truly, like a battalion
a waffling white flag, holes oppugned
by the critical inquisition of the woods.

The white flag, a bandage, blood-spotted and needing to be changed
but never was; the white flag, the snowy landscape
sparse as a haiku but never as beautiful;
the white flag, my body contorted to imitate, skilled at method acting
while I kneeled and pleaded and gave whatever was meaningful to me
that lay plentiful by virtue of my eagerness to please
in the top drawer of my bureau where meaning would multiply
according to the law of supply and demand.

Accordingly I wrote notes, many note-cards long, of my love
of my apology, of my unworthiness.
But the atonement never came.
But the snowy landscape remained sparse and unlike a haiku.
The snowy landscaped was indeed ugly and without hope even amongst the animals.

I wish that, in the way the snow was not ultimately responsible
for its ugliness, I too could relinquish myself from that responsibly
in the gesture of lying down, clothed, with you.
I wish that the internal raving that may always rave
(as with the shell-shocked it often does),
the sentry inside me who still clocks the woods,
suspects even the quintessence of a starry night
would on another occasion, allow the tranquility a starry night
might provide, just in its night-time starriness.

I wish that I could turn these symbols of sorrow over in my hand
like expired coins that increase in value,
hock one one day and buy something special for you,
partly deft have I become to discerning bombs from animals
partly desirous like a flurry, flustered and excited to lie down with you
as if snowed-in, and hold you
undisturbed like a house, undisturbed.

Without Saying

The felony of rain delineates the spring from a crass rendition,
the divine from the myth of its intervention.

What is divine, imperfect as my body or your clear eyes
that look at me without diverting themselves
longer than I can return; though my attention goes nowhere else,
sleeps with no one else,
my glance moves briefly, self-consciously from cup to neighboring table
to traffic to the henna horizon of the Palisades.

The misshapen pearls of them become more misshapen, protrude further
with my projection, my dissemination of you in everything
that reverberates continually, like aftershocks, back to me—
variations of you and what you mean to me
until action and repercussion become one and the same and the world
is never still again.

Please, don't think less of me, think it means I think less of you,
but forgive me anyway, simply because I'm asking you to.

Whether I have something to be sorry for or not
I'm forced down on the floor, to a humbler place
a humiliation, if you will, where selfishly I'm more in sync
with what resembles this feeling: flawless but misshapen pearls,
baroque facsimiles, felicity, a fer-de-lance, fetterbushes,
fetlocks, and forget not the carved wooden fetish, Dahoman.

I know eventually I'll be able to gather in my pearly gaze
these monstrosities, and be less ashamed, less in need of apologies,
less attached to such ghastly architecture I so identify with,
that ornamentation which succeeds in busting out from within,
which insists itself upon the silken air, a cow's ear, like gargoyles.
How compatible delicacy and vulgarity appear.
How I envy their compatibility, envy most enviously, to tears.

Don't we all grow, though, in staggered juts like economic charts
drawn impartially from dream to digression?
Like these over-crafted, audacious, self-entertained poems,

an adverb fanatic happily lost in its own mazes,
mesmerized by opiated myoptics of azaleas.

The body is born, a misshapen pearl, a girl! a girl!
Even if it is, indeed, a boy—a boy with the heart of a girl
and the body of a man stuck in a manly world;
Where all around busts and bellies and buttocks protrude
like baroque architecture or baroque music.
Double violins in opposite ascension scale up and down,
economic charts within the misshapen pearl of their concerto.
The hourglass body of the violin and the voluptuous sorrow of her voice
collide in the unconscious where no penetration, no music
can undress, unearth, all the illicit, misshapen secrets.

Don't we all want to listen and be fully listened to
to what we haltingly say and add on to and add on to
until we find inbreed in such articulation
the very architecture where ornamentation breeds like beats
bulbous as if bruised, busting out, exclamatory, from within;
while deep inside this palace we are walking a long and lapping stride.
We are breathing deeply in the way of genuine relief
since its been such a long time, long and lapping
that we harbored this certain feeling way down inside of being en route toward something
you really love, albeit misshapen, flawless in your mind.

What I wouldn't give to receive an arm for a leg,
a violin for a violin, a cow's silken ear to breath like that again.

Don't we all sometimes sense the overwhelming
misshapen pearls well up inside, bulge out in confrontation of our denial
so that we're forced to eat beats for dinner and dreams of palaces at night?

And then notice with relief a lack of fear of the grotesque,
of our misshapenness, even acquire an appreciation for the clash
the way one anticipates great music in an orchestra's tuning.
Of sharp digressive and diverting scratches
haphazardly scrawled, ekes out our shaping
understood as essential only in their belated designation,
(yet how else is the essential to be understood but belatedly?)

What ornamentation is honest as no ornamentation,
belies itself as only, as set apart uncontrollably,
only busts out eventually
as only, only a lie.
But what are lies, but more misshapen pearls?!
More excuses
for the asking of one's pardonance:

more double violins,
more dramatic digressions, more ornamentation,
more liturgically beautiful trinkets,
more fey, ambling, self-centered and interminable poems,
more likewise monstrosities,
more desecrating arguments, more waffle irons,
more manly bodies,
more gargoyles,
more pink and violet stones,
more girlish hearts, pink and violet stones that are soft in the center
more facsimiles,
more orifices (all shapes and sizes, please!)
more economic charts,
more lace panties,
more fer-de-lances,
more sacramental chalices,
more taxis,
more exquisite acquisitions, more tenderly felt phrases,
more insistence, more insistence,
more concertos,
more bellies,
more unheard grievances,
more elicited secrets,
more extenuating circumstances,
more pleasantries for the middle class,
more crap,
more Crustacean,
more Harlequins,
more exit signs,
more pardonances,
more forgivenesses.

Black Pebbles

Its raining copper and purple beads on a red, red beach.

Who are you?

I am on the beach and I'm crying. The rain and the wind pull at my gown and it's hard to keep my balance. I's wearing a shawl which is strange since I never wear shawls. I seem to be screaming, calling out, but my view is obscured by my tears and by the rain, copper and purple.

Who are you?

I am on the copper beach and there is only a little breeze, very dry but peppered it salt air. My gown is still wet, though, purple and red and copper streaks continue to flow hallucinogenically down my bodice to my feet. I watch, afraid, and notice they are my tears falling involuntarily from my eyes, from my face without a grimace of sorrow, but poker and somewhat amazed as I stare at my gown, heavy with tears, buffeted, though only slightly from the dry, salt-spat breeze.

Who are you?

I notice black pebbles scattered along the beach, black pebbles like the anonymous ballets cast for an execution, or on a less violent level, for the exclusion from a circle or club. I notice that in fact they do form a kind of circle around, though helter-skelterly drawn. I feel as if there has been made some kind of decision, a passing of judgment, or perhaps just a passing involving me. A decision has been made, involving death or exclusion, a veto of something or someone now absent. I check my gown and it is white now, pristine even, as if freshly laundered and ironed, not starched, but soft in texture as it laps against my legs in the slightly stronger breeze. I notice that I listen, my legs shapely and secure on the almost equally white beach.

Who are you?

I'm sitting crossed-legged on the pale pink beach. The black pebbles are still scattered around me though in more of a uniform arrangement and I realize that they are there to protect me. The black pebbles form a circle of protection. I stare out at the ocean, running at its normal narrative pace, waves systematically rising like days, peaking for a time in the distance, at first pretending not to, then arching over to stretch lionically, androgynously, its last words silly and frivolous foam like an inside joke. Sometimes the sea seems taunting to me, so self-contained, rather arrogant actually, overly mature and out of sync with what I'm feeling so completely it just accentuates my isolation. Why do I expect more from the sea than say trees or rocks or even mountain ranges that only deflect your feelings like a Freudian. The sea is animate, fleshed out and filled to the brim with itself, so scorpion in its secretiveness, so Piscean in its servitude, so otherworldly with all its fish and depth and danger and tragedy. I'm longing for something, for someone I guess, sitting cross-legged, my gown stretched taut across my knees and the sea finds its way, has its way with me, pours over my ankles and up between my legs, my vagina, my spine, my heart my brain. I long for something, someone I guess, and the sea has it, something integrally mine like my own remains, cremated and jettisoned as stated in my will, from a coffee can, preferably a brand I never drank like Saverine. It jettisoned into the ocean some sea-weary Lobster fisherman elected for his indifference, someone to whom my remains mean nothing so that dumping them into the ocean brings not even a twinge of pain, no real introspection. At the most the gesture might form as an afterthought, a bizarre detour to his day that looking back was distasteful and therefore a nuisance. Its only value lies in its potential for an antidote he recuperates later that afternoon at the bar to another fisherman who unresponsively listens then eventually comments, lips nearing the head of his beer, something appropriate like "Well, that's weird!"

Who are you?

I long for something but not nostalgically, not as if I truly missed something, but more along the lines of feeling freaked-out by the sense of unfamiliarity. It's a little bit of a lost feeling to know that your ashes are out there dispersed in the ocean, perhaps having settled in the crevices of a sunk ship, atop a trunk of buried treasure or perhaps still descending, very, very, slowly, a hundred years taken to reach the ocean's bottom, or floating forever, suspended eternally as the metamorphosized properties of the ocean's psyche, save for a few particles gulped up already by a ravenous fish or a ravenous school of fish.

Who are you?

I am wearing an exquisite gown, incredibly chic of aquamarine chiffon. It's more of an Isaac Mizrahi creation than say Oscar de la Renta. I am at the water's edge, not standing but flying, propelled by the velocity of the ocean's wind and sea spray yet the action is of my own doing like the ability to glide a plane or fly a kite only I am both the kite the kiter. I'm arched like a dolphin over the surf, laughing and incredibly proud of myself. You are standing on the beach, exclaiming, "Wow, Tory, that amazing," and I'm exclaiming, "Look! Look at me, look!"

Dot to Dot, Dear to My Heart

At different points in the night, behold
 the stem of my glass that turns from wine
to whiskey, then to armagnac. Blessed are these changes
caught in time, carefully set by a mother's hand,
a passing glove—whether it be really hers
or a brief hallucination, she was there, there for you
now beginning to disappear, exiting like an actress
from the silent era into a snowfall of soap flakes.
Only a little heather dust is left behind, trails of iris
and yellow, spurned. The scene kicks in,
the scent bends the mind like a tranquilizer
and you know you're helpless: to be no longer falling
but to have fallen
like in love, like an empire,
a spiraling column set down on its side.
The blue salts in your system swiftly pare her image
to only a profile, to a Polaroid of her profile,
and that way conveniently she can stay inside, overnight,
like a refrigerated rose.

Even if sleeping your past keeps waking,
the angle of your elbow guiding you like a mantra
back to your cot, your original bed
where you once slept, where you meet her again.
There upon your pillow your two childhoods meet,
and like yearlings you're both free
set loose inside a ring.   But tomorrow you can leave
with hopes of reaching the volunteer of your dreams;
someone in front of which you're allowed to be afraid
even if what looming looms lovely overhead.
The Côte d'Azur becomes a coat of arms upon a shield
rushing to your side, and by your side, to your defense,
while the free arm
drops its double-edged sword
to hold you close as a ray of sun.

Think of all your plans:
the expanse of your life in your glance from earth to sky.

Marvelous ruins await almost anywhere!
Or the way faces circle in one's sexual imagination,
let countries and cities travel toward you.
For tomorrow you can leave
or tomorrow you can stay, like a tree
very tall and in being tall, very brave.
And if late at night it's impossible to sleep
wildly let regrets plunge--*saltimbanques* at your feet.
Carry your losses like a guitar on your back
when their weather wins you over
pulling the covers to your neck.
So much like the passing a of a mother's careful hand
who smoothed your hair like sleep itself,
leaving your door ajar, leaving you what has left.

The Cathedral

Like veins in marble my sorrow and my sorrow lessened
share part and parcel like ore and glass
the windows and walls as vast as an individual,
the floor, the staircase, where down each mindful stair
I'm taken as if led by a paranymph palliated in blue
one peg then two to a leveless, heinous land.

I'm left to stand at the foot of a path, an aisle
more than a mile in length, aligned with heirlooms, trees and pews.
Between my path and its hereditary stance
gutters run like rain pipes or some rudimentary irrigation system
a sewer as I look closer at the water, tepid but rising
overflowing with debris, excrement and skulls of household vermin.
Welling up as well in its bubble and hiss tows
doll's clothes and other remnants discarded with efforts, impulsive:
photographs, jewelry, postcards and letters
I recognize unflinchingly to be my own.
As if somewhere up ahead some changeling were cleaning out, mercilessly,
my home, pulling rank and ransacking throughout my belongings
dividing them up according to their value without sentiment,
the way relatives devour the estate of the deceased.
I can hear them chewing greedily even though more than a mile away.
I can feel them rifling though impatiently thing after thing.
I only wish I had a long stick so that I could retrieve just one
already bobbing past me in the river of things now gone.
But things they were, albeit lovely, as the cathedral
made up of things is a thing in itself, very large, very opalescent
like the stained glass that casts shards of colored light on my path
chameleon-like as carp in the pond of a pagoda.
The path itself stretches out, a note sustained in operatic soprano.
Marble and veined, an open mouth, the watery song, the pagoda pond
suspends and shivering, multiplies within its own vibration
like notes in a xylophone or marimba.

You might think I would feel anger but like the trees, like the pews
my anger has become a thing of the past, an heirloom,
a photograph, a postcard, an engagement ring flowing past me into the gutter.
All that I'm attached to, or was, crescents and wakes to my left and right,
and when briefly synchronized with my step, thing and I,

one moves ahead and the other further behind.
The symbolism having reached a bursting point in my head
suddenly depresses the way a novena muttered releases into what has been said.
What has been lived I enter and exit to enter again, as a needle threads
or song breaches when taking a breath
but never ending except when it does like breath or a finished dress.
The song etymologized as if a Latin verb
roots to a child's cry from a child I've never met.

Gallons of tears (and not all from children) flow to my right and my left,
buoying up my belongs that in their buoying loose themselves
as objects of possession.

Only the song channeled like a gutter is, for a moment, entirely mine,
watering like my mouth from desire, from frustration
like the rain that splashes outside
in sympathetic reaction to my own crying
as if the god's were as frustrated, as desirous as I'm.
My mouth procreates its tears like children, a vagina, it takes in, takes in,
then gives out, my great tongue undulating outward, serpentine in its approach
to lick the cross slowly like ice cream, just the way you want.
The gutters swell up to the brim, nearly overflowing, until they do
lightly grazing my path with missives and swirls of urination.
And as if taking on the sobs of the world
babies burst from my mouth like fish from a half-drowned sailor.
Tremulous the weight increases of colored rain on the cathedral roof.
It buckles just an inch. Buttresses protrude from their niches.
The gargoyles, animated and fettered, alight from their stoops,
circle above with prescient accuracy, vultures in the desert.
They adumbrate the eventuality of the half-drowned sailor
to drown completely in a sea
as disclaiming, as erogenous, as mercenary as it appears to be.
Eventually my flesh too will dismember exactly, the debris
that now, comparatively speaking, babbles by me so innocently.
Like excrement from my body, my flesh will separate itself from my bones,
and my bones from their long-standing commitment to each other.
Somewhere my blood will resurface in a pool, like an oil slick,
which in the minds of others, will be referred to as "spirit"
recognized as ascending, unbeknownst to the atheist
to whom, like an oil slick, like a pool of urination
my blood will be that and nothing more.

So be it. So be it.
To all those healthy attitudes may my steps steadily amend,
such minor steps, sliding upon the tears I shed.
Lush like tears be the forest of colored rain that flays against the windows.
I'll take in the utterances from the twelve-pipe organ,
with equal aperture, as a birth cavity opens to take in
in order to give out, knifed open to a wider width still.
Mouthfuls of music spew from my lips, cadaverous as a cathedral
my jaws pried apart, unhinge, flap like a screen-door at whim of the wind.
And out of this assemblage, this accompanying bent, I'll rant
rat a tat a tat tat a rat a tat a tat tat a rat a tat a tat tat a rat a tat
a tune more pure than its purpose, than tears,
no matter how opaque they be made by their emoting,
sullied as the water floating in the gutter,
the great guttural Thespian of my throat.

They came like Latin verbs from a source pure as infants,
as Moses, swathed and basketed to be sped down the river.
Soft as him, bequeath the dark recessing of their inceptions, always.
To the tunneling intrusions of the phallic organ,
may its music splay out into space like its antecedent, silence,
may its semen splay out into space like its antecedent, absence.
Give me, give me, give me, antecedents, give me semen, give me music.
Give it to me, one by one, by one, purposefully, methodically,
candles lit then candles singed, left behind in the chapel.
Like the velveteen worn thin and vulnerable on the praying stools,
line my mouth with velveteen, worn as thin and as vulnerable.

Velveteen, velveteen, unroll the song, a blue-red carpet running up the aisle
until it reaches the cross then rises, a wave, a tongue
that licks slowly like ice cream then swallows it whole
with a viscous, ever-widening mouth; no teeth (that's right) no teeth at all
just lips, encompassing, encasing like a dome, an endearing mother
the cathedral that accommodates one worshiper after another,
impaled by semen, impaled by song,
the monolithic organ feeds on schedule a multitude of open mouths.

Shelling

Deplorable, the devi's draw back ceremoniously
as a tea ceremony the infinite poem that pools outward, overwhelmed;
an unassuming brook caught in a downpour.

Like a depth charge implanted in my body the infinite capacity
to fill overflows a bathtub or submarine gushing
throughout its labyrinth of rooms.
The sealed doors warp toward me, the black tape bulges out
and like a broken pipe the water jets into the chamber
ringing the walls with its demarcation as it wells higher to the ceiling.
The walls, dripping with scrawled obscenities, adolescent loves
and other graffiti, write and then erase themselves immediately
like messages on an answering machine.

Within me the recording, the remodeling reconstructs cavalierly
my guts made up of many miniatures like a lego set
snapped together and pried apart to another's content
until an ennui with the remnants sets in like daylight savings
and once a rushing, stagnates to perfection,
a surface almost synthetic in its stillness, almost godless,
even in my fingertips where the pain, shelled, fully fleshes out.

I dip them mechanically, hands of a Barbie doll, in the standing water
now bogged and murky in the basin of my bathroom.

There in my reflection I recognize my debasement, my chastity,
my desire to change, my desire to save myself from my desire to drown.

All that is left is the chair I sit in, although ready-made
is the floor, tiled or planked, spread before me, cornerless and thus unending,
merging neatly with the landscape, ever-widening in its parameters.
Its infinite capacity, like mine, to absorb sorrow leaves me no alternative,
but to capitulate to what we have in common.
The clouds deflect empathetically their own version of bereavement.
Within the wild grasses their wild crying feels with me,
this sense of wallpaper torn insancly by the fingertips still swollen
apparently with some malice for my plummy interior, soon deplumed
and moth-ridden, stuffed as if with forked hay or wild, crying grasses.

A scared pheasant alights suddenly, ascends, an omen
swallowed up in the wake of its own prescient trajectory.

The blind sky remains aloof, swaggering its long stick as it threshes
to the other side of the world and with it the clouds and the light
and its subsequent illumination, all linked in a procession like elephants
or cars in a funeral, one by one, driving slowly with their headlights on,
or blind men who continue forward
with their hand on the shoulder of the blind man before them.

Then darkness drags itself out with routine gesture
to the middle of the room, piles up as if several throws or blankets
into a makeshift bed where stretched out in this solitary discarding,
my immediate future mediates, palpitates, like a mewing foghorn,
discloses briefly in camera's shutter the warning, a wailing
within the quiescent night into which I've been backed, a tamed lion,
my voice another form of the silence as ice is of water.

All has been pared down scrupulously as a principle,
vodka from alcohol, distilled, distilled; intensified, purified
multiplied in proof so looped by the silence in the silence as listen
to the silence uttered immeasurably like Tibetan chanting.
No more and no less kelly green than the dale dallies the vowels, dilly, dilly.
No more and no less fugitive than the catwalk's riddles the unanswerable riddles.
No more and no less than a medley of bedding that grows like a man-eating plant over
my belly does my spine, unroll
chink by chink, upon the many mattresses
under which sits like a Buddha the infamous tender pea.

No more and no less within my body as muscle tissue that wraps wound our skeleton,
is the isolation, sputtering one word, one inflection,
a fire cry as the bed, doused with kerosene, ignites
like a birthday cake and the little flames procreate instantly up the rafters.

The roof, as if a hand started campfire, begins to smoke and waft.

The burning house wreathes outward, an electrifying October foliage.

It spits and seethes and puffs and wheezes
inside the hearth of a hapless evening.

Eventually the embers just glow, blown glass spun slowly in a kiln
then dies in spurts without witness on the well-intentioned
but bellicose land.

Yet no more and no less than the charred foundation
does the cry anachronistically prevail;
no less than the melted belt buckles and picture frames, the stubbed leg
of the dining room table;
no less than the twisted chandelier and the cellar sunken
like a bathtub or emptied swimming pool,
does the sound exalt as if the one element extracted in time from the defunct.

No more nefarious than a whilom wind, shook sheet metal when there were windows.
No more oceanic than the ocean, a school of dolphins, jetting and jet black.
No more jet black than this darkness blasted as if from behind a plastic veil.

No more spontaneous than the scattered embers that like welding sparks
revive then fail.
No more and no less resilient than they or pine needles,
sea-spray or liberated pearls that disperse their negative ions
like snow-making machines upon the candescent terrain.
No more and no less sober is snow than snow,
is pain, are the candescent tears from whence came snow;
that sift into the spotlight of moonlight then out again into shadow,
snowing invisibly on the feverish embers as well as on the moribund deray,
where no more and no less persistent than the definition of "deray"
exists disorder than merriment.

Face Value

And the two dark forces like two large men with dark eyes held her down
by her wrists and forced her to be quiet.

The moon watched unwilling to get involved from the corner.

Goblins rose in droves like steam swarming on the lit ceiling, winged beetles
fixated in their stares and gossiping—
she could hear the rustle of their whispers.

And the two forces penetrated her, one shoved down her mouth,
one up her vagina.

She squeezed her eyes shut, tightly, tightly, begging to be rid
of her brain, her heart, her clitoris.

Then she would be free to stumble, nomadic as an idiot
her feet flattened and swollen, her hair matted and nested
with little bugs that laid eggs in her ear while she slept
but she didn't care.

She liked it. She liked being blitheful as a leaf.
She was free as a leaf. She would lead the life of a leaf,
twitch and flex according to the weather, sit static as a stone
on a stone and stare out all day at the deadly still sea.

She would twist around, flogged pirouette, eating mouthfuls of grit
from the road in the wind and wear a fancy shirt and matching pants
soaked with rain, their threads stretched to their limits.
Frayed at last, their fabric would deteriorate into fag-ends,
lost as a last semblance of stability, springs popping out from a mattress.
Like a mattress, like a shirt, her focus on the road would fray,
would like a spring pop out of her head.
She would wander off into the bushes and further into the forest
filled with thickness and staggering height
and the smoky abyss of directionlessness.

But she didn't care. She liked it.

She liked being lost but not lost, because leaves are not lost, are they?

And the forest thick with leaves, thick with rain that poured at last
like her frayed clothes
on her hair and cheeks and eyes filled with rain
were now leaves, exactly, that twitched and flexed, twitched and flexed.

She watched them from her delirium on the bed.
She watched her own eyes dripping with rain and blood pressing, smearing
against the window. They were panicking.

She wished that she could help them.
She wished that they could help her.

She wished as hard as her eyes were shut, tightly, as the power that penetrated
her finished up, turned her over, and began again, over and over,
caressed and assaulted,
over and over
and over
and over and over and over
and over and over
and over and over and over and over and over and over
and over and over and over and over and over and over and
over and over and over and over and over and over and over
and over and over and over and over and over and over and over and over and over

and over

and over

over the tops of the birches she would be hauled, fingernails
scraping across her belly
over and into a dale of grass she would feel for a moment really, really, loved
over a whitecap way out at sea she would be ostracized
like an elderly Eskimo no longer of use to the community
over the table and chair where she sat as a child and peered sadly into the
white oasis of her dinner plate
over the stairs one by one where pushed she plunged over and over like a leaf
that floats dreamily until it dies on the pond
or a leaf that tumbles eternally, over and over, down a well
over the marital bed where she recognizes herself
playing the part in a long-standing desire
where a strong hand holds her roughly and a strong hand touches her very lightly

where a strong hand sidles like a spider up her thigh
over a car scrapped and destroyed in one crunch
over and over its junkyard, a graveyard
where like a soul she would circulate throughout the headstones
ceaselessly, over and over
like the leaves drenched with rain that were now her eyes.

She watched them as if they were her children from her bed.

How her longing rose up like a snake from her guts,
a goblin in the form of a snake,
and wrapped its great long body, green and cold, round and round the house
squeezing tight as her shut eyes that begged to be rid of it all

but nothing changed.

The Origin of the Comedy is the Feast of the Stones

1.) The Origin

And those that lived in the village besieged by plague, who prayed again to their deities, who placed fruits and delicacies at the feet of their statues, at last brought no more grapes or rancid meat. They wrenched their gods from their secure homes in the temple and dragged them into the streets and made them stand up upon the table left empty for all to see. The people prayed no more to the stone feature. They felt betrayed. They mocked their faith with all the fervor with which they had once believed. They took their betrayal into their hands and threw it back at their gods. They had feared and they had prayed, and prayed desperately and the plague only continued. Some of them died by themselves without their gods and some of them endured without their gods and some of them still secretly prayed anyway.

2.) The Comedy

And those the livid on the island couldn't understand why it had happened, why he had waited so patiently outside the house with a rope and his gun for the boyfriend to arrive. They just couldn't wrap their minds around the fact that quietly he had entered the house while his wife and her boyfriend were watching television, while his six-year-old daughter slept peacefully upstairs, and ordered his wife at gunpoint to tie up the boyfriend, not to make any noise that would wake their daughter. The islanders still burst into tears at the general store, at the post office, the only places open in the winter besides the bar, when they think of what happened. He ordered his wife at gunpoint to drive the truck with himself and the boyfriend tied up to the deserted house he had been contracted to build, where he had written earlier that evening obscenities all over the walls, the black letters still wet and dripping down to the floor. He pushed the boyfriend bound and gagged into the basement. Everybody on the island had their own version, only vaguely different, of how he then ordered his wife at gunpoint to drive him back to the house where their daughter still slept, how getting out of the truck told her to drive directly to the police, to get the rescue squad and the fire department, how he told her quietly but venomously "this will be a night you will never forget for the rest of your life." Left alone in the house while his wife sped out of the driveway, he climbed, perhaps slowlly, the staircase and entered his daughter's room. Everybody in the town knew how much he loved his daughter. He was the only person who understood her, who could control her, for she adored her father and everybody knew that too. He and his wife had been arguing over custody rights and a restraining order had been about to be put in effect for once when their daughter was a baby he had kidnapped her so afraid was he of their ever being separated. He was a strong believer in the afterlife, one person told me. He was a very religious man. He must have thought, everyone imagined, when he entered her room that night, the tears streaming down his face as some people visualized, he must have thought, being such a strong believer in the afterlife, that no one would ever be able to separate them again as he aimed his gun at his daughter while she was sleeping and shot her in the head and then himself, also in the head, curling up half dead next to his dead daughter in her bed until he died.

3.) The Feast

And those that turn in the tyrannical night, who feel the darkness penetrate them as if by process of osmosis, who soak up in fact the black paint that is cold and oily and claustrophobic and starless and the tears that continue on as if they cannot stop, as if the sobs were governed by someone else. They cry as if their heads will crack open any moment from the retching, their bodies imploding from the emotions and left to a fragmented deterioration, an infantile heap and like a vegetable, without recourse to be whole again presuming that they were whole in the first place. They plummet down through the hollows of their despair they reach the vortex point, a pinprick of light like a match lit suddenly in the oily darkness, a sense of hope that sobers them slightly, frighteningly bright so that the head adverts itself immediately from the upheld hand that serves as a visor to deflect the beautiful beam. And seeing more clearly within the meager shade of this deterrent, they somersault suddenly and swim upward swiftly, though with measured strokes as a diver must be cautious amidst the ocean's pressure not to burst his lungs. The measured strokes, the desire to surface becomes a kind of strength that comes from sinking, the psyche that comes to know its power and thus its embodiment from allowing itself to be overwhelmed. By then realizing that they are not overwhelmed, they survive, and are resilient and steadfast as the rocks of the waterfall that do fall apart but only instead become more immovable by the water that surges, and they like rocks come to know survival, the water that surges through them, for what are events in life, really, if not the feelings attributed them, the tyrannical night disappearing in droughts part and parcel of the violet haze.

4.) The Stones

And those confined to their beds that look upon the doctor who arrives sometimes late at night to check on the neighboring patient, offering nonchalantly though ingenuously his advice "How's it going Leo? If you want something for the pain just lets us know," and Leo, in the advanced stages of his cancer writhes and groans and never sleeps and never knows an escape from his pain and the doctor arrives sometimes late at night to offer nonchalantly though ingenuously his advice, "How's it going, Leo?" until Leo dies. From your side of the room you listen to Leo's last days that take place during the week of your chemo treatment, and make a pact with yourself that it will be different in your case, that you will refuse to lie alone in a dark corner of Sloane Kettering while shots of morphine barely dint the pain and the doctor arrives sometimes late at night to ask you how its going until you die. Until you die you will come to know the doctor within and you will stand unaccompanied like a seagull and kill crabs and hop in the sunlight crying plaintively to the sun bathers. You shall leave the large hospital as you promised yourself, beige and vast in its false promise to you, and standing unaccompanied, veer toward the both opaque and transparent sky, crying plaintively and laughing as if on a joyride at the nothingness from which you know in the back of your mind you will again materialize.

Ask Me No Questions

The last time the ceiling pivoted toward the sky like a lean-to,
mothering us from burnishing rain and black bits of reality from
the outside

The last time you fell deftly, limb by limb, on top of me, while I
lay fallen on the bed, atop a pile of leaves, me, a lost, fallen thing:
O glove, key, O leaf

The last time the lights dimmed in the same environment, the melancholy
grass swayed on the mooring, where flute and drum held you down by me;
and though you were about to leave, I wanted you to stay, that way I mean;
on the verge of leaving, but with me, with me, with me, with me, with me

          a bullet hole, this precise space
          you can see right into the room, a keyhole
          pieces of material flap flagrantly
          where the wind tunnels clean through
          where mugs, penknives, matchbooks
          whiskers, Kleenex, blown kisses,
          mini-batteries, Limericks, and other
          earthly paraphernalia, man made or not
          are caught in the suction of winding homeward
          as they veer with increasing velocity toward
          the end, but flung instead! Pell-mell,
          sown from the wheat sower's sack,
          onto the unfamiliar land, biodegradable
          as the body and fertile as its waste.
          Recycled, a rock is this longing.

Is it your lips I crave or simply the kiss?

      Your kiss laid upon me like a knighting sword
               or poisonous ink I lick from the vellum of your lips.

                   I'll never know
To what extent my memory plagiarizes itself.
               (Not unlike the tabloid of one's mirror
               no matter how hard I stare at it, it
               will never become uncensored).

Soften everything, please,
            to pleasant sentences and insensible hands—

   The kaleidoscope of names, arms, and faces,
            a flabellum of love laid out from the start,
                        an astrological chart,

or soldier's graveyard . . . grid of my misread heart.

                        So bury the boy on the hill!
Bury him with his gun to his side
            despite the protests of his mother

Let the solemnized notes of the flute
                        fly over head
         and shed petals (how about yellow?),
   into the erotic confinement of his grave.

                        Suicidal lovers,
            now they will never part
He and the dark women of the glen.
He, deep inside the damning shoal of her.

                  Back and Forth
                        in the long box I wait with you
and sleep in the stationary kayak of your bones
and talk to you, but in fact to myself
                        inside your skull,
                              drafty bungalow;
      of thrashed bamboo are the slit spaces
            where you teeth still clench.

While I, with my love suspended in my breast, indefinitely,
      levitated, like the hypnotized patient:

            thinks of you and of my desire for you, and thinks,
            maybe my desire just inhabits you (or me),
                        like a poltergeist.

But, so what?
                If I care not send for the exorcist?

If upon a bed of Sweet William they be a bed of nails,
I still smell the Sweet William
                        when I lie down, full-length, on a bed of nails.

Still into your marbled eyes that flagellate me with expressionlessness,
        upon their two-dimensional depth I won't economize.
                I've wrought urn from everyday cup.

And followed red the scent to the root of my nervousness.
        to the virgin origin, the following, my metaphysical deflowering.
                        (O not again).

The favorite song obsessionally plays,
             never the same, never changed.
        And with the intension to preserve what we mean to us,

                from the very act of playing, I guess,
meaning is lost in negligible drops (O.K., like tears), negligible
                    by virtue of their abundance.

Its gain,
        a blank metaphor for gain, or song,
            the gap filled with a slide projected

the optic effect, my expectation,
                on what is has been fed:

        1.) Tombigbee Waltz.

        2.) The bruised winter sun.

        3.) A little pencil note oblivious to placement.

        4.) Your arms (both being held and how they look).

5.) The plastic wall we talk through like prisoner and visitor,
and the frail scratch in the surface we spot simultaneously
and subsequently, cannot tear our eyes away from.

6.) The closed room we writhe in, we writhe in.

7.) That weird pocket of air we caress between our hands,
a silver-lined vacuum.

Poem

Ah! Androgynous night!
You are both rough and slow
Your arms aloof like the contemptuous woman
Or distracted like the man in a "distant" mood,

But now your attention approaching
Silently yields as wheat does from wind

Carry me tenderly
Like a pitch in your memory to vertigo,
Hubris rising, a stable of flowers!
Sleep with me
There, insistently, heartfelt before me
Your passive arms overlapping amply, calmly, as you speak to me
Evenly, insistently, *legatissimo*
The hours dilating with an owlish cry
                    rising, rising, in their lavender stride

Elegant as the deaths that let them fall.
Let them fall!
Let them fall!
Falling instantly absent from memory
Falling intently like the truths we marry, let them fall…
Recognizably mine.

****

Waking,
It is over with you.
It is black, but never black enough.
The daylight is still humid and clumsy.
In my head you still move like music trembling.

Where are you in this city?
In a dream I pass you in the street.
A white sail reels next to me, and I touch your arm. You look at me,
Your eye sinks like a bone
In the pleated blue.

****

There is no place away from you.

In the night you are, of course, everywhere, caught in the trees
Like a kite, or walking independently...
Coming into my room and leaving the door ajar
Your pale hand, your pale hair
Leaning against me like a yellow theatre

Undressing for me
In the stairwell
The rain in the streets
Outside the office
The avenue and Pole Stars
Seen at noon
The limit of winter cantering away
A linen tarp
Filled with violets renewed
And thunder lifting
Like an eyelid
In Battersea!

O Stairwell! Office! And Avenue!

****

Deft score
Of nightly curtains drawn
Seek me out and out of your intention
I'll appear

Wakeful as a cloud
The arched terrain of both sea and sky, a teal wing
This landscaped arm of mine
Climbing like glee or bravery

Everywhere entering and descending near
A graceful voice pressed against the air

1981

Peter the Great

for Sharon Olds

I never wear tampons because they remind me of my mother.
I only wear pads which she wouldn't be caught dead in.
I remember her leg craned like a neck over the silk basin for shaving
Her upper thigh, webbed with black hairs and pockmarked with cellulite,
shook slightly with each stroke like flesh protruding from a plaster cast.
I remember the two strings hanging between her legs, entwined like rope
half saturated with blood, a thermometer reading.
It was as if her womb were running a fever.
Because she had done the favor of having three children
her vagina was so big it could fit two supers
her belly, yellow-white, with its stretch marks like water stains
stuck out permanently as if she were still with child
still pregnant with us children, I being the runt,
a favor for which she'd never forgive us.
And I'd sit obediently at the edge of the bathtub
while she shaved her legs, only an inch above the knee
just up to where fashion demarcated the appropriate skirt length,
and lectured me, as she put it, staring indirectly into the mirror,
never meeting my eyes:
"A person like you Tory, will never be happy. Even in college,
I think you'll always be miserable."
Those words though deflecting like street noise you get used to
wormed their way anyway into my flea-infested soul,
the miserable nest she referred to nonchalantly, matter-of-factly,
vehemently in the cold, cold bathroom.
I would stare at the two strings hanging
and hate the fact that I was a woman
because I never wanted to be like her.
I'd wished I'd never come from that gappy hole
stuffed with wads of bloody cotton.
How can I begin to tell you what happened?
I've talked my head off for twelve years, more, and still people
don't really believe, can't entirely imagine, get the idea, the whole picture
nor can I figure out myself the discrepancy
between what I feel and what I saw and what I'm able to express of it.
It took me more than three years in therapy to confess it, to say
yeah, she hit me, all the time, she hit me,
that's right she even pushed me backwards down our staircase;

although I had been trying so hard to say it, I swear I'd said it already
trying to beat the clock of what I refer to as *neurosis rigor mortis*,
Because I believe, that like Lyme disease, mental illness burrows in
with a disfiguring virus, eats away and leaves rotten the wood of the brain,
irreversibly: not everything in life is built with resiliency.
We think because we see the cycles of nature, the seasons come
and go like a tourist season, that we, being tourists of nature
will go 'round with it, but no, it's not like that: we're witnesses,
that's all; activity or passivity, that's our only choice
and every minute counts in that choice-making.
You have to really, *really* want it
for your life to be different, to change.
You need something to strive toward and something else to react against
like two notes held in suspension, your life becomes their sonant difference.
You need a feeling, even stronger than a vision
You need a revulsion, a vivid idea of hell.
You even need to have once visited there.
So I suppose I should thank you, here's my thank-you note, Mother
for the hell-hole of your vagina, a snake-pit
for your breasts, rubber gloves hooked to your chest
with which you compared their former life
to my pre-pubescence one day in the mirror.
I was brushing my teeth in my underwear when you entered without knocking (as usual)
surveyed my nakedness with ruthless estimation and dryly said
"I don't know how you inherited those breasts, Tory. Mine were always round and full
and all the men loved them!"
Then you whipped up one of your bona fide social smiles for the mirror
(I don't believe I ever saw you smile naturally)
and loitered there, flushed and expectant, as if posing for the subtitles
of that worn-out story about the debutante parties
that you would force my father to recoup at the dinner table.
"Tell them," you would demand, "how the men would line up to dance with me . . ."
My father would blink, then recite mechanically,
as a waiter does the evening specials.
Thank you for the hell-hole of that social smile, mother,
the cavernous imagining of your throat that lead's 'to your stomach
your intestines, your asshole—
my hate turned you inside out, attempted to dissect you
like the generic frog in ninth-grade biology, I pinned back your legs and arms
to render you as helpless and as victimized as I felt,
to demystify, de-sublimate your enormous power,
which had always eluded me in terms of its source, dog-eat-dog

in its ability to excuse itself—the self-justifying mentality
of those devoid of a consciousness convinced of the morality of their motives
like Klansmen, like McCarthyism.
Years later at some perfunctory birthday celebration
you posited a subtext in order to provoke from me a forgiveness
or rather to make the case that forgiveness need not be required.
Your name via posterity has been clean from the start.
"After all, Tory, Peter the Great, for whom we have to thank for all that
is beautiful in the Russian Empire, would burn his cavalrymen at the stake!"
So via the posterity of the scorched soldiers, Mother
I've visualized my mutiny in their honorarium and in mine.
I've saved up for it, saved up for it
so that I could get out of it, the Russian empire for your maternal love,
away from the Peter the Great in you,
from the social smile stuck to me like the history of your invidious clit.
O, you know, it's your cunt I hate the most, Mother,
because that's where it all started from.

Now you have no control over me
the offspring you let loose upon the world, an idiot,
with nomadic shoes, with matted hair, like Lizaveta in *The Brothers Karamazov*
I'd like the world to be my witness when you said on my thirtieth birthday
in response to my explanations as to why we hadn't spoken
or seen much of each other in over a decade;
to my recountings of the abuse, to my spare statement
that I just didn't trust you;
when you spoke from the very essence of your soul, from the origin
of a personality beyond their flesh and bones, beyond their emotionality
as if from eternity itself:
"There are no witnesses, Tory. It is your word against mine."
Let the world be my witness, let god then, as it were,
but a different god than yours, Mother,
that watched over Peter the Great and surveyed his torture.
It's your word against mine, your word against mine
Let our words fight then, Jarndyce vs. Jarndyce,
Let our words fight, mind over matter, eye for an eye,
let the best man win, Satan vs. Christ:
the ruddy dwarf with a single lock of hair standing
perpendicular like a unicorn's vs. the anorexic pale-faced academic;
the Bloomsian stud vs. the virgin-breed transvestite.
Let them wrestle in the mud, in the antiquated air of St. Petersburg.
I'll reserve a box seat and risk

standing in the corner for the rest of my life.
I'll eat my dinner in the garage (I'm used to it),
be bruised again by the plastic doll you beat me with from head to foot
because I stole a stick of your chewing gum!
There was no hiding place, we were too rich
to call 911 and make use of police intervention.
Let our words fight, the Devil vs. Our Savior, let the best man win,
survival of the fittest, I'm in top condition.
I bet you thought when I tested HIV positive you had me beaten
that you would tend to me the way Joan Crawford did to Bette Davis in
What Ever Happened to Baby Jane?, fool all the nurses and even the doctors
would be duped by the afterglow of your debutante days.
And only I would know, me mute, me dying, me wasting away
with no fight in me left, your face my last sight.
Maybe even the words *I love you* would be bullied from me in my last breath
by your determined jaw, your grizzly brown eyes,
the protruding vein in your forehead.
So weak I would be, so small, so regressed to the brokenhearted child of four
so tired, so frightened so desperate to believe that you loved me after all.
It's true I loved you once, so much, I'll never let myself love again.
When you left for a party I would sleep with your sweater
smell the perfume (Norell), and configure a narrative, although desultory,
contrived and glued together with the stuff fairytales are made of,
of a good mother, but I failed because I couldn't apologize enough.
What witchery took place between us? Were you the witch
or were we singled out to combat some hex? O not we,
it was I, the bad seed, or so you would say.
I couldn't help myself, I was evil through and through, so rotten
that when I loved you, it made you hate me instead.
i.e., remember when I complimented you and said you should be god's wife?
Your hand came down so hard it knocked me out of bed.
I couldn't understand except that I was bad.
Only apologies, as numerous, as heartfelt, as pious as possible
could purify the sinful, could reverse the blackness
that metastasized each year inside me, but I only got worse and worse.
Finally I got so bad my apologies couldn't be apologetic enough.
Nothing I owned was precious enough, dear in possession for me to give to you
give up to you, no sacrifice great enough when I tried, night after night
and laid at the threshold of your master bedroom compartment
a better present than the last along with a note
to supplement the gift. I wanted no stone left unturned
in my begging for forgiveness.

"I'm sorry," I would write, "I'm sorry," I would say, I would chant, "I'm sorry,"
I would cry myself to sleep, "I'm sorry," I would dream, I would repeat until
it's become a kind of stuttering stumbling block to this day.
When people tell me not to apologize I don't know what to say
save for apologizing for apologizing.
I would do anything to get you back, to be nice to me again.
But "Sorry" isn't enough you would say.
I'd made a mistake so big I couldn't make up for it.
I'd made the mistake of being the love-child you never wanted,
doubly disappointing since you had wanted another boy.
I was a mistake, and you would say so without hesitation
such a mistake you wished I were dead, and never thought twice in telling me so.
"O how I'd like to take you out and shoot you, Tory!" you would yell
at the top of your lungs. And I believed you, believed you completely
that some nights, crying myself to sleep, I wished you would,
like a lame horse just take me out and get it over with.
How some nights, even now, I wished you had.

Now that I'm positive, you just might get that wish after all, Mother.
Isn't that ironic, as if your god had listened and executed your prayer.
Well, my god listened too, and hence I'm still here.
So you can forget it, you can forget it.
It's that very vision, that goddamned nightmare,
that keeps me ticking, kicking against the odds,
shadowboxing for the hell of it
with the hell-hole of that hospital scene that reminds me of my childhood.
Let our gods fight then, vice vs. virtue
I've got strength to spare.
Over my dead body, it's a fight to the finish.
Over my dead body, I refuse to die if it means having you there.
Right from the get-go I've been on top of it, so there.
But how can one so ungrateful, rebellious, neurotic, angry, obsessive,
pick any word, Mother, arbitrarily with care.
I'll spit back I'm healthy, spit back I'm healthy,
spit back I'm healthy, 'til there's nothing there
for you to hit, or criticize or abuse or whip or order about my Father
like a subordinate to carry out your orders: Whip her! Hit her! Get her!
The only time he said no was when with a broken leg he declined to hit me
with his crutch.
Now there's nothing left to control, nothing left but your own despair
and I've got no heart for it, nothing to lay at threshold of your door
because I know you would leave me behind like a Nazi.

I know because it happened, it's happened all right,
when you kicked me out into the street when I had shingles in the
cornea of my eye and chances were I'd lose my eyesight.
It happened when you tried to lock me up; told my teachers I'd lost it,
that my personality was borderline.
It happened when you ordered me out of the house past midnight to take a train
back to New York a million fucking times;
when I was twelve and a horny football player tried to rape me;
when I got mugged at knifepoint;
when I had an abortion.
Your only words of consolation were that I'd just regret it if I had children.

It's your word against mine, your word against mine.
I suppose I should thank you, Mother, so here's my thank-you note
for fucking me over so many fucking times
it's filled me brim-, top-full with direst cruelty like Lady Macbeth.
It's fed me intravenously with bitterness until I ODed
and learned the hard way to crave the methadone of love.
It taught me to be alone, utterly, utterly alone
to survive the worst of circumstances, and I've done all right
with no help from you, Mother, not one lousy, loving hand—
Thanks to you I should thank you, so here's my thank-you note.
I won't end up at St. Vincent's in some windowless room,
listening to my dying neighbor while
dreaming up ways to kill myself; with your face above me, illuminated
as the holy ghost's, so that later you can say to yourself, to the world
in that perverse shrink-like setting you pretend to have with god,
that you tried to save me, you did all that could have been done.
O no, it'll be just a *little* bit different:
I won't have put my feet up on a patch of grassy pine-needled earth
nor aspersed my soul like a fistful o' sand
o'er the vast slate-blue tableau we call the sea.
I'll have the satisfaction of watching my god win.
He may trip on his dress when he tries to stand up, but it'll be my god,
my god who wins—I'll watch my savior, muddied and thin
stagger to his feet with staggered resilience,
but on his feet he'll be nonetheless, while your god lies flat out
stars spinning, a halo of defeat, a faux crown of thorns,
ready to be sent D.O.A. to the morgue.
I'll be watching from my box seat, suckling the baby you swore I'd regret,
while *you* tee off, Mother, in that great eighteen-hole golf course in the sky.

[Fragment]

Marigold leaves already falling; October's entering insensitive to present circumstances. Rice paper moon pasted ornamentally on disseminating daylight and an agate gray-blue partisanship tints everything. I'm driving slowly, another medication haze. Memories of past medication hazes, melancholy pleasure begot regardless from similar leaves loosing their color. The beauty of dying. It's their dying that's so ravishing I realize. Driving through the countryside of blazing plague. Ford trucks pass impatiently. Strong accelerator sound then the fall of nothing. Virility against failing. Left alone with the silent landscape, like white farmhouse vacant. Inlet water tideless and shiny, reflects neither moon, nor shore pines, nor farmhouse. I search for reassurance in its unflinching iris. There must be something beyond its thousand-mile stare, that look of the refugee child. The act of searching an act of optimism, I deduct. Hopelessness, a kind of starvation, though nature's routines make us all seem negligible.

The Baby Chick [Fragment]

One strangely sunny day so clear all objects appeared as if newly sanded and filed, refined and formal and thus wanting to have nothing to do with me. I held in my hand a baby chick, still jelled in its embryonic encasement, quivering slightly though the chick had long past died, perhaps never having been alive.

I stood somewhere inconsequential, a quiet street perhaps, or park. A tuft of land. It may have even been sandy. I have such problems remembering because I was focused so intently on the baby chick I held, the myopic perspective almost of an obsession when everything outside you drifts into the blurred, insignificant sphere of your peripheral vision. I guess you could say I was obsessed, but obsession to me implies a kind of insatiability, a greediness of passion, a rioting impatience. I felt none of those things.

When I felt was more of a frozen feeling, of being gripped by a sense of poignancy and tenderness. I felt as well a fascination that seemed prescient, as if I stared long enough at the baby chick. hidden meanings I couldn't yet fathom would surface and I would finally come to understand something about my future and my past that might give some coherence to my long-term perspective that is often referred to as "peace of mind."

Looking back now I see I had a lot invested in obsessing about the baby chick, so much so that my expectation couldn't possibly be fulfilled unless by some miracle the baby chick began to breathe and stretch its wings with its transparent cocoon, which I knew intellectually it never would. But I searched anyway, unconsciously I now realize, for little signs of movement particularly in the head region. I concentrated on the wet cowlick of pale yellow fur nearly white that swept upward above what appeared an abnormally large eye, humanistically closed. Her lid was so fragile. Yes, I gave the baby chick the sex that was mine because I felt she was mine, or rather a part of me, even me *per se*, selfishly and narcissistically interpreting her presence as symbolic of my existence, even though she had no existence of her own. I even gave her a name, "Susan." I felt guilt and even remorse about this narcissism at times, and a little even now, this guilt perhaps perpetuating my infatuation beyond whatever life span could be deemed, however insanely, appropriate.

I knew, no matter how I imbued Susan with my will, with in fact, my love, she would never come alive. Still, I kept her in my hand and staring at her, tried. Sometimes, in moments of paranoia, I thought of it as a failure on my part, deliberately so due to a secret desire of not wanting her alive, of liking, of admiring the eerie beauty of her still born state. It represented for me my mysterious beginning and doubly mysterious end that bookended, so to speak, my life, in such a delicate and innocent form, as if the unknown if discovered were after all, after all my fear, just like that, just like her, incredibly sweet in appearance, and in intention as benign.

Predictably, there came the day when it was clear, no matter what argument I could come up with to counter my reasoning, that this had to stop, that the time spent searching for symbolic revelations in Susan was futile, or more optimistically put, had come to fruition. There was nothing more to be found or experienced aside from the continued depth of my own emotions since I had grown so enormously attached to Susan that the thought . . . .

[Fragment]

and somewhat of an oddity to the world.
I pierce with precision and learn to distinguish what's sharp and silver
from that which is deep blue and diving to the surface, paradoxically
by what lands, delicately, in slow motion, and continues to exist
among the silt and mud and loveless leaves at the bottom of a nondescript pond.
A penny tossed not fragrantly into the fountain.
My faithful wish, pulled like a skeet, rewinds its wishful intention,
spins upward, catapulting its wisdom back to its origin
to the palm of my fearful, irretrievable hand.
From the bottom of the pond, clear as a cornea, you look up, all pupil,
all desire, to remind me of what we said, of what you gave me,
of what I have, what I have, what I have, what I have:
my wrought iron desire, an infant kitten, the vacant swing set mews
up ahead where unkept and rudimentary the acre idles like an engine
beyond the gate. Way, way off, beyond the gate.
Raw as potential or your pubic hair, the pebble floods upward
and the wistful penny bursts inside my lungs to no avail.
No departures, no arrivals occur in the alien sky
wrought in the lone night air like iron,
taupe-gray beneath the streetlight as my grandmother's hair
or headdress of the hateful goddess.
Or how like the clouds lit from the back by the moon
the way projection screens are and x-rays of one's interior
lit up from the inside like a jack o'lantern or happy home or master bedroom
inside such a happy home happily ensconced in the lone night air.
I want to be there, the wrought iron gate our headboard
reaching up in Gothic tribute to the alien sky; to my grandmother's hair,
to the headdress de-hexed and all ours, to the gate
from which in each other's arms
we can safely speculate and mitigate its influence;
to the candid moon that shines benevolently down, all pupil, all desire;
on us glowing, levitated with love above the rumpled sheets;
on the pulse of a kitten that strobes within us as the moon itself
surveys protectively, a searchlight
our dark room, minute and oceanic, wrought iron and welling to the brim.

A Poetics of Resistance: Tory Dent, Sylvia Plath, and "The Moon and the Yew Tree"[1]

by Nicole Cooley

1.

In her poem "What Calendars Have Become," Tory Dent describes her poetics: "I refer to the world but I speak of the body" (35). Diagnosed with HIV at age 30, Dent has written three books of poetry—*What Silence Equals* (1993), *HIV, Mon Amour* (1999), and *Black Milk* (2005)—which explore AIDS and its range of social, political and personal implications. She is, to my knowledge, the only woman poet in America to publish multiple volumes of poems about living with HIV and AIDS. Yet all of Dent's work resists being classified as "representative" poetry about AIDS. In fact, as I will explore here, her work resists representation itself and continually underscores the inadequacy of language to describe the experience of living and dying with AIDS. With its reliance on strategies of Language Poetry and the New York School, its long Whitmanesque line structure, its web of allusions, and its complex syntactic patterning, Dent's poetry challenges our assumptions about writing about both the world and the body.

The body Dent refers to above and elsewhere in her work is always a female body, but here again Dent resists easy categorization: it is a female body identified with gay male bodies, a female body suffering as those bodies suffer. And it is not a private, individual body. In her final volume, *Black Milk*, which is my focus in this essay, Dent titles her poems about HIV and AIDS after poems by such writers as John Donne and Paul Celan, and employs the other poets' language within her own to show how the body under siege exists throughout history. Dent's individual body in these poems is always a social body.

In this essay, I will frame Dent's poetics of resistance through a reading of her work in terms of these contradictions that surround her evocation of the body. Specifically, I will look closely at her poem "The Moon and the Yew Tree," which explicitly locates Sylvia Plath's poem of the same name as an intertext. Dent's use of Plath's work is interesting because it asks us to consider gender and the female body so directly.

---

1   *Pilot Light: A Journal of 21st Century Poetics and Criticism.* December 2011.

Just as her work does not fit easily into the category "AIDS poetry," Dent's writing does not comfortably align itself with dominant traditions of "women's poetry." For the most part, her poems appear not in anthologies of women's writing but in volumes of AIDS poetry (such as *In the Company of My Solitude*) and experimental work (*The Exact Change Yearbook*). The one "women's anthology" in which Dent's work appears is *Bearing Life: Women's Writing on Childlessness* (edited by the late Rochelle Ratner). In this book, Dent has contributed a selection from an unpublished memoir, titled "The Deferred Dream." Dent writes:

> Writing about my living with AIDS is always painful for me. But it is—always—what I write about; I can't think of anything else to say. In the desire to write is the desire to communicate, I believe. I'm sharing with someone and in that process trying to understand myself what I'm thinking or feeling . . . . By writing I hope to feel closer to the world. It's what I want. It's more and more what I want as I lose slowly, incrementally, unpredictably and of course unfortunately my physical grip on the world. It is AIDS weakens my grip . . . My organic body, born into this world and made up of this world as its by-product, is the rejecting factor (122).

Yet the experience Dent evokes in her work is crucial. Although current literary criticism seems oddly uncomfortable with Tory Dent's poetic linking of the female body, the gay male body, the social body and AIDS in her work, it is important to remember that AIDS is currently the third most deadly disease for women in the US. And women now make up 25% of all new HIV/AIDS diagnoses in this country ("Women and HIV/AIDS: An Overview," Elinor Nauen and Bonnie Goldman). Paula Treichler writes, "Despite documented cases of AIDS from almost the beginning of the epidemic, AIDS was assumed by most of the medical and scientific community to be a 'gay disease' or a 'male disease'—assumed, that is, to be different from other sexually transmitted disease" (42). Even in 2011, more than twenty years after the epidemic was first named, I have seen this disbelief about women and AIDS in the college classrooms without exception every time I begin a discussion of Dent's work. And as soon as we start talking about women and AIDS, my students always want to know how Dent contracted HIV. I ask them why this matters, which often leads to a conversation about stigma—what it means to be an AIDS "victim"—that can be valuable.

Finally, while Tory Dent's work resists categorization as AIDS poetry and women's poetry, it also resists in another ways that have to do with her linguistic strategies. Her work investigates real, material bodily experience but does so through a poetics of resistance. Her poems constantly expose language's formal limits and yet it is at every moment a project of bearing witness to atrocity. For example, Dent continually challenges writing as a mode of discourse through her invocation of other art forms. Her work is not simply ekphrastic but it borrows the techniques of music, film and photography. In Dent's first book *What Silence Equals*, music or sound is the dominant trope that signifies writing (several poems are noted as being written to songs and one poem is titled "Poems in American Sign Language"). And in her second, *HIV Mon Amour*, photography and film play a central role as she deploys jump cuts, frames and cropping of images to make her poems, In Black Milk, the poems offer very direct poetic intertextualties; Dent titles them after well-known poems and employs the other poets' language within her own.

My reading of Dent's work follows several recent literary and cultural studies that look both back and forward at the AIDS epidemic in the context of multiple kinds of writing. Paula Treichler's assertion in *How To Have Theory in An Epidemic: Cultural Chronicles of AIDS* that AIDS is an "epidemic of signification" (19), that AIDS cannot just be read by language but that it is constructed through language, in particular the language of biomedicine, and that an understanding of AIDS' multiple and at times contradictory meanings is crucial to our understanding of the disease. "Signification" and its relation to disease is a central focus for Dent; her poetics are inseparable from AIDS and its significations. As well, in *Untimely Interventions: AIDS Writing, Testimonial and the Rhetoric of Haunting*, Ross Chambers notes that "witnessing" is usually understood through ideas of legal testimony—as "honest and direct, straightforward and unproblematic—the simple report of a reliable eyewitness" (18). This is exactly what Tory Dent's work complicates and at times even refuses.

Dent's poem "The Moon and the Yew Tree" from *Black Milk* is illustrative of her poetics of resistance and offers an important way to think about that resistance in terms of gender and the gendered body. The poem adopts Sylvia Plath's title "The Moon and the Yew Tree" and situates Plath's poem within Dent's own framework. As I noted, *Black Milk* is comprised largely of poems that use this format, which invoke, embed and translate lines from canonical, older (i.e. non-contemporary) poems. Notably, the use of Plath's poem within Dent's own marks the only instance of a woman poet as model and intertext within the book. (Other poems Dent uses are by Rilke, Hopkins, Donne and Celan.) The question arises: why does Tory Dent invoke Sylvia Plath? I don't mean to position Plath here as a kind of literary mother figure or to trace a clear line of influence. Indeed, many contemporary women poets would probably assert Plath's importance for their work. Nevertheless, Plath's use of tropes of death and dying, the ways in which her speaker's female identity is often performative, and the way in which her work functions as a testimonial are all significant for Dent's poetics.

Dent's use of Plath is not simply a one-to-one correspondence. From the poem's first moment, Dent makes Plath's image of death both metaphorical and highly literal:

> This is the light of the mind, cold and planetary. The trees of the
> mind are black. Their irregular branches, like broken arms back-
> lit from MRI dye, offset by yearning. They take form in ways only
> experts can decipher (22).

Here, Plath's "trees of the mind" open the poem, and Plath not Dent is the first to speak. Yet Dent immediately concretizes the abstract image, moving from the "mind" right to the ill body (the MRI). A similar rhetorical move occurs in the fourth stanza: "The moon is no door. It is a face in its own right. / White as a knuckle and terribly upset. I identify with its nausea." Again, the moon as metaphor is grounded in the body, in illness's bodily sensations, as "upset" becomes, for Dent, "nausea."

If, as Treichler maintains, AIDS is also constructed through language, then Dent's use of the vocabulary of biomedicine (the MRI, for instance) read through Sylvia Plath's representation of the "cold and planetary" mindscape is a way to describe a female experience of living with HIV and AIDS. Refracted through the words of one of the foremost—and most famous—twentieth century American women poets who wrote so openly about death, Dent's poem takes on a new valence. Death, in Dent's version of the poem, is always resolutely physical while she extends Plath's metaphors and weaves them with her own. The poem never flinches from its depiction of the material dying body: "the scraped out bottom of a uterine nothing" (22) and "someone suffocated who suddenly stops struggling" (23).

Throughout the poem, Dent re-writes Plath's "O-gape of complete despair" into a world in which her body is being "whittle[d] down to horse feed pellets" (23). Towards the end of the poem, Dent's testimony departs from Plath's metaphors and offers her own:

> I have fallen a long way. I lie at the bottom, smashed
> Like a dinner plate against kitchen tile, china cups and jagged bits.
> I lie at the bottom, shattered and dangerous, looking up

With a baby's stunned engrossment. I'm moving closer to Pluto and Mars.
Clouds are flowering blue and mystical over the face of the stars, —
It will not be quick. Death drinks me in, slow syrup. (24)

In these lines, Dent literally abandons the moon of Plath's poem to approach "Pluto and Mars." The moon as mother from Plath's poem shifts to the speaker as the child, the "baby" lying "at the bottom, smashed." And here, Dent offers an explicit contrast with Plath: "blue and mystical" and "flowering" clouds are juxtaposed with the declaration "It will not be quick. Death drinks me in . . . ." There is also a sonic echo here, as "mystical" and "drink" and "syrup" link together. On the one hand, Dent analogizes clinical depression and AIDS. Yet at the same time these lines could be read—to extend my claim here—as Dent taking Plath's evocation of the death-in-life that is depression and turning the death into something imminent and physical.

The fact that Dent places "a baby" in Plath's poem is also significant here. One of the first woman poets to write about motherhood (and daughterhood) in all its complications, Plath does not position her speaker as a mother in her poem but rather as a daughter: "The moon is my mother" (18). Reading this poem against the essay I quoted earlier, about Dent's abortion because of her disease, her use of Plath becomes more complex. Bringing the baby into the poem is an act of resistance, and through metaphor, the speaker becomes the baby not the mother.

Unlike her other uses of other poems within her own throughout *Black Milk*, in "The Moon and the Yew Tree" Dent positions Plath's poem as the frame for her own: Plath's first line opens Dent's poem and her last line closes the poem. It is as if Dent's poem occurs within Plath's poem. The interior lines quoted from Plath work like jump-cuts in film, both connecting yet exposing the seams between pieces of texts. Plath interrupts Dent. Dent interrupts Plath. The beautiful surface of Plath's poem is continually disrupted. Dent builds on Plath, Dent bears witness to Plath, Dent turns Plath's bleak, cold despair into a terrible series of bodily sensation.

Finally, and most importantly, the death in life that Plath describes in "The Moon and the Yew Tree"—and in so many of her late poems—is a state of contradiction and resistance. This contradiction is central to Dent's representation of living with AIDS. As Dent asserts in *Black Milk*'s title poem, "I will not say I'm fortunate, I will not say I'm lucky / traitor to the living, traitor to the dead" (51). These lines again underscore Dent's poetics of resistance. Her writing is dependent on the collapsing of every binary opposition we might want to use to think about her poems.

Works Cited

Chambers, Ross. *Untimely Interventions: AIDS Writing, Testimonial, and the Rhetoric of Haunting.* Ann Arbor: University of Michigan, 2004.

Dent, Tory. *Black Milk.* Riverdale-on-Hudson, NY: The Sheep Meadow Press, 2005.

_____ *HIV, Mon Amour.* Riverdale-on-Hudson, NY: The Sheep Meadow Press, 2009.

Plath, Sylvia. *Ariel: The Restored Edition.* New York: Harper Collins, 2004.

Treichler, Paula A. *How to Have Theory in an Epidemic: Cultural Chronicles of AIDS.* Durham, NC: Duke University Press, 1999.

Greg Miller is the author of *The Sea Sleeps: New and Selected Poems* (Paraclete Press 2014) and three books of poetry published by the University of Chicago Press Phoenix Poets Series, as well as critical essays and books of literary scholarship and translation, with a particular focus on George Herbert. Miller is a professor emeritus of English at Millsaps College.

Nicole Cooley is the author of *Breach* (LSU 2010) and *Milk Press* (Alice James Books 2010), as well as two other poetry collections and a novel. She has received the Walt Whitman Award, the Emily Dickinson Award, and a National Endowment for the Arts Grant. Cooley directs the MFA Program in Creative Writing and Literary Translation at Queens College, New York.

INDEX OF TITLES

More Praise for Tory Dent

Dent's "metaphysics" is her own extravagant creation. The sense of emergency crossed by the objectionable truth leads to a style "livid" and "mad" in both senses. Polysyllabic words trail through the fingers of her long, let-loose lines like hair that is turning to sand. Breaking the rules, which are made to be broken, many of these verbal horrors end inly, not to mentionity, and - ness. "Hideous and addictive," pushed and pushed so as to come to "seem" "magnetic and good" ("Listen"), subjected to tics and slams of repetition, the language seeks catharsis through freakish excess, the run of the words corkscrewed from normal, now stilted with albeit's or subjective he's and jawbreakers that would be pretentious if they weren't weirdly beautiful on the little rollers of their many syllables, and now course in an Anglo-Saxon way. The great thing is to flow "extemporaneously, forever," reaching "like a river across the rioting fog" ("Death as a Material"). Not that it isn't all a joke, almost, "like paint thrown against a wall with anger in in the arbitrary gesture, / anger at arbitrariness itself, for you're jealous of its freedom" ("Ash"). In all, a style that loves to hate itself. There has never been a poetry quite like this before, so passionately and understandably barbaric in its deployment of uselessly learned words. And, withal, stormily beautiful, at the border where beauty tolerates the sublime.

—Cal Bedient in *Parnassus* (1995)

In *HIV, Mon Amour*, one thinks of the long line as a near classical conceit, a life-line tethered to in-depth meaning and breathless pursuit. This collection is a whirlpool of energy that seems to be reaching for cinematic clarity, driven by a need to confront modern psychology and anthology until there's a focus of certainty. Here's a map where ideas and experiences collide, and what rises out of the landscape and underneath is a poetry that is painful and truthful, beautiful and terrifying, lyrical and narrative, always engaging the intellect and the body politic. *HIV, Mon Amour* seems relentless, a long-breath engine that propels the urgency of this spell-binding collection of poems at the end of our millennium. The voice here is not stingy; it as a full-throated singing that demands a passionate response because it has compassion for the reader. This book is brave, and a bold sophistication is in the heartbeat of the truth telling.

—Yusef Komunyakaa,
1999 Laughlin Award Judge

Tory Dent has astonished me with a courageous, heart-breaking poetry . . . it is not for nothing that the almost unbearable tones remind many of Plath at her best. These extreme poems should shock and comfort many. They tell us how to use affliction in the service of more than poetry. Dent is outraged, angry, and alive, and her poems mean to survive.

—David Shapiro on *What Silence Equals*